The Argyle Sweater

The Argyle Sweater

**A Cartoon Collection
by Scott Hilburn**

**Andrews McMeel
Publishing, LLC**

Kansas City

09 10 11 12 13 RR2 10 9 8 7 6 5 4 3 2 1

ISBN-13: 978-0-7407-7695-3
ISBN-10: 0-7407-7695-9

Library of Congress Control Number: 2008937975

www.andrewsmcmeel.com

www.theargylesweater.com

―――― **ATTENTION: SCHOOLS AND BUSINESSES** ――――

Andrews McMeel books are available at quantity discounts with bulk purchase for educational, business, or sales promotional use. For information, please write to: Special Sales Department, Andrews McMeel Publishing, LLC, 1130 Walnut Street, Kansas City, Missouri 64106.

To Maddie and Emma.

I hope that this life becomes everything you'd ever imagined it could be.
No matter your plight, through your proudest and most victorious moments,
as well as through your most painful defeats, I'll be at your side
to lift you up, set you straight, and keep you going.

At least until I die. Then you're on your own.

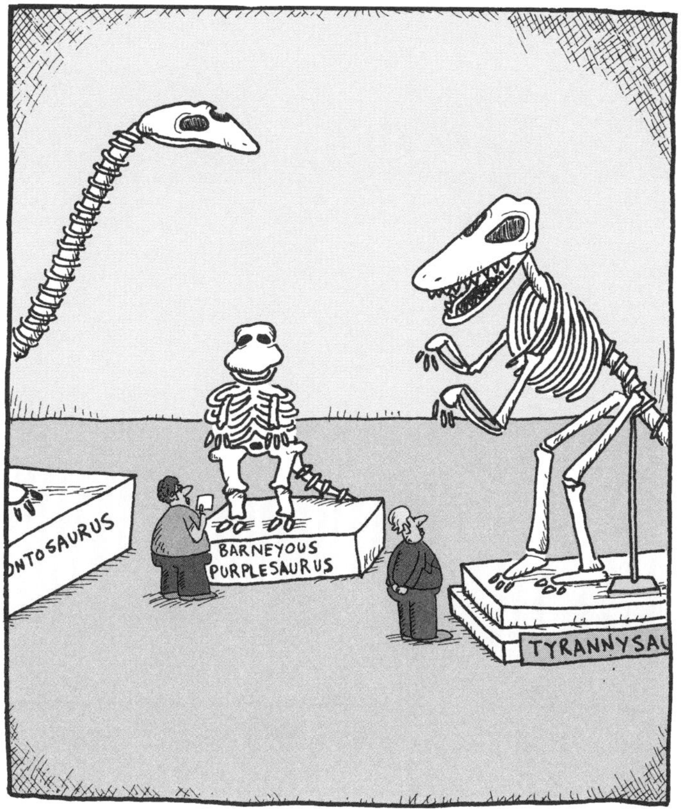
ONTOSAURUS
BARNEYOUS PURPLESAURUS
TYRANNYSAU

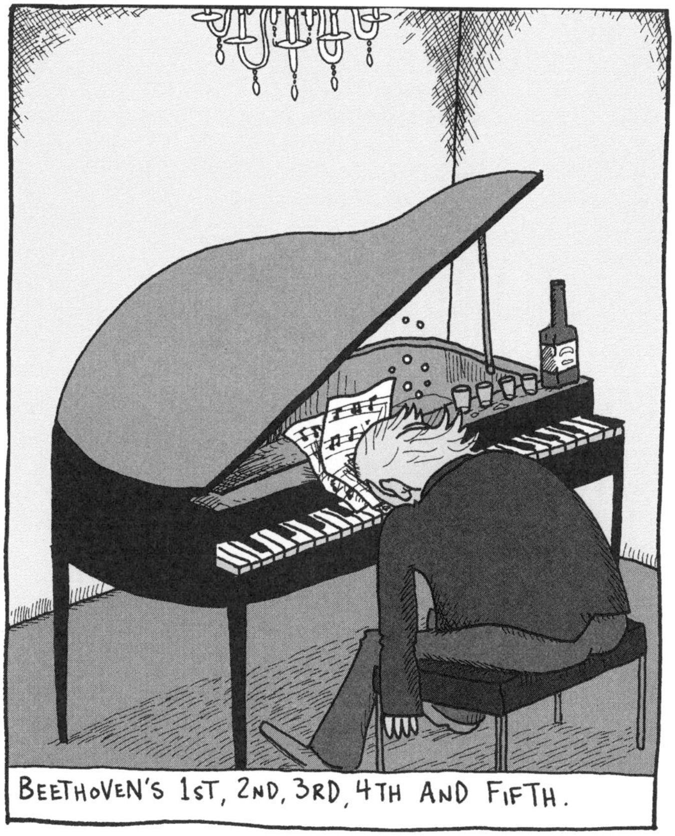
BEETHOVEN'S 1ST, 2ND, 3RD, 4TH AND FIFTH.

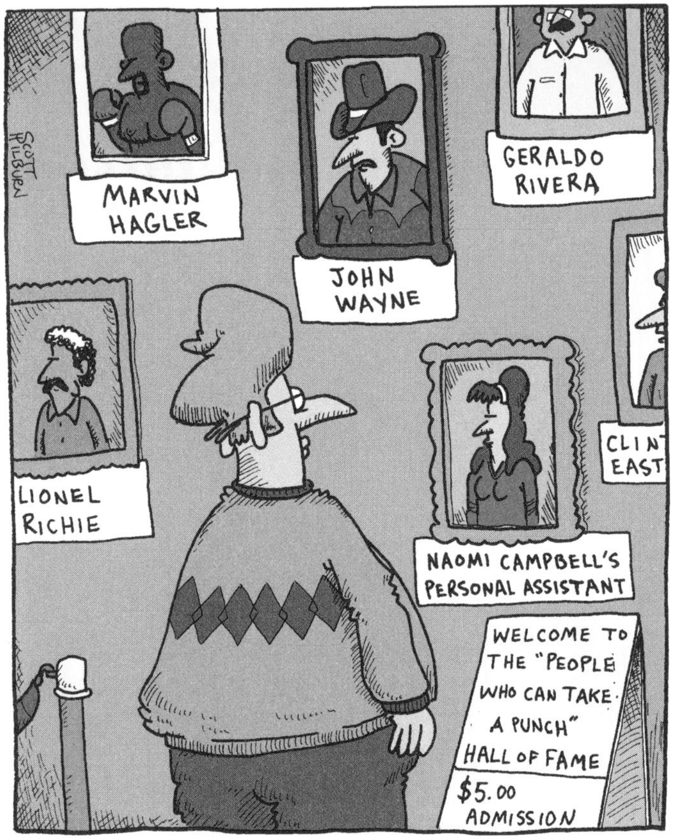
SCOTT HILBURN
MARVIN HAGLER
JOHN WAYNE
GERALDO RIVERA
LIONEL RICHIE
NAOMI CAMPBELL'S PERSONAL ASSISTANT
CLINT EAST
WELCOME TO THE "PEOPLE WHO CAN TAKE A PUNCH" HALL OF FAME
$5.00 ADMISSION

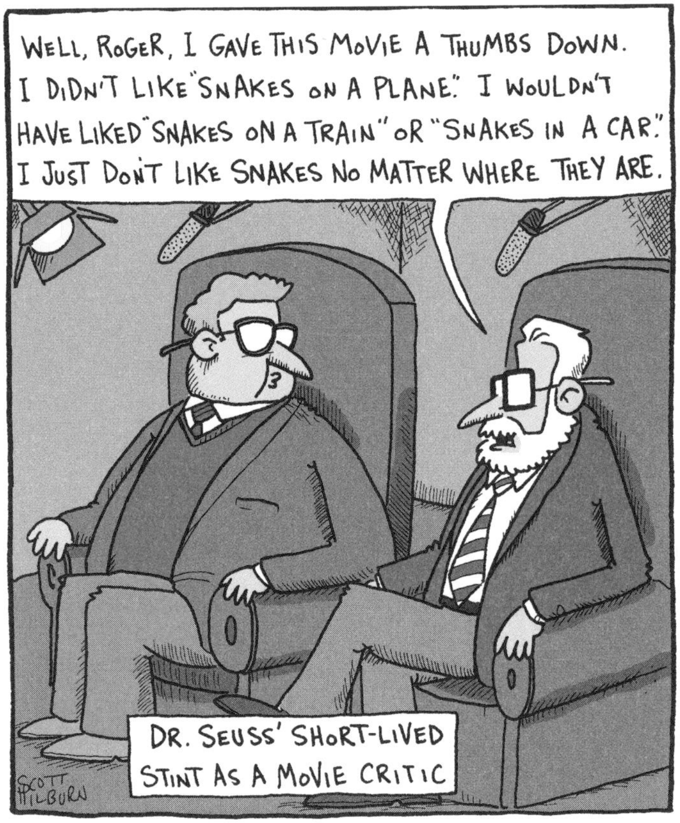
WELL, ROGER, I GAVE THIS MOVIE A THUMBS DOWN. I DIDN'T LIKE "SNAKES ON A PLANE." I WOULDN'T HAVE LIKED "SNAKES ON A TRAIN" OR "SNAKES IN A CAR." I JUST DON'T LIKE SNAKES NO MATTER WHERE THEY ARE.
DR. SEUSS' SHORT-LIVED STINT AS A MOVIE CRITIC
SCOTT HILBURN

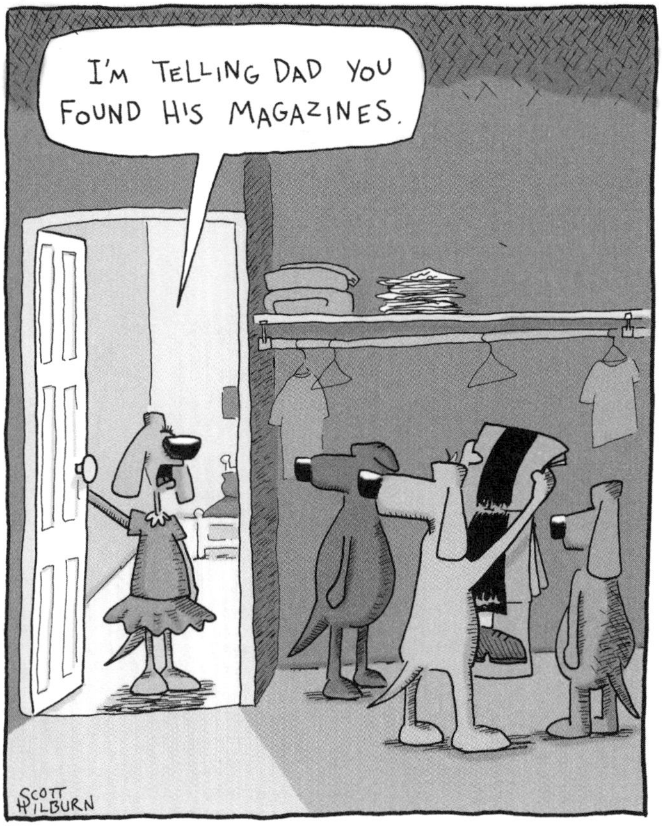
I'M TELLING DAD YOU FOUND HIS MAGAZINES.
SCOTT HILBURN

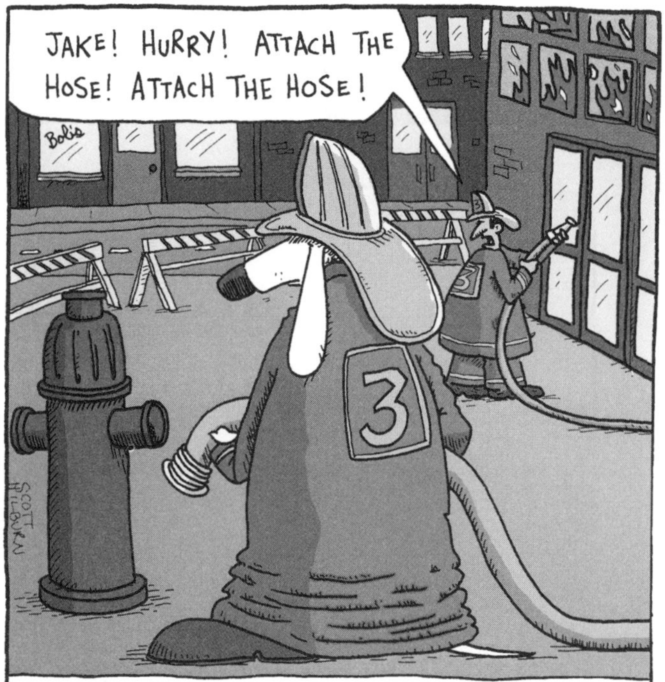
JAKE! HURRY! ATTACH THE HOSE! ATTACH THE HOSE!
Bob's
3
SCOTT HILBURN

JAKE IS TORN BETWEEN UPHOLDING HIS RESPONSIBILITY TO THE COMMUNITY AND SATISFYING HIS CANINE URGES.

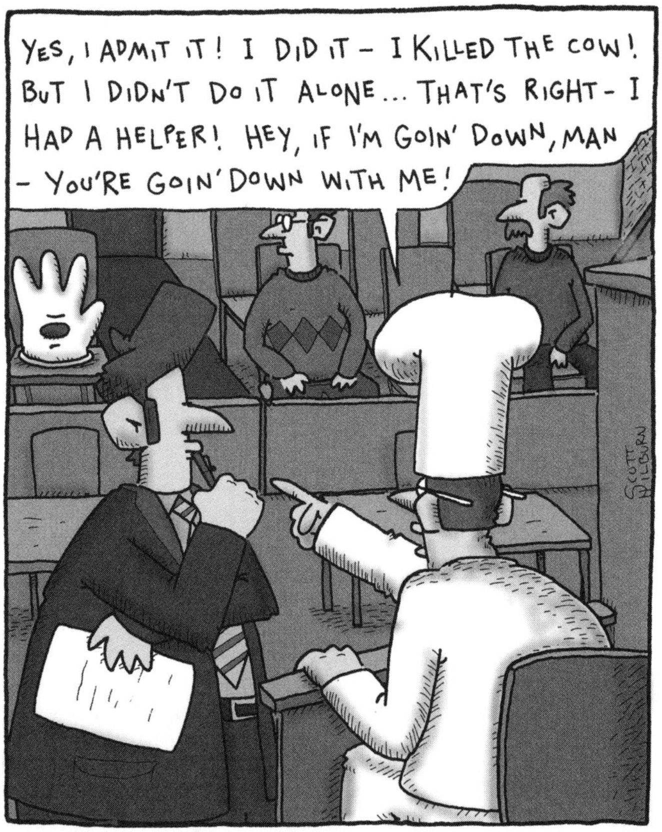
YES, I ADMIT IT! I DID IT – I KILLED THE COW! BUT I DIDN'T DO IT ALONE... THAT'S RIGHT – I HAD A HELPER! HEY, IF I'M GOIN' DOWN, MAN – YOU'RE GOIN' DOWN WITH ME!
SCOTT HILBURN

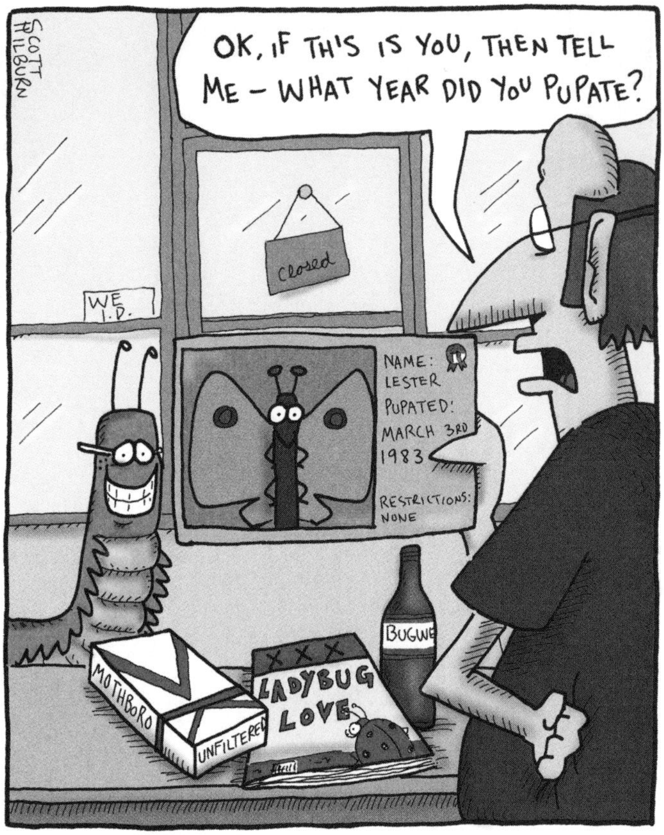
OK, IF THIS IS YOU, THEN TELL ME – WHAT YEAR DID YOU PUPATE?
SCOTT HILBURN
WE I.D.
Closed
NAME: LESTER
PUPATED: MARCH 3RD 1983
RESTRICTIONS: NONE
MOTHBORO
UNFILTERED
XXX
LADYBUG LOVE
BUGWE

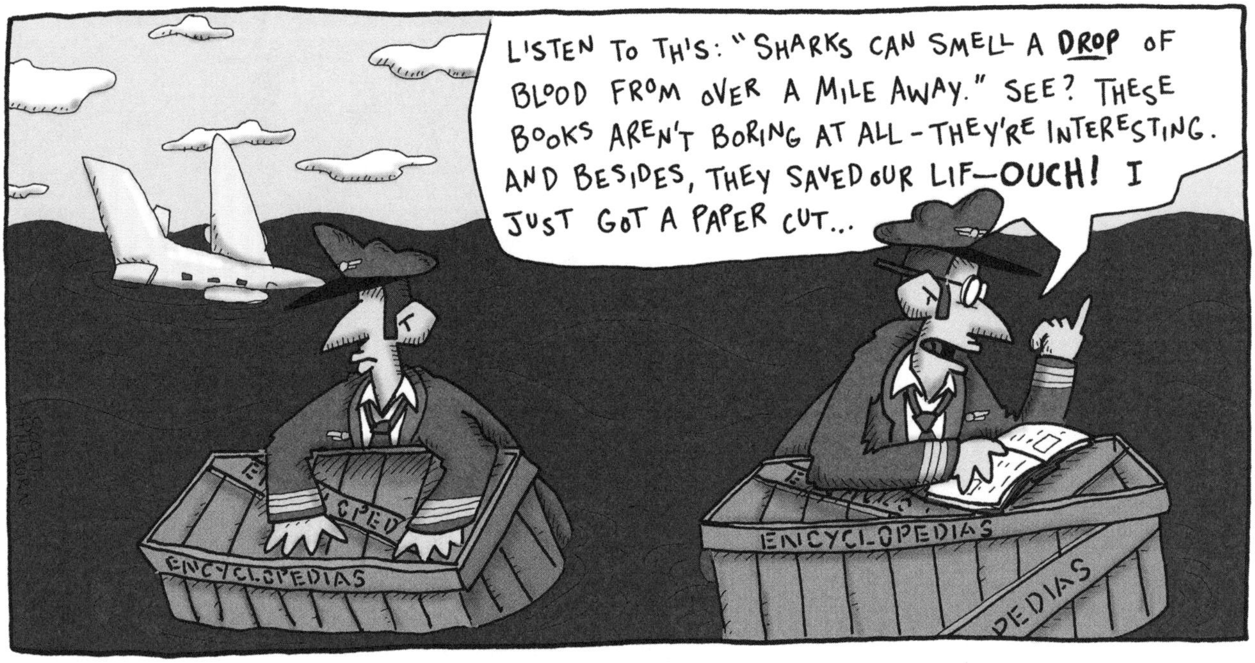
LISTEN TO THIS: "SHARKS CAN SMELL A DROP OF BLOOD FROM OVER A MILE AWAY." SEE? THESE BOOKS AREN'T BORING AT ALL – THEY'RE INTERESTING. AND BESIDES, THEY SAVED OUR LIF—OUCH! I JUST GOT A PAPER CUT...
ENCYCLOPEDIAS
ENCYCLOPEDIAS
PEDIAS

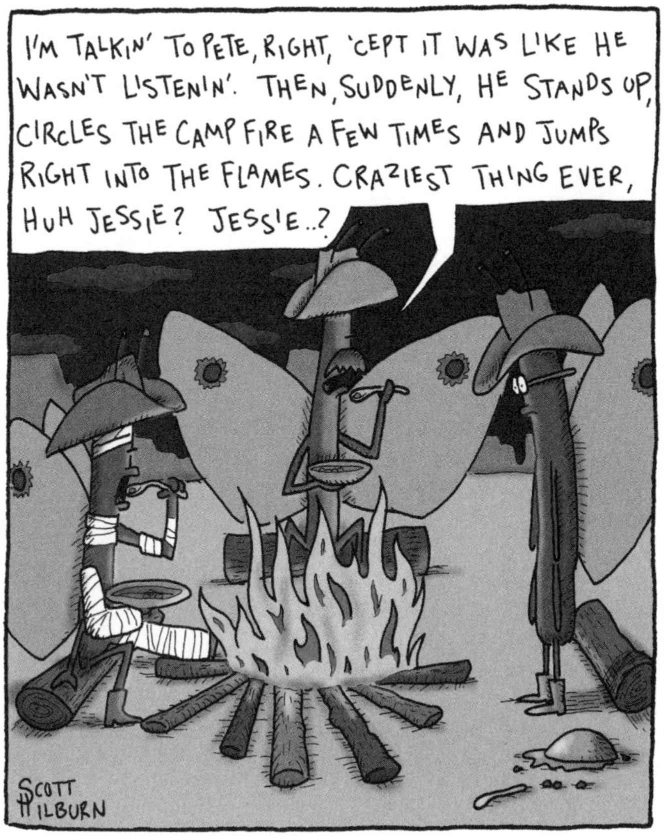
I'M TALKIN' TO PETE, RIGHT, 'CEPT IT WAS LIKE HE WASN'T LISTENIN'. THEN, SUDDENLY, HE STANDS UP, CIRCLES THE CAMPFIRE A FEW TIMES AND JUMPS RIGHT INTO THE FLAMES. CRAZIEST THING EVER, HUH JESSIE? JESSIE..?
SCOTT HILBURN

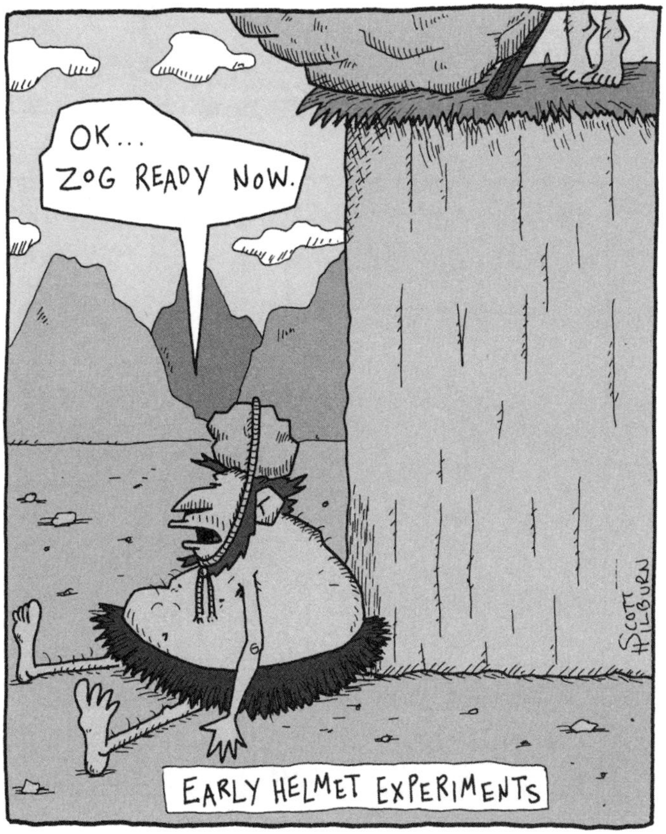
OK...
ZOG READY NOW.
SCOTT HILBURN
EARLY HELMET EXPERIMENTS

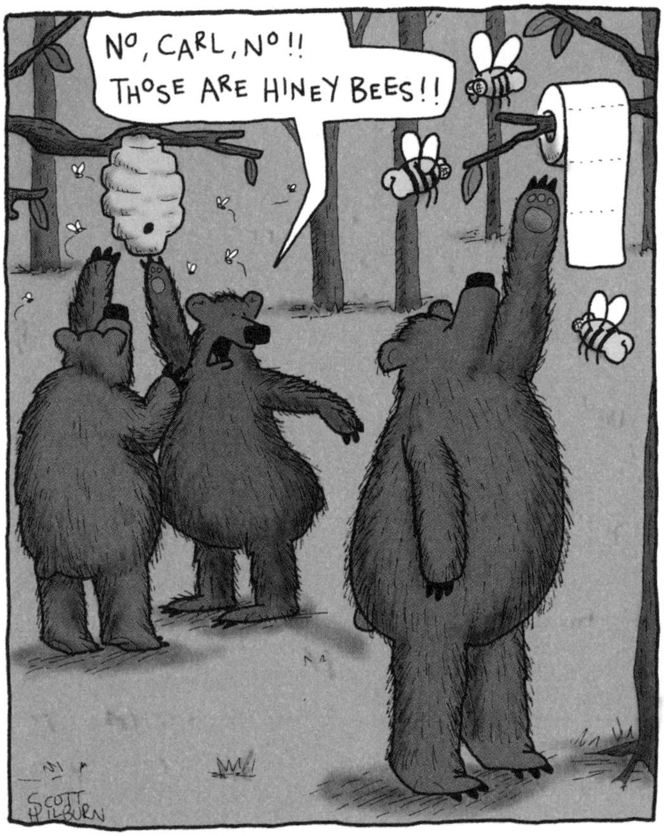
NO, CARL, NO!!
THOSE ARE HINEY BEES!!
SCOTT HILBURN

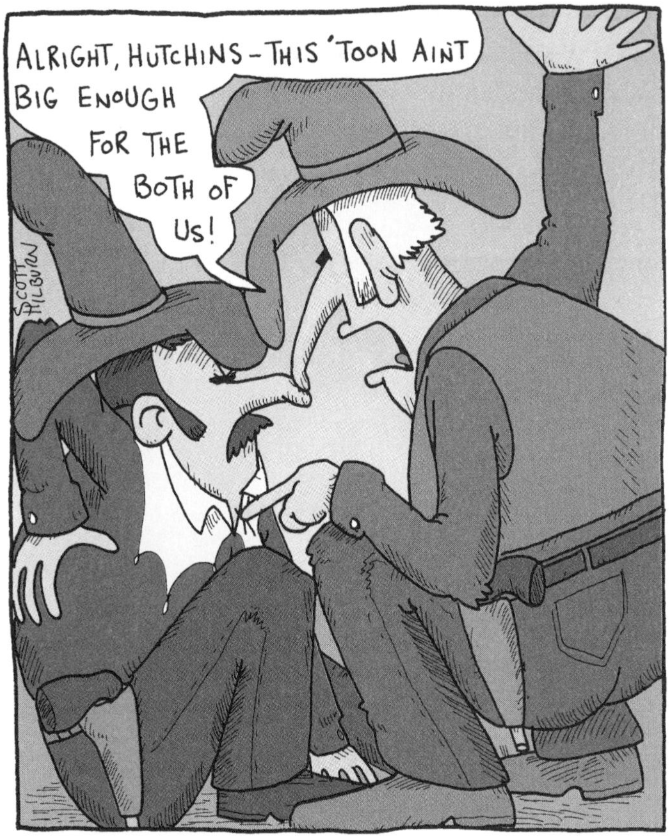
ALRIGHT, HUTCHINS – THIS 'TOON AINT BIG ENOUGH FOR THE BOTH OF US!
SCOTT HILBURN

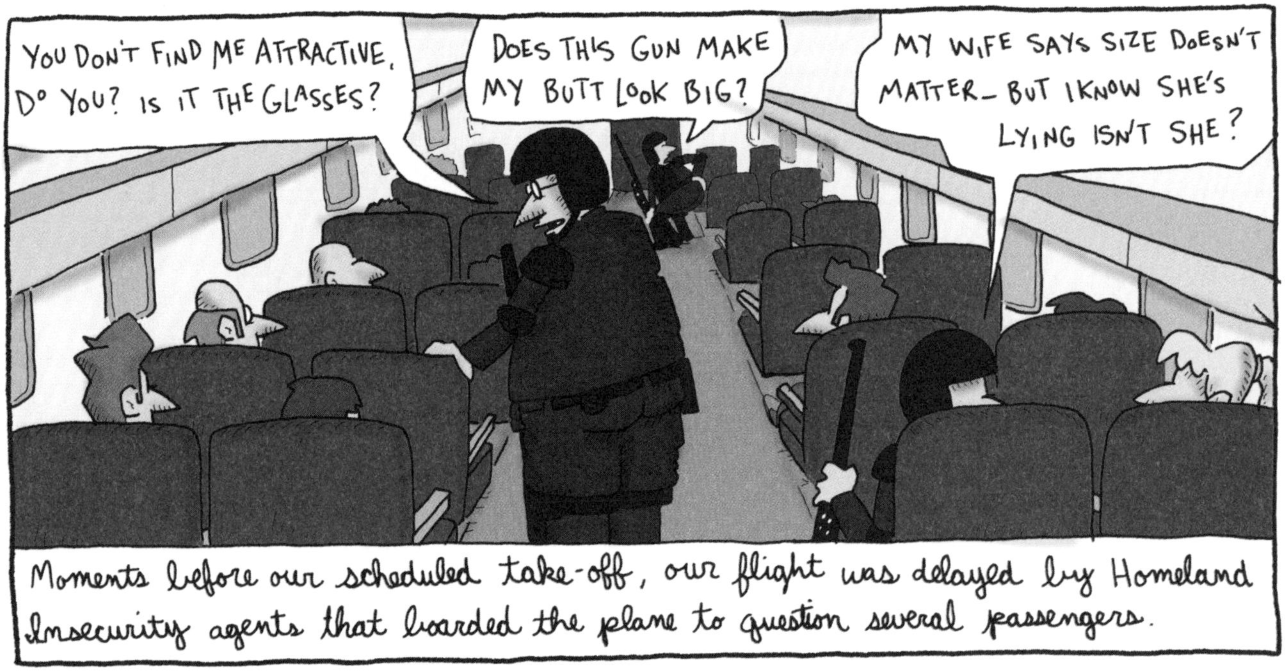
YOU DON'T FIND ME ATTRACTIVE, DO YOU? IS IT THE GLASSES?
DOES THIS GUN MAKE MY BUTT LOOK BIG?
MY WIFE SAYS SIZE DOESN'T MATTER – BUT I KNOW SHE'S LYING ISN'T SHE?
Moments before our scheduled take-off, our flight was delayed by Homeland Insecurity agents that boarded the plane to question several passengers.

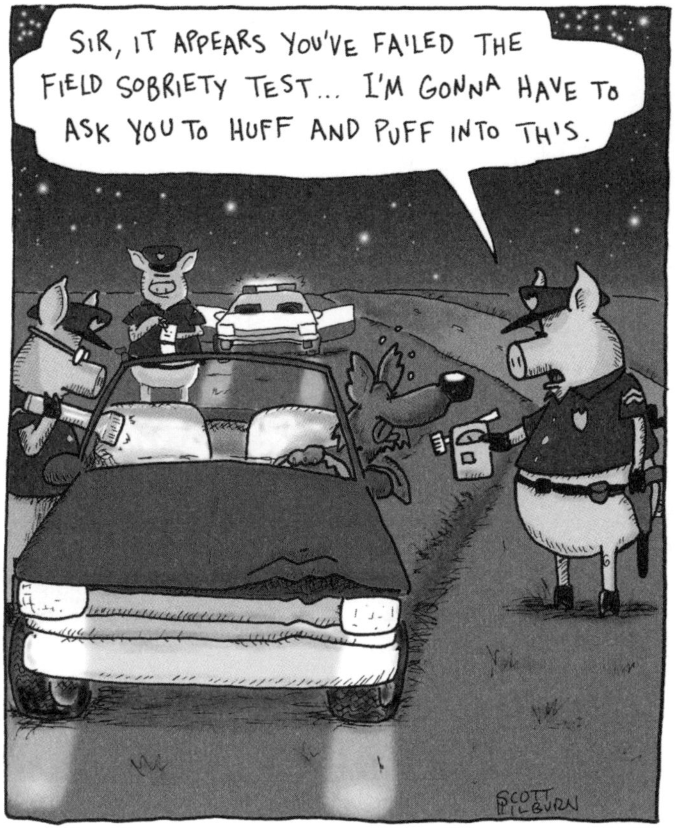
SIR, IT APPEARS YOU'VE FAILED THE FIELD SOBRIETY TEST... I'M GONNA HAVE TO ASK YOU TO HUFF AND PUFF INTO THIS.
SCOTT HILBURN

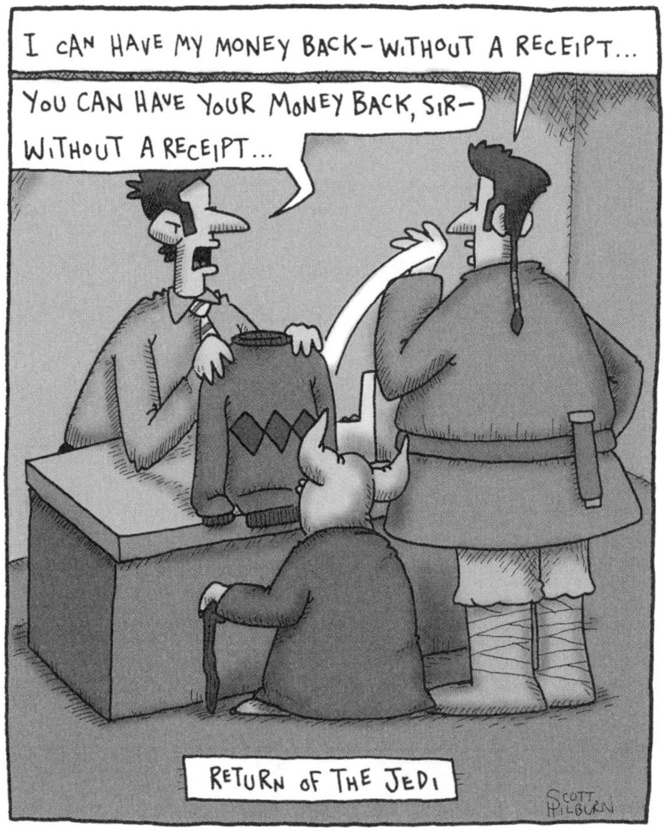
I CAN HAVE MY MONEY BACK- WITHOUT A RECEIPT...
YOU CAN HAVE YOUR MONEY BACK, SIR- WITHOUT A RECEIPT...
RETURN OF THE JEDI
SCOTT HILBURN

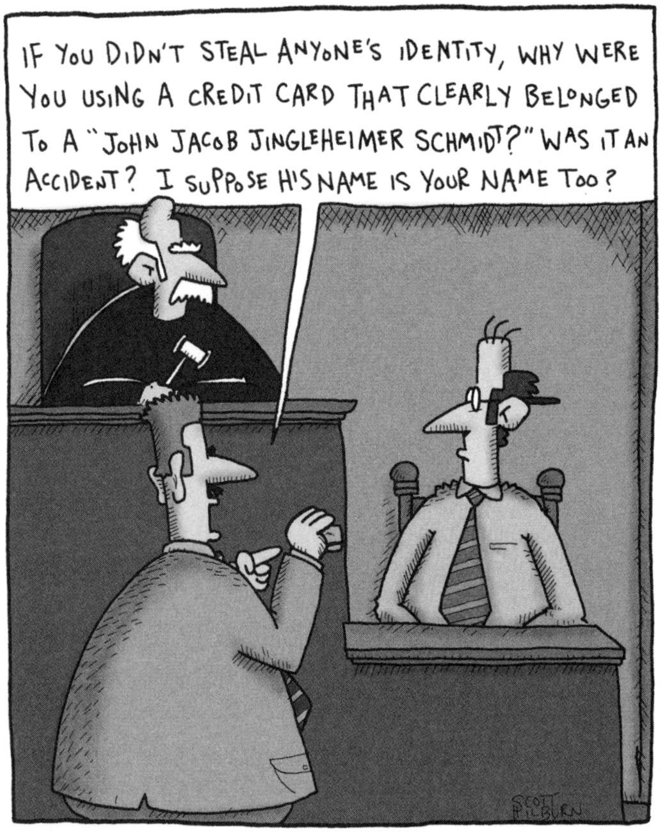
IF YOU DIDN'T STEAL ANYONE'S IDENTITY, WHY WERE YOU USING A CREDIT CARD THAT CLEARLY BELONGED TO A "JOHN JACOB JINGLEHEIMER SCHMIDT?" WAS IT AN ACCIDENT? I SUPPOSE HIS NAME IS YOUR NAME TOO?
SCOTT HILBURN

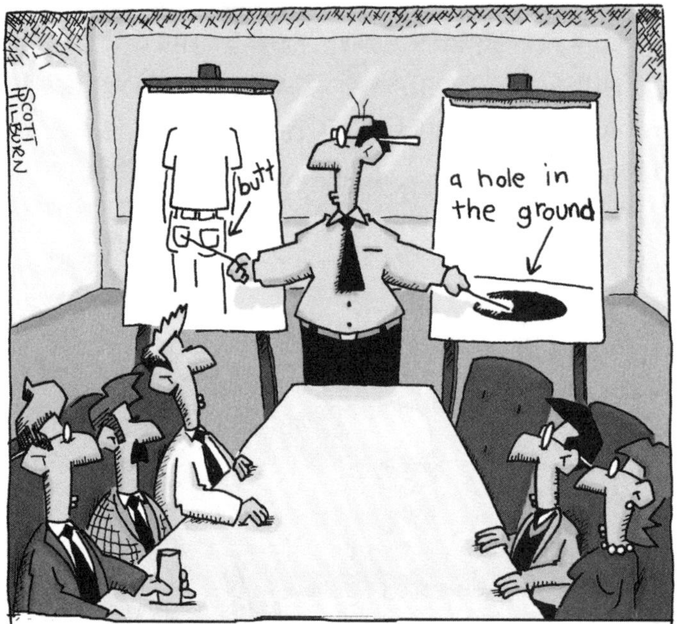
SCOTT HILBURN
butt
a hole in the ground

TAKING ADVANTAGE OF THE COMPANY'S "OPEN DOOR POLICY," ELTON PROVIDES THE COMPANY BRASS WITH <u>HIS</u> ASSESSMENT OF <u>THEIR</u> PERFORMANCE.

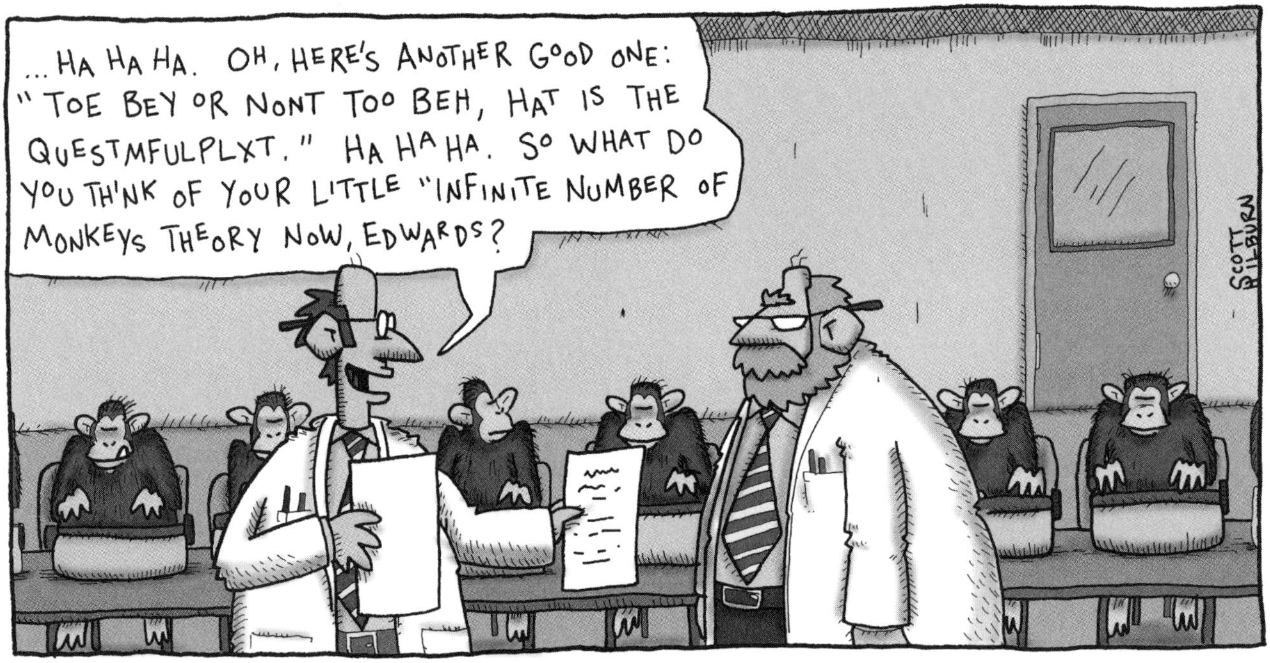
...HA HA HA. OH, HERE'S ANOTHER GOOD ONE: "TOE BEY OR NONT TOO BEH, HAT IS THE QUESTMFULPLXT." HA HA HA. SO WHAT DO YOU THINK OF YOUR LITTLE "INFINITE NUMBER OF MONKEYS THEORY NOW, EDWARDS?
SCOTT HILBURN

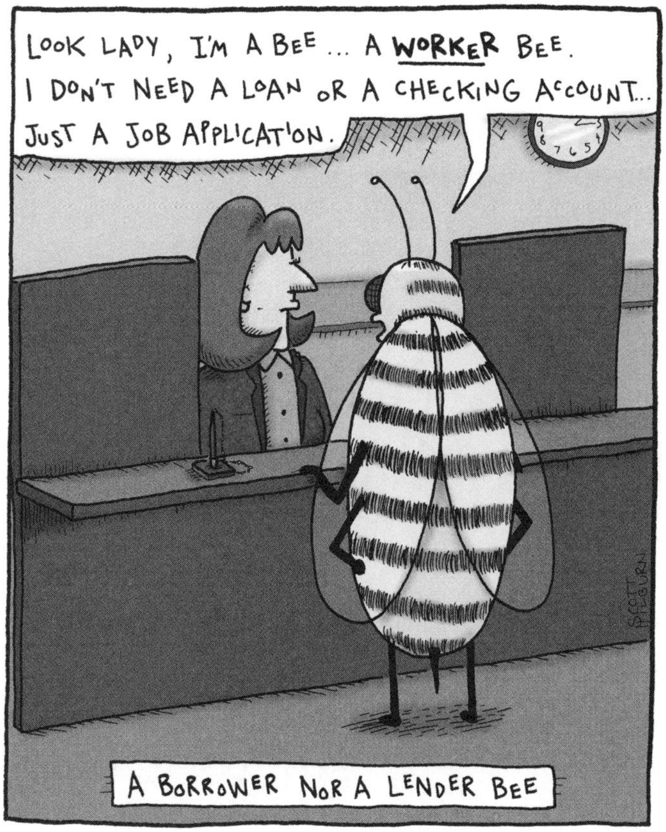
LOOK LADY, I'M A BEE ... A WORKER BEE.
I DON'T NEED A LOAN OR A CHECKING ACCOUNT...
JUST A JOB APPLICATION.
SCOTT HILBURN
A BORROWER NOR A LENDER BEE

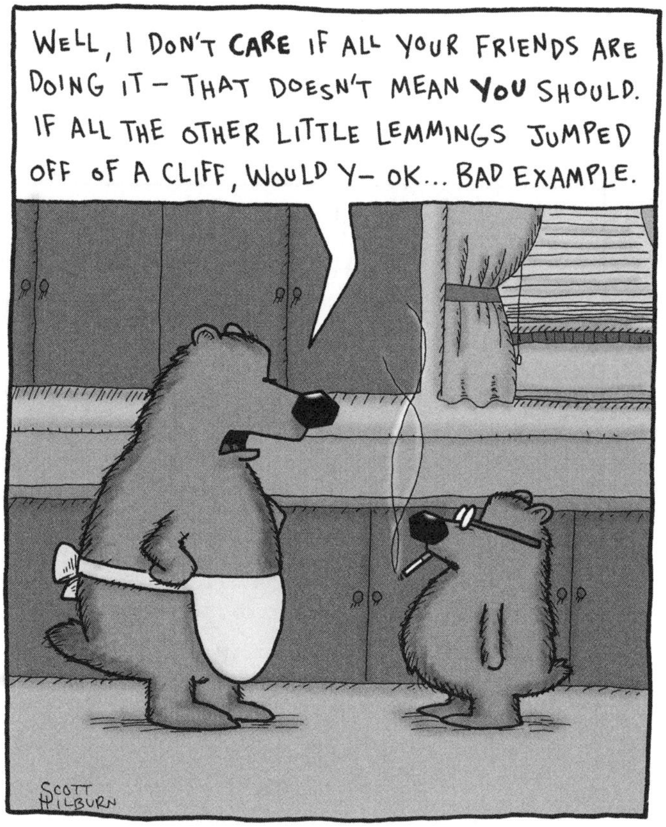
WELL, I DON'T CARE IF ALL YOUR FRIENDS ARE DOING IT – THAT DOESN'T MEAN YOU SHOULD. IF ALL THE OTHER LITTLE LEMMINGS JUMPED OFF OF A CLIFF, WOULD Y– OK... BAD EXAMPLE.
SCOTT HILBURN

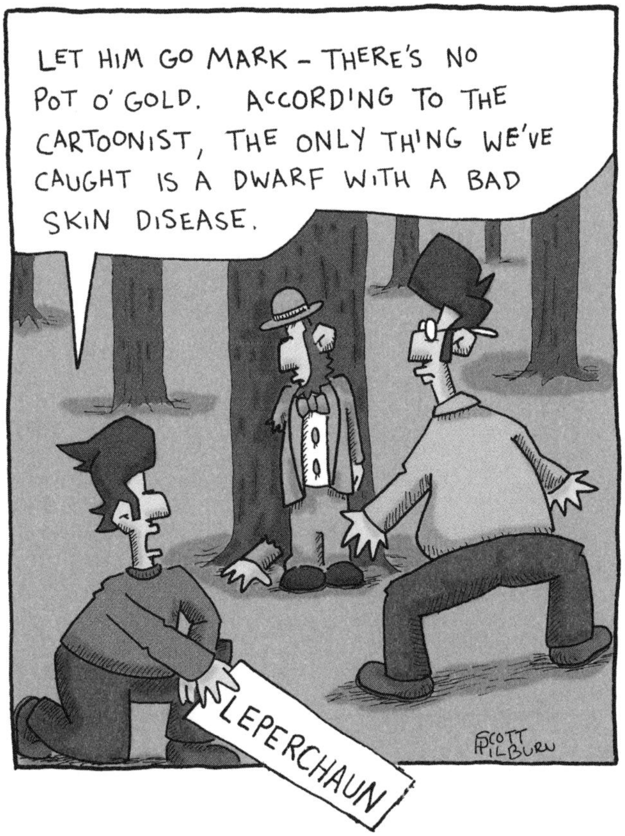
LET HIM GO MARK - THERE'S NO POT O' GOLD. ACCORDING TO THE CARTOONIST, THE ONLY THING WE'VE CAUGHT IS A DWARF WITH A BAD SKIN DISEASE.
LEPERCHAUN
SCOTT HILBURN

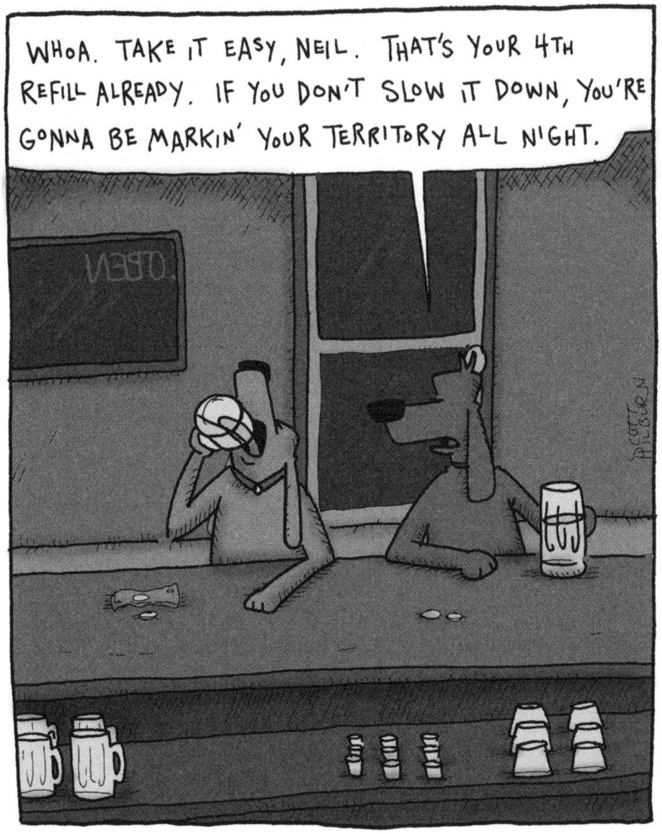
WHOA. TAKE IT EASY, NEIL. THAT'S YOUR 4TH REFILL ALREADY. IF YOU DON'T SLOW IT DOWN, YOU'RE GONNA BE MARKIN' YOUR TERRITORY ALL NIGHT.
OPEN
SCOTT HILBURN

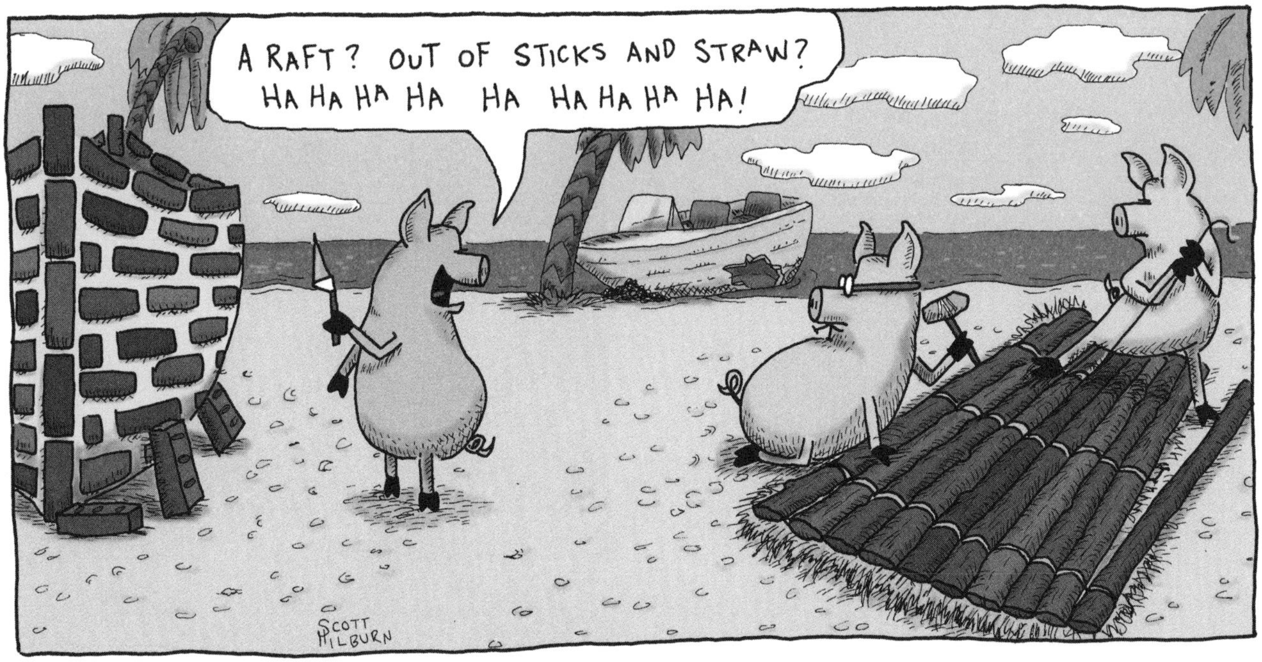
A RAFT? OUT OF STICKS AND STRAW? HA HA HA HA HA HA HA HA HA!
SCOTT HILBURN

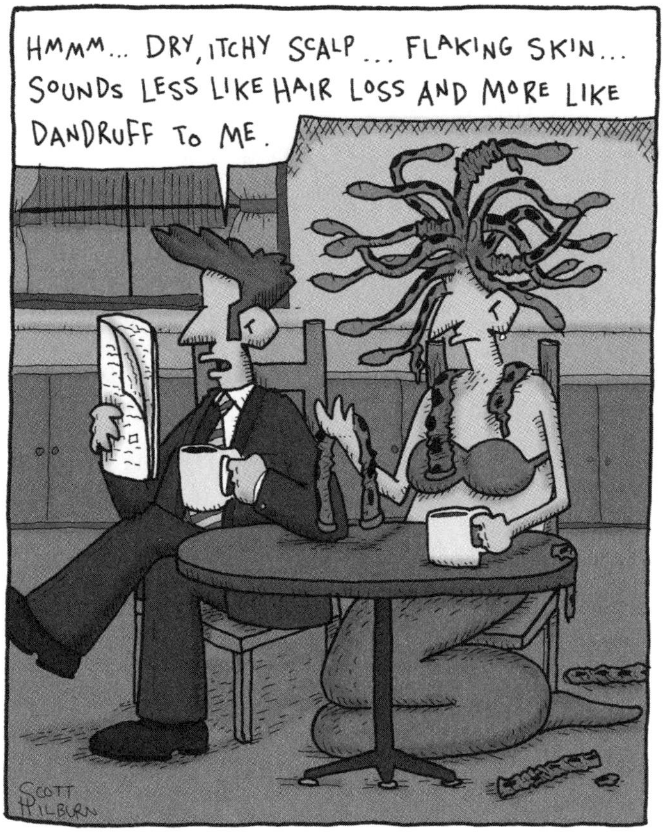
HMMM... DRY, ITCHY SCALP... FLAKING SKIN... SOUNDS LESS LIKE HAIR LOSS AND MORE LIKE DANDRUFF TO ME.
SCOTT HILBURN

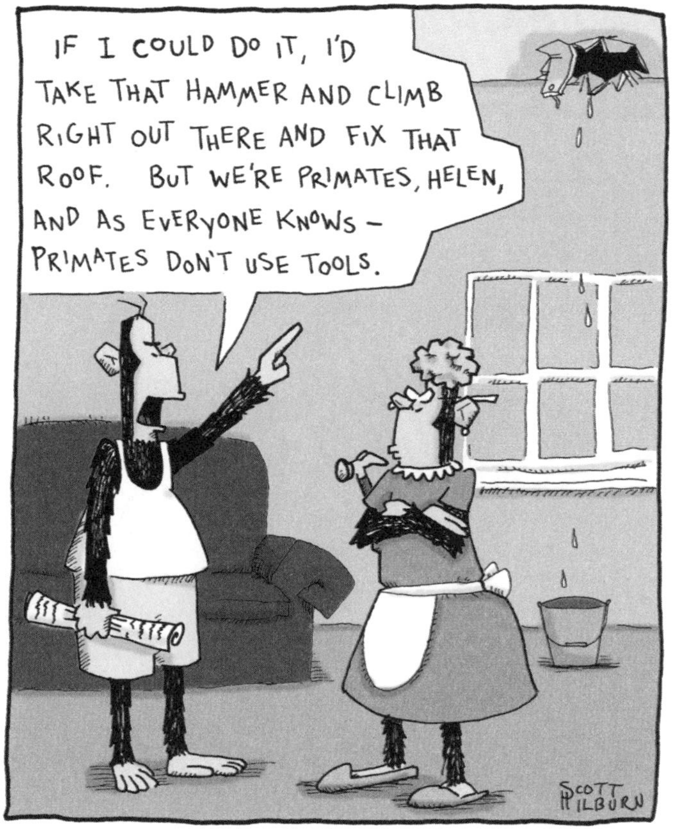
IF I COULD DO IT, I'D TAKE THAT HAMMER AND CLIMB RIGHT OUT THERE AND FIX THAT ROOF. BUT WE'RE PRIMATES, HELEN, AND AS EVERYONE KNOWS – PRIMATES DON'T USE TOOLS.
SCOTT HILBURN

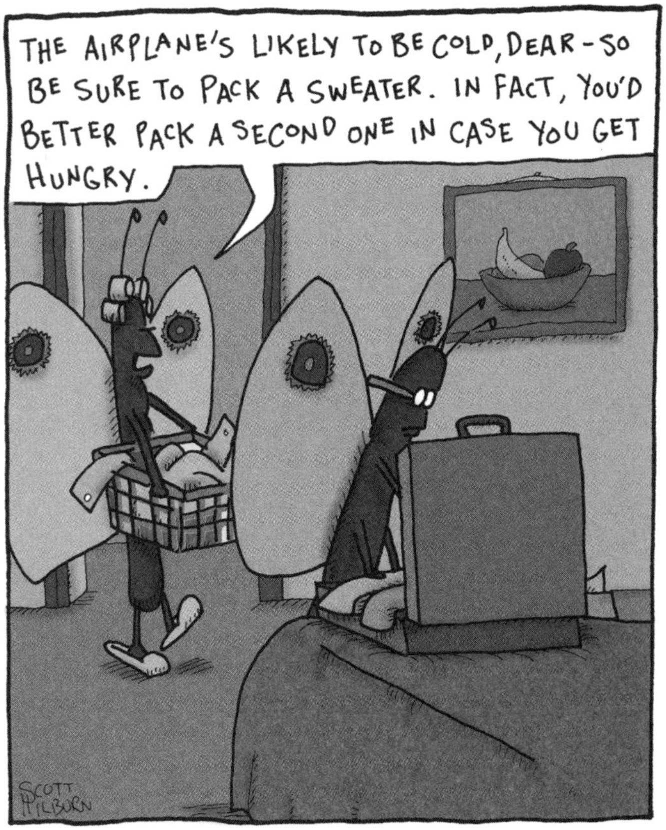
THE AIRPLANE'S LIKELY TO BE COLD, DEAR - SO BE SURE TO PACK A SWEATER. IN FACT, YOU'D BETTER PACK A SECOND ONE IN CASE YOU GET HUNGRY.
SCOTT HILBURN

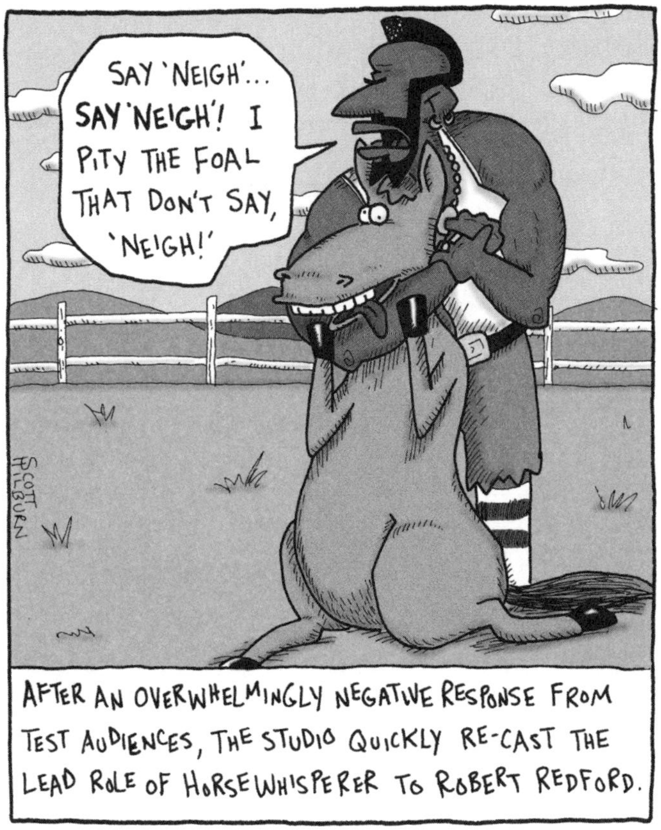
SAY 'NEIGH'... SAY 'NEIGH'! I PITY THE FOAL THAT DON'T SAY, 'NEIGH!'
SCOTT HILBURN
AFTER AN OVERWHELMINGLY NEGATIVE RESPONSE FROM TEST AUDIENCES, THE STUDIO QUICKLY RE-CAST THE LEAD ROLE OF HORSEWHISPERER TO ROBERT REDFORD.

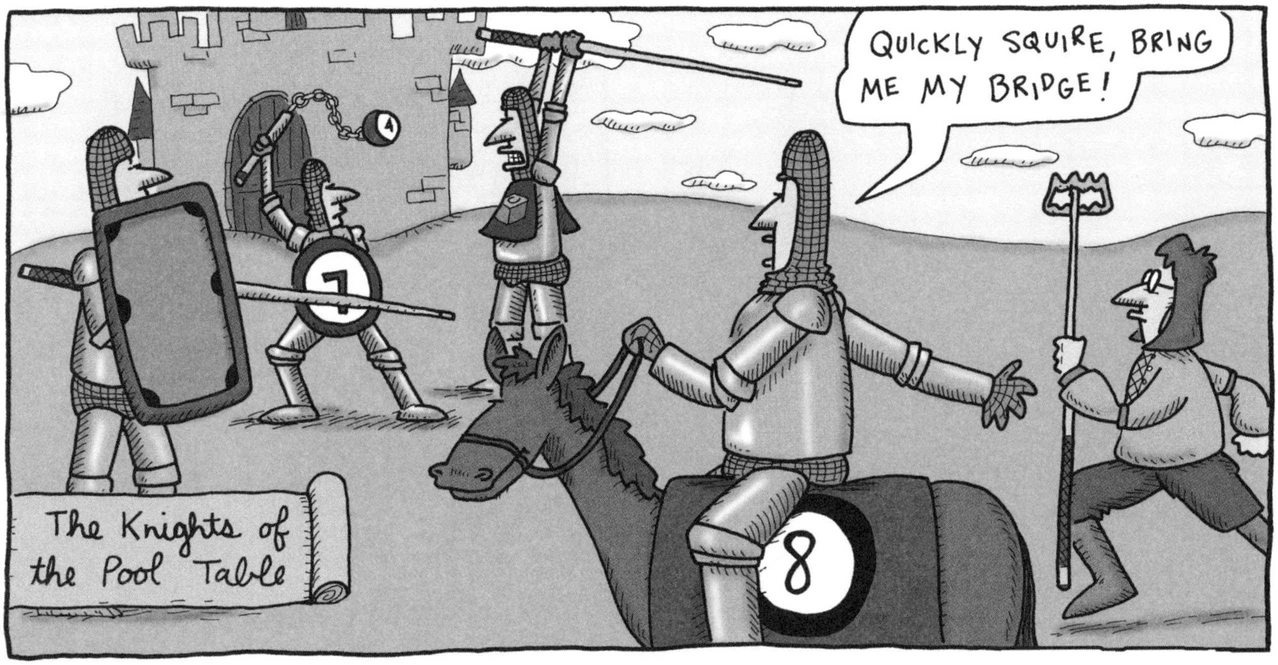
QUICKLY SQUIRE, BRING ME MY BRIDGE!
The Knights of the Pool Table

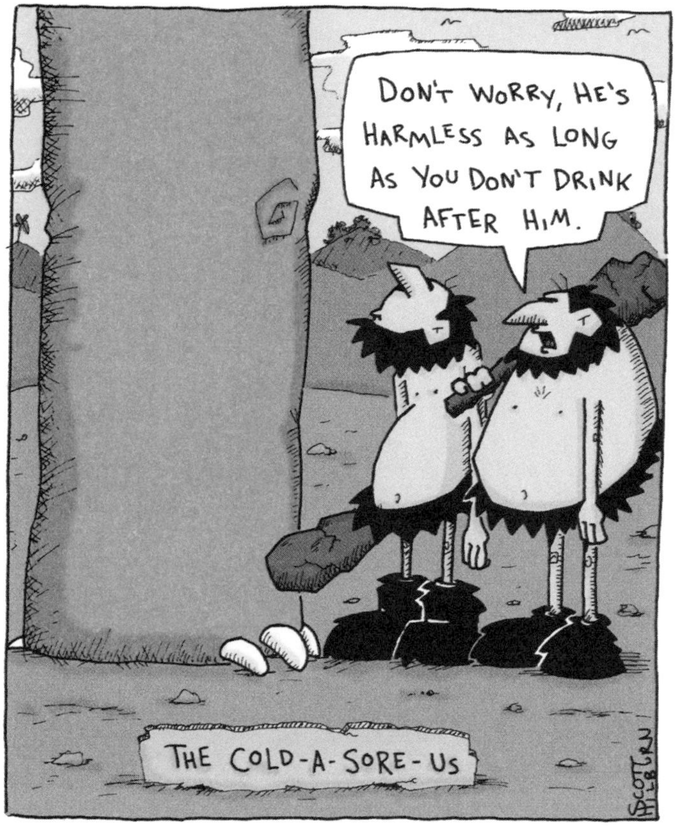
DON'T WORRY, HE'S HARMLESS AS LONG AS YOU DON'T DRINK AFTER HIM.
THE COLD-A-SORE-US
SCOTT HILBURN

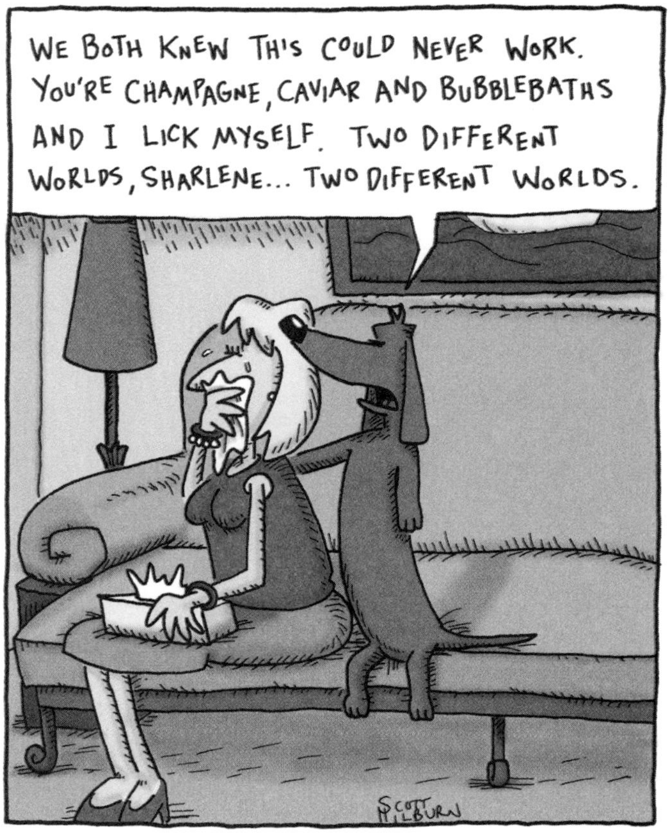
WE BOTH KNEW THIS COULD NEVER WORK. YOU'RE CHAMPAGNE, CAVIAR AND BUBBLEBATHS AND I LICK MYSELF. TWO DIFFERENT WORLDS, SHARLENE... TWO DIFFERENT WORLDS.
SCOTT HILBURN

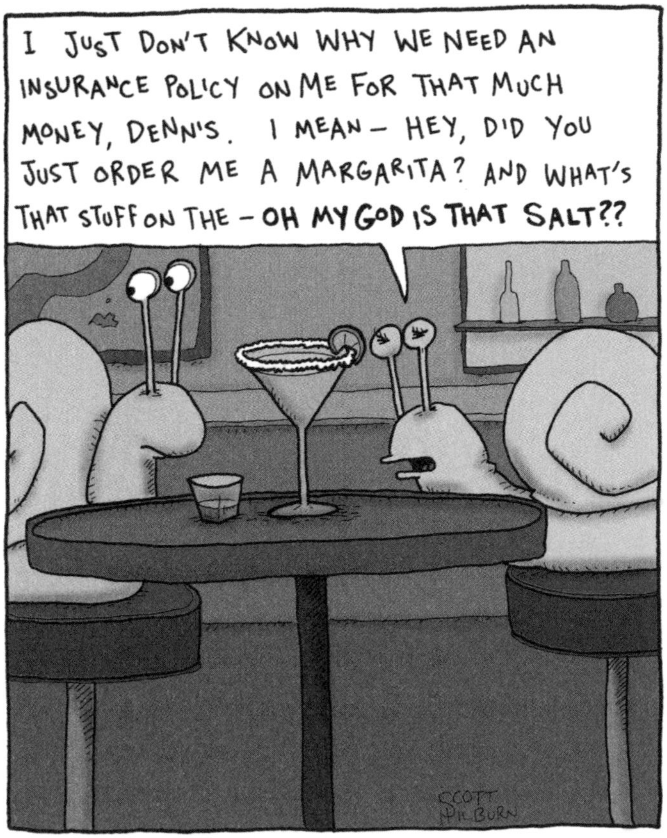
I JUST DON'T KNOW WHY WE NEED AN INSURANCE POLICY ON ME FOR THAT MUCH MONEY, DENNIS. I MEAN – HEY, DID YOU JUST ORDER ME A MARGARITA? AND WHAT'S THAT STUFF ON THE – **OH MY GOD IS THAT SALT??**
SCOTT HILBURN

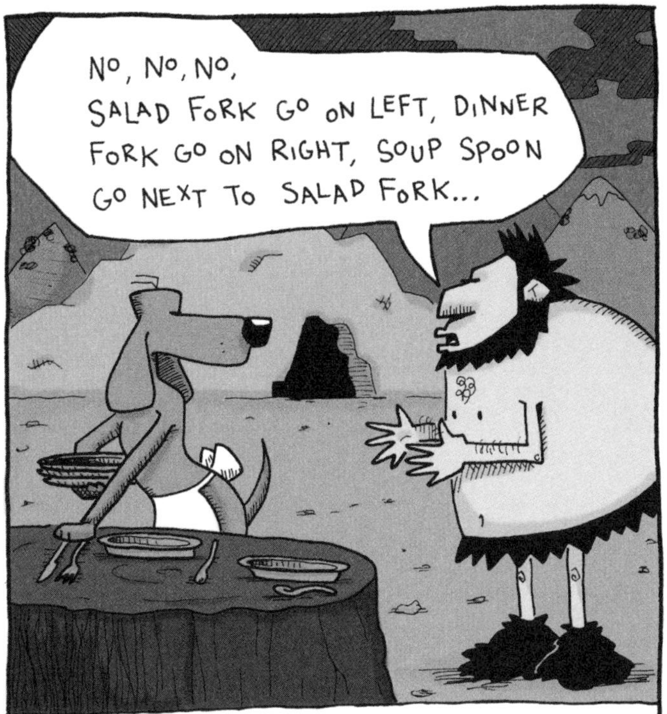
NO, NO, NO,
SALAD FORK GO ON LEFT, DINNER FORK GO ON RIGHT, SOUP SPOON GO NEXT TO SALAD FORK...
SCOTT HILBURN

EARLY DOMESTICATION OF THE CANINE

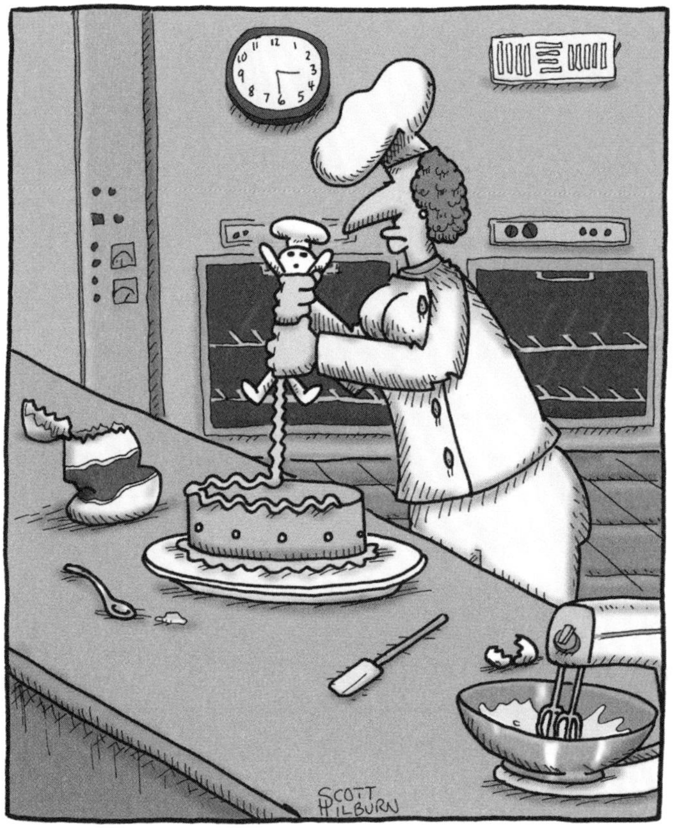
SCOTT HILBURN

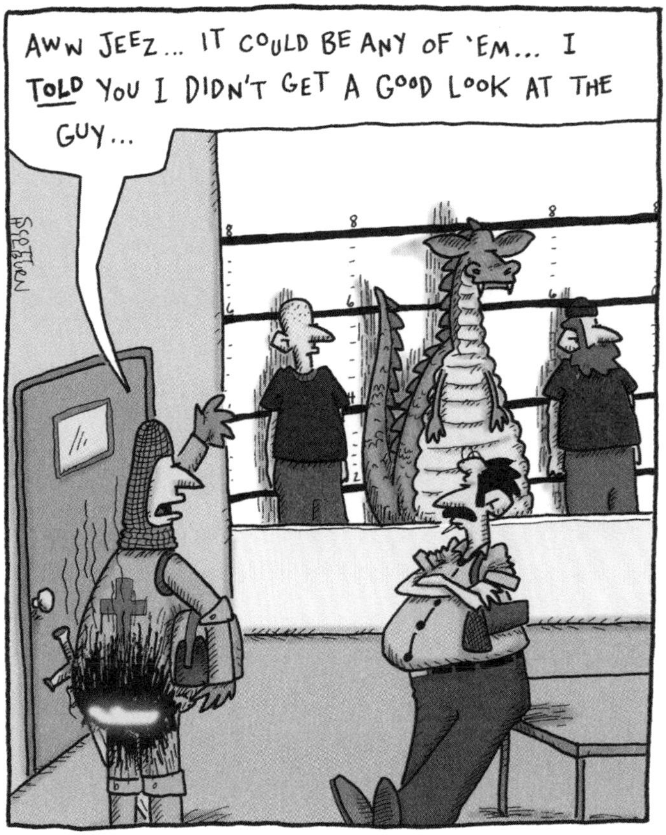
AWW JEEZ... IT COULD BE ANY OF 'EM... I TOLD YOU I DIDN'T GET A GOOD LOOK AT THE GUY...
SCOTT HILBURN

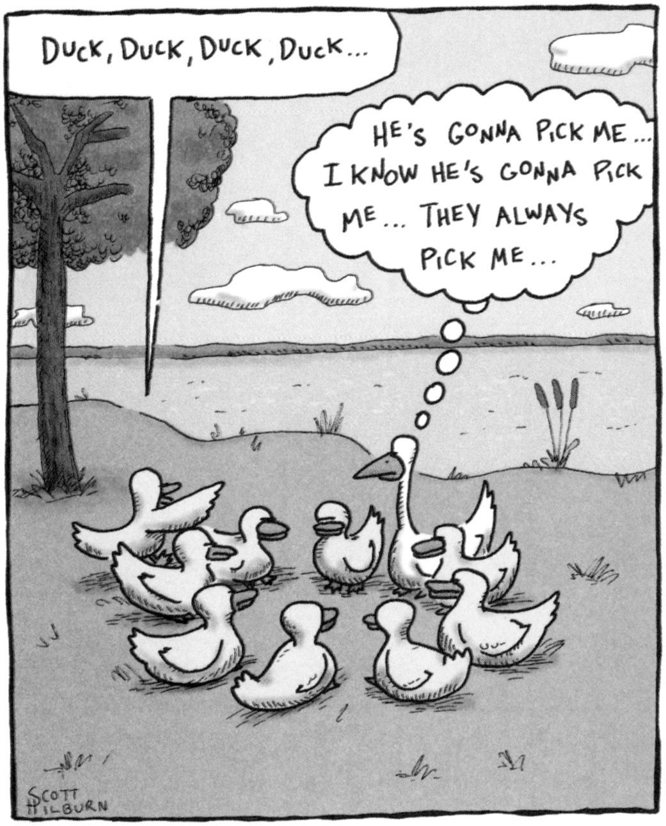
DUCK, DUCK, DUCK, DUCK...
HE'S GONNA PICK ME... I KNOW HE'S GONNA PICK ME... THEY ALWAYS PICK ME...
SCOTT HILBURN

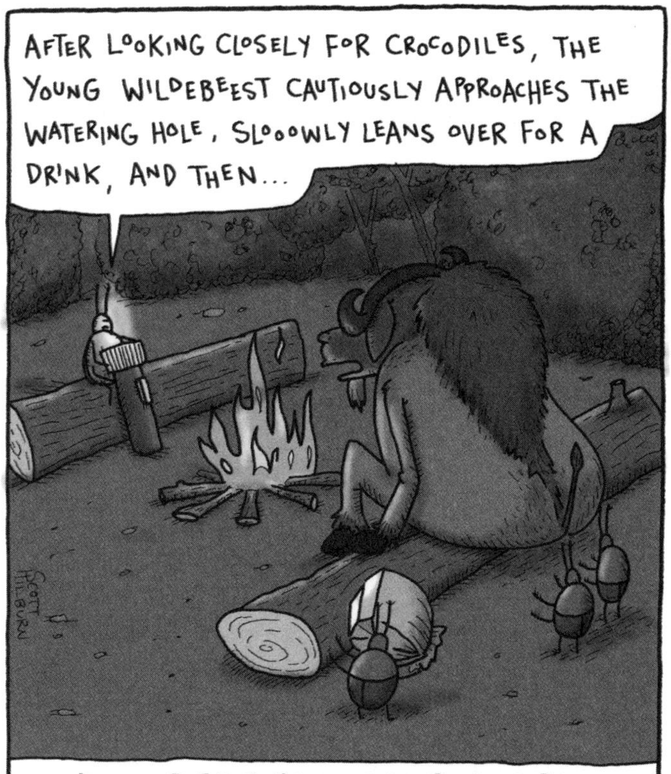
AFTER LOOKING CLOSELY FOR CROCODILES, THE YOUNG WILDEBEEST CAUTIOUSLY APPROACHES THE WATERING HOLE, SLOOOWLY LEANS OVER FOR A DRINK, AND THEN...
SCOTT HILBURN

DUNG BEETLE HARVESTING STRATEGIES

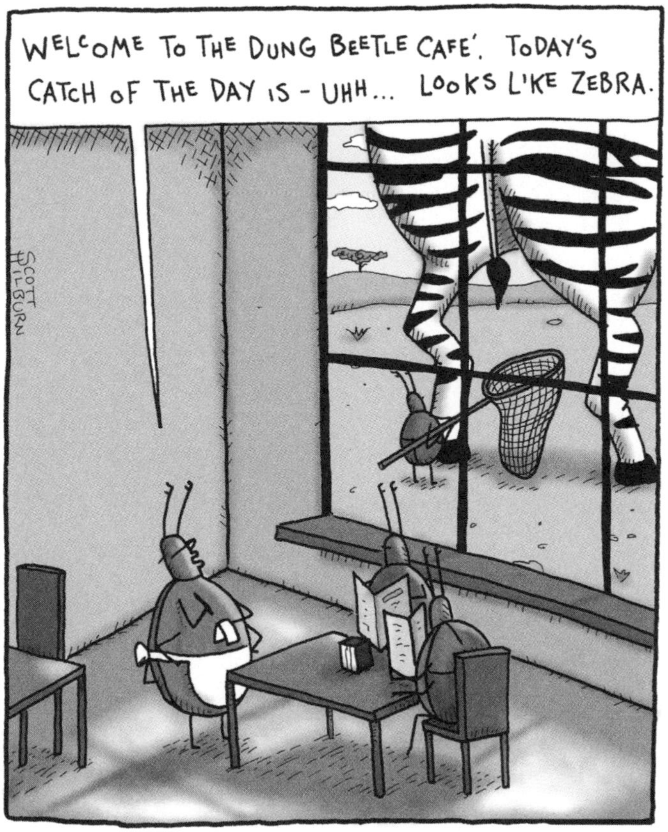
WELCOME TO THE DUNG BEETLE CAFE'. TODAY'S CATCH OF THE DAY IS - UHH... LOOKS LIKE ZEBRA.
SCOTT HILBURN

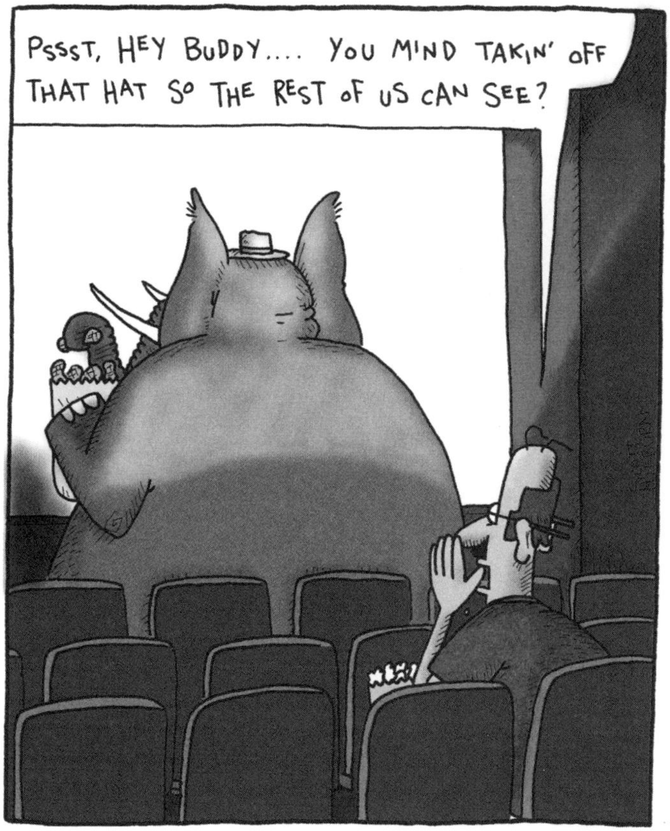
PSSST, HEY BUDDY.... YOU MIND TAKIN' OFF THAT HAT SO THE REST OF US CAN SEE?

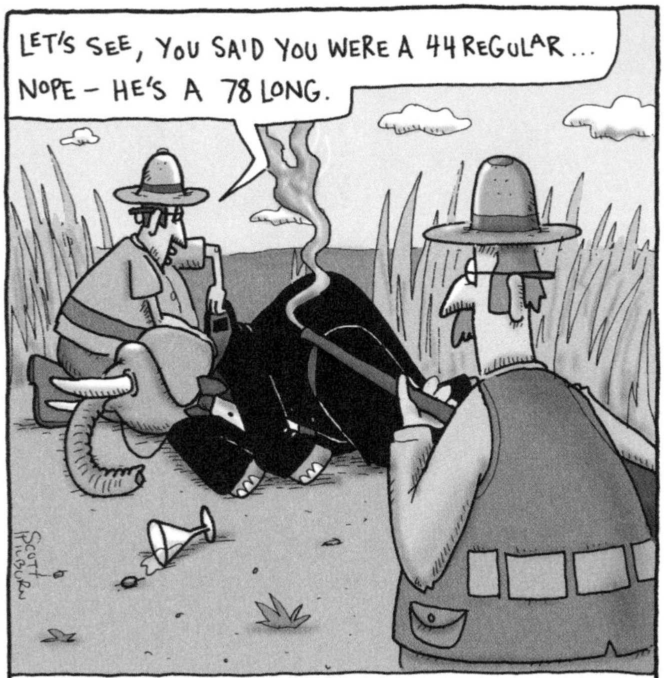
LET'S SEE, YOU SAID YOU WERE A 44 REGULAR...
NOPE – HE'S A 78 LONG.
SCOTT HILBURN

BEFORE THERE WERE LAWS IN PLACE TO PREVENT IT, IT WASN'T UNCOMMON FOR HUNTERS TO TRACK AND KILL WILD ELEPHANTS FOR THEIR TUX.

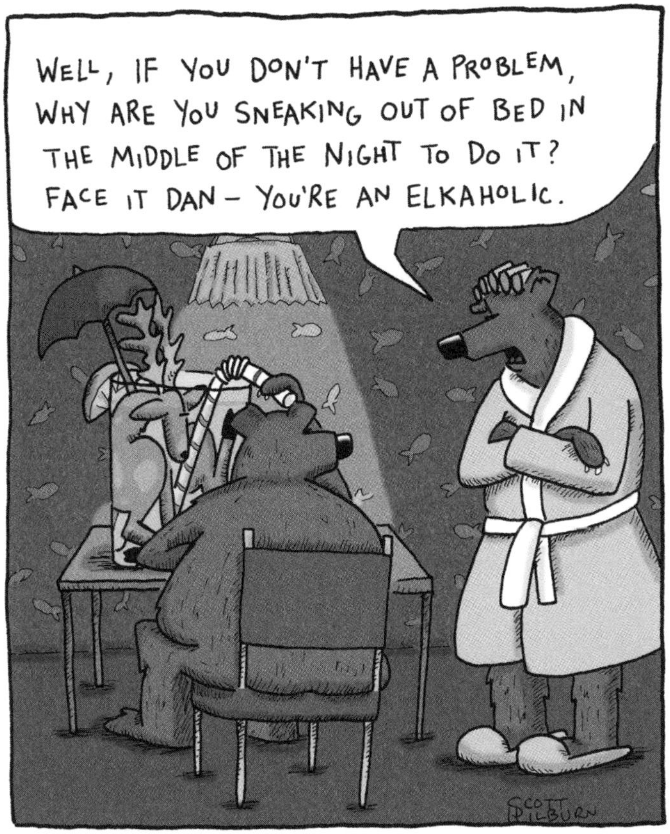
WELL, IF YOU DON'T HAVE A PROBLEM, WHY ARE YOU SNEAKING OUT OF BED IN THE MIDDLE OF THE NIGHT TO DO IT? FACE IT DAN – YOU'RE AN ELKAHOLIC.
SCOTT HILBURN

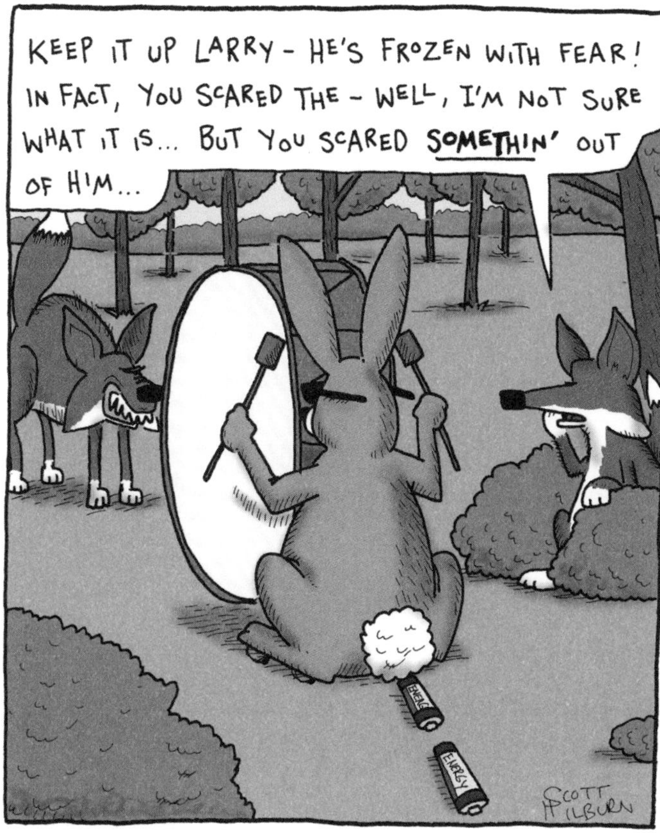
KEEP IT UP LARRY - HE'S FROZEN WITH FEAR! IN FACT, YOU SCARED THE - WELL, I'M NOT SURE WHAT IT IS... BUT YOU SCARED SOMETHIN' OUT OF HIM...
ENERGY
SCOTT HILBURN

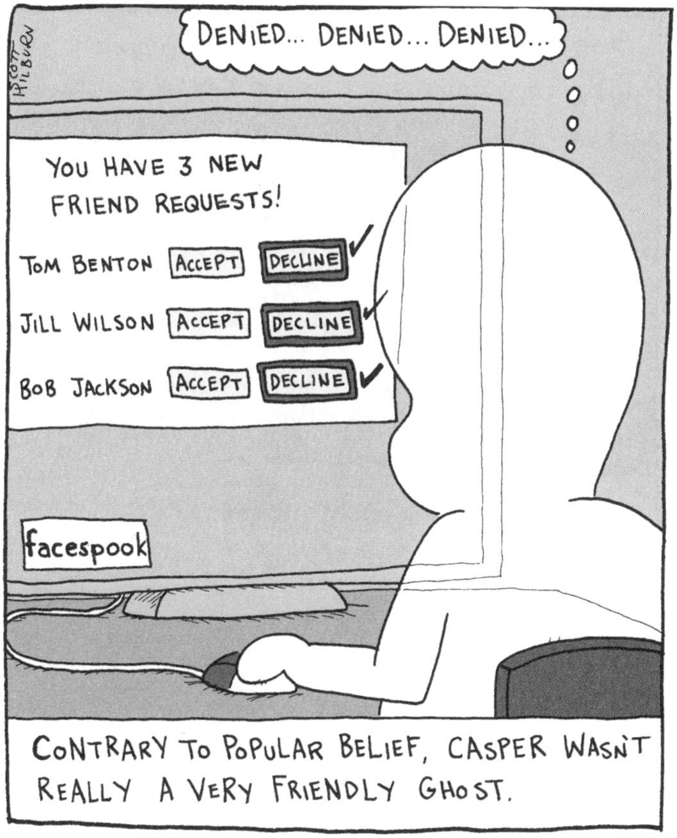
DENIED... DENIED... DENIED...
YOU HAVE 3 NEW FRIEND REQUESTS!
TOM BENTON ACCEPT DECLINE
JILL WILSON ACCEPT DECLINE
BOB JACKSON ACCEPT DECLINE
facespook
SCOTT HILBURN
CONTRARY TO POPULAR BELIEF, CASPER WASN'T REALLY A VERY FRIENDLY GHOST.

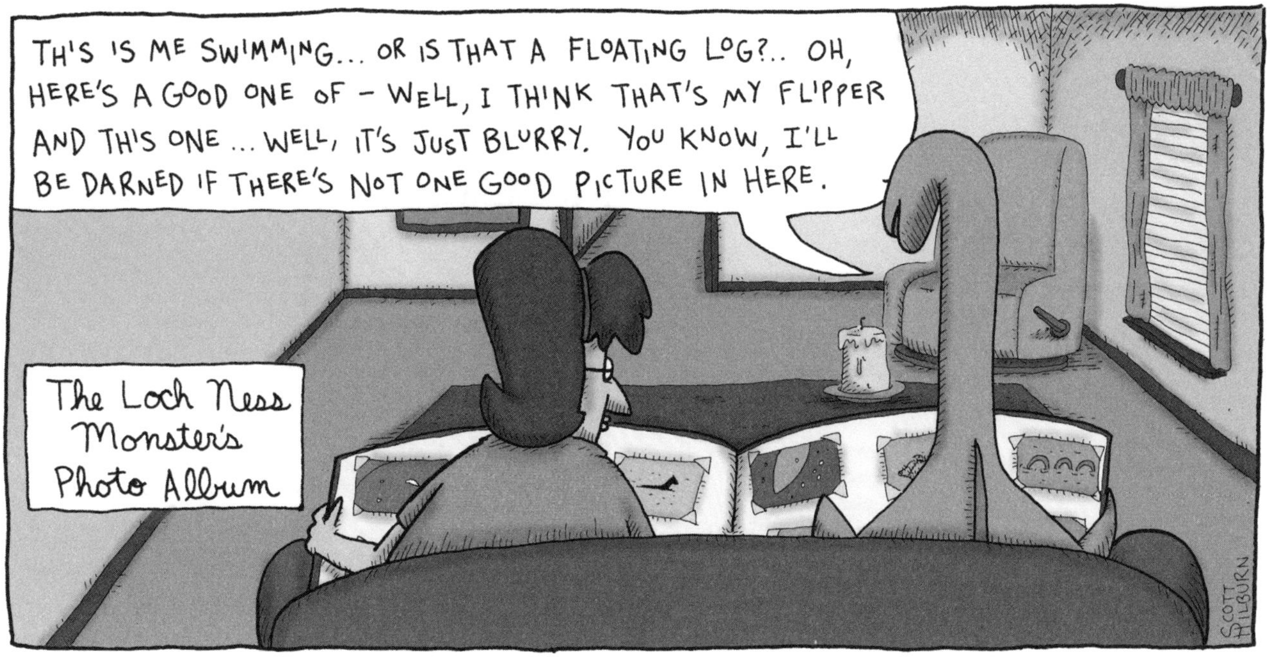
THIS IS ME SWIMMING... OR IS THAT A FLOATING LOG?.. OH, HERE'S A GOOD ONE OF - WELL, I THINK THAT'S MY FLIPPER AND THIS ONE ... WELL, IT'S JUST BLURRY. YOU KNOW, I'LL BE DARNED IF THERE'S NOT ONE GOOD PICTURE IN HERE.
SCOTT HILBURN
The Loch Ness Monster's Photo Album

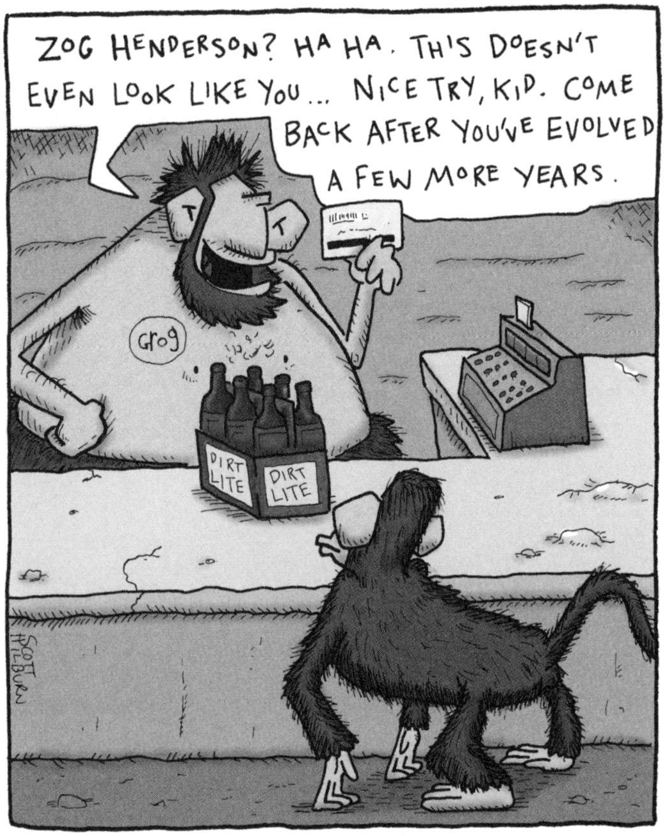
ZOG HENDERSON? HA HA. THIS DOESN'T EVEN LOOK LIKE YOU... NICE TRY, KID. COME BACK AFTER YOU'VE EVOLVED A FEW MORE YEARS.
GROG
DIRT LITE
DIRT LITE

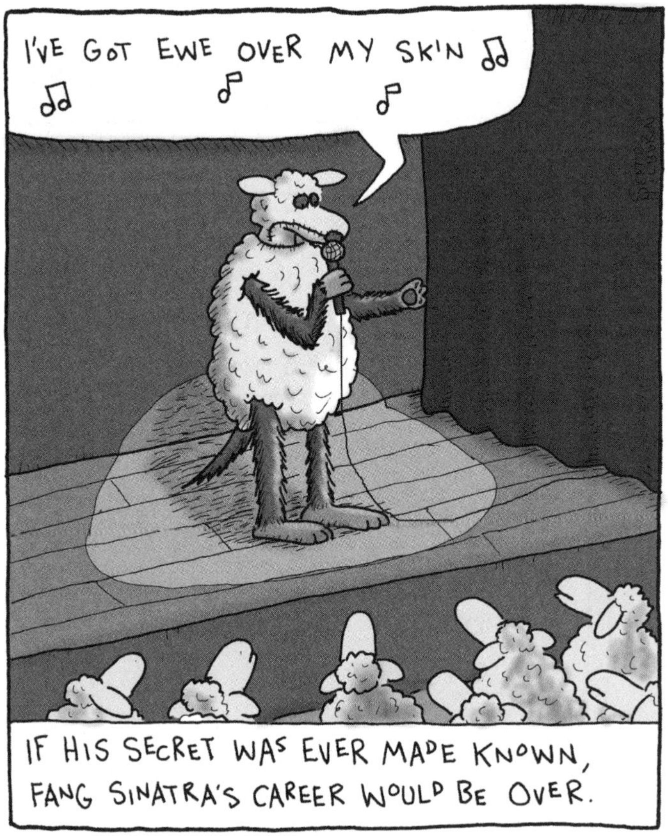
I'VE GOT EWE OVER MY SKIN
IF HIS SECRET WAS EVER MADE KNOWN, FANG SINATRA'S CAREER WOULD BE OVER.

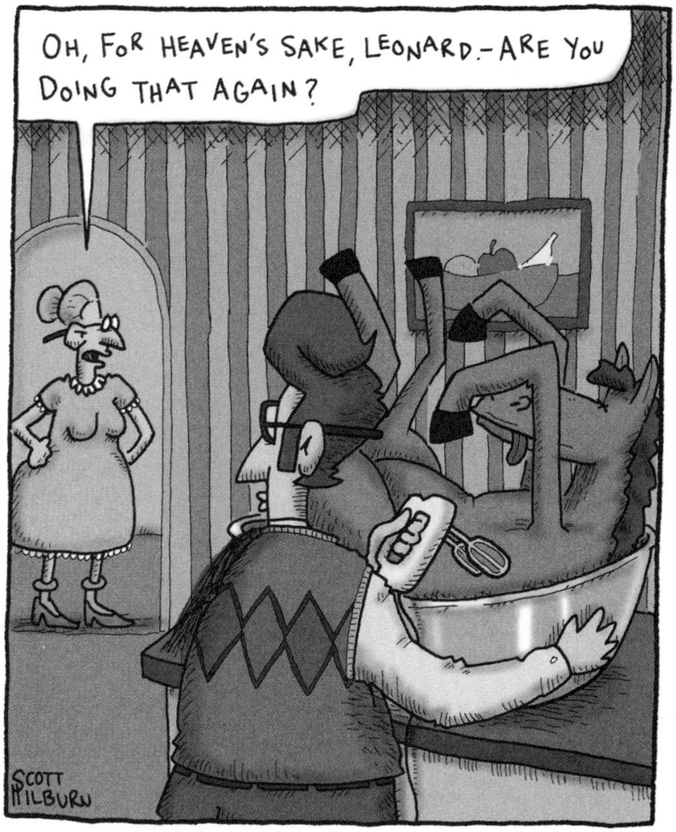
OH, FOR HEAVEN'S SAKE, LEONARD.—ARE YOU DOING THAT AGAIN?
SCOTT HILBURN

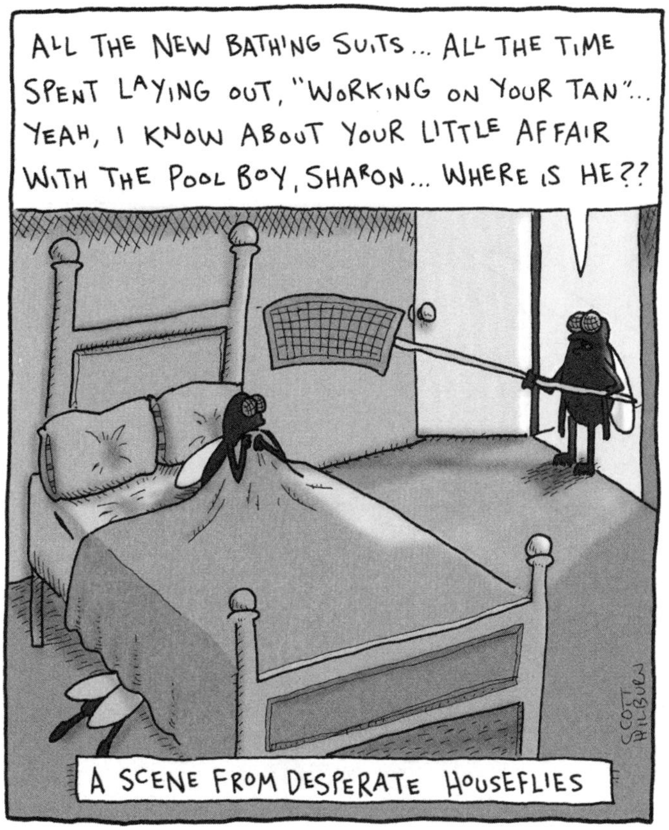
ALL THE NEW BATHING SUITS... ALL THE TIME SPENT LAYING OUT, "WORKING ON YOUR TAN"... YEAH, I KNOW ABOUT YOUR LITTLE AFFAIR WITH THE POOL BOY, SHARON... WHERE IS HE??
SCOTT HILBURN
A SCENE FROM DESPERATE HOUSEFLIES

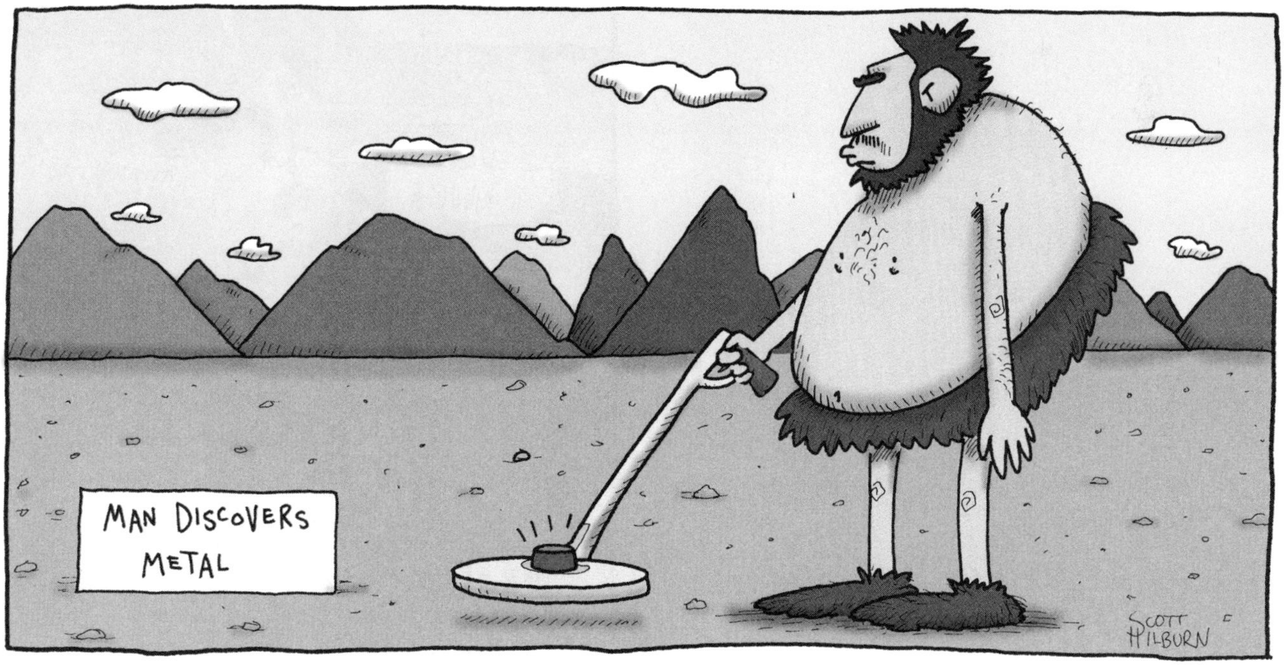
SCOTT HILBURN
MAN DISCOVERS METAL

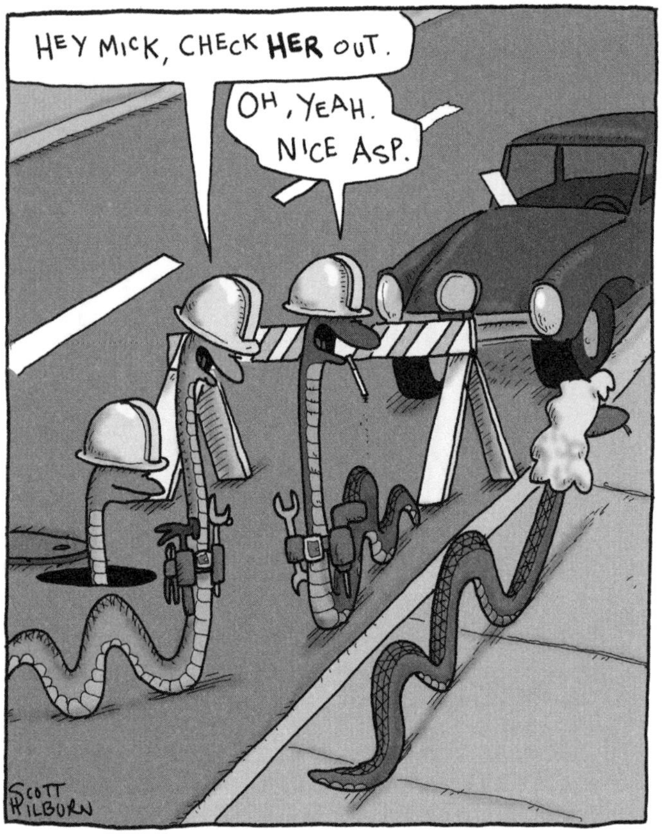
HEY MICK, CHECK **HER** OUT.
OH, YEAH. NICE ASP.
SCOTT HILBURN

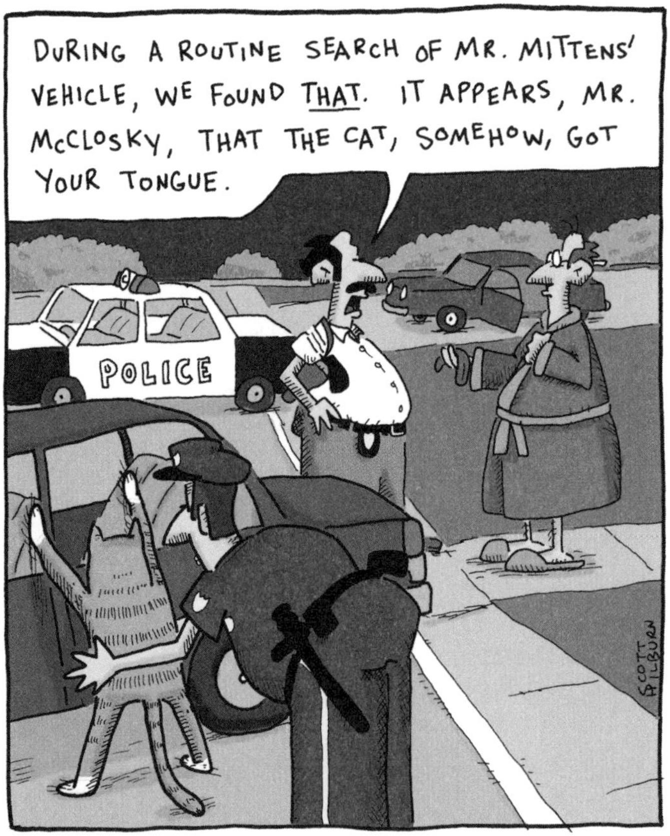
DURING A ROUTINE SEARCH OF MR. MITTENS' VEHICLE, WE FOUND THAT. IT APPEARS, MR. McCLOSKY, THAT THE CAT, SOMEHOW, GOT YOUR TONGUE.
POLICE
SCOTT HILBURN

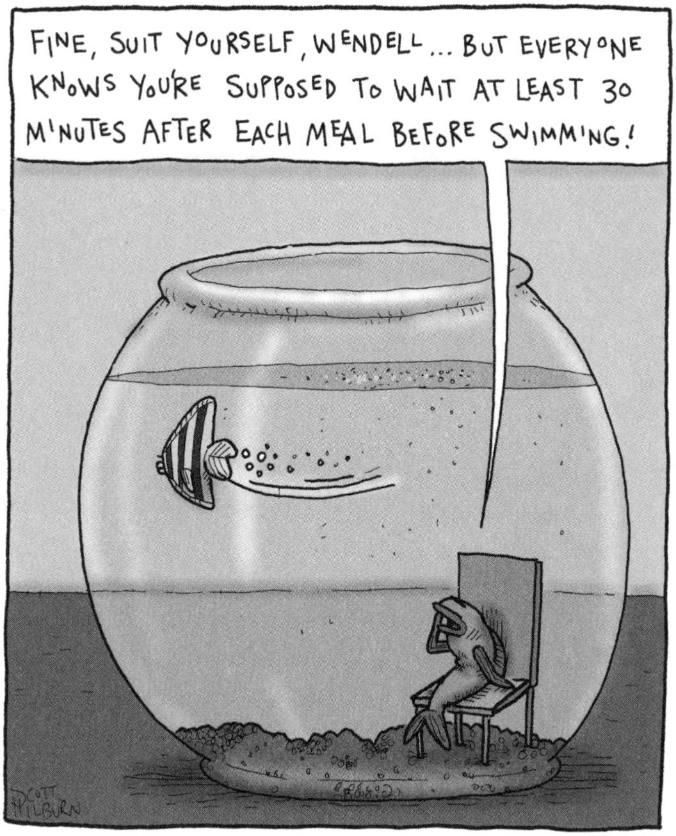
FINE, SUIT YOURSELF, WENDELL... BUT EVERYONE KNOWS YOU'RE SUPPOSED TO WAIT AT LEAST 30 MINUTES AFTER EACH MEAL BEFORE SWIMMING!
SCOTT HILBURN

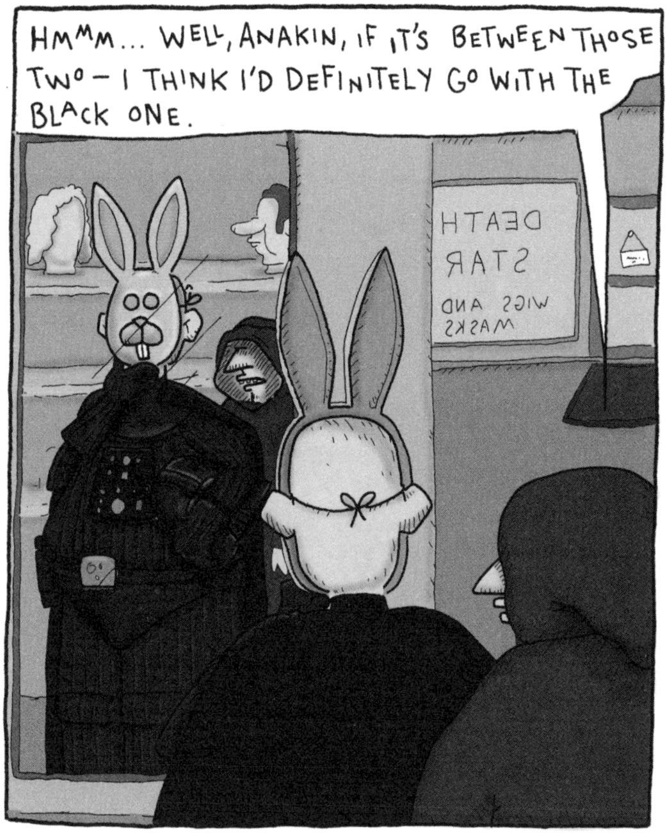
HMMM... WELL, ANAKIN, IF IT'S BETWEEN THOSE TWO – I THINK I'D DEFINITELY GO WITH THE BLACK ONE.
DEATH STAR
WIGS AND MASKS

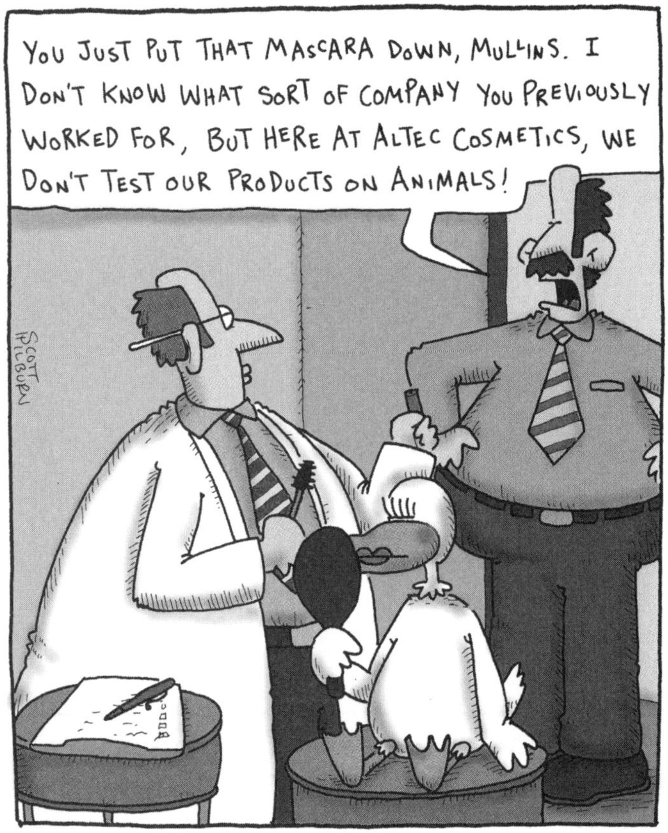
YOU JUST PUT THAT MASCARA DOWN, MULLINS. I DON'T KNOW WHAT SORT OF COMPANY YOU PREVIOUSLY WORKED FOR, BUT HERE AT ALTEC COSMETICS, WE DON'T TEST OUR PRODUCTS ON ANIMALS!
SCOT PILBURN

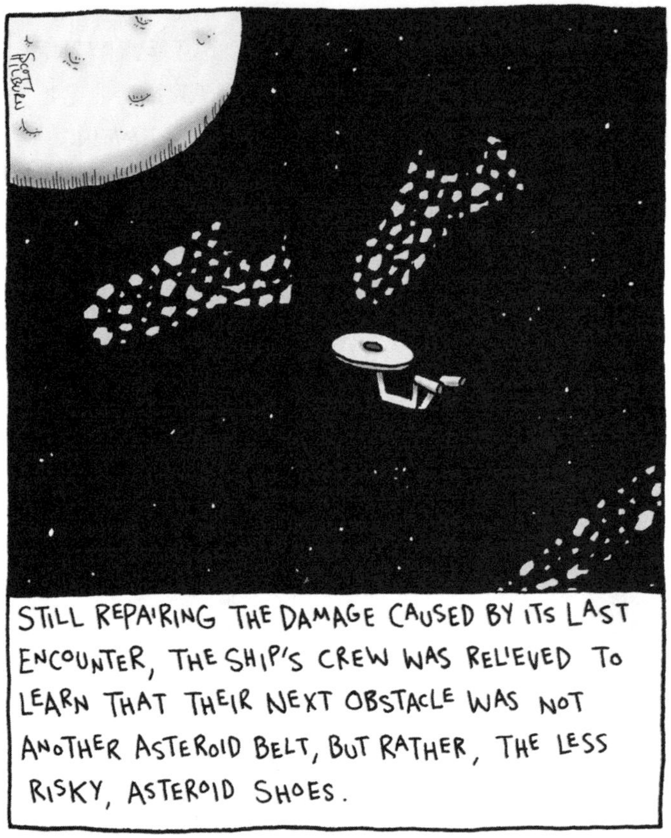
SCOTT HILBURN
STILL REPAIRING THE DAMAGE CAUSED BY ITS LAST ENCOUNTER, THE SHIP'S CREW WAS RELIEVED TO LEARN THAT THEIR NEXT OBSTACLE WAS NOT ANOTHER ASTEROID BELT, BUT RATHER, THE LESS RISKY, ASTEROID SHOES.

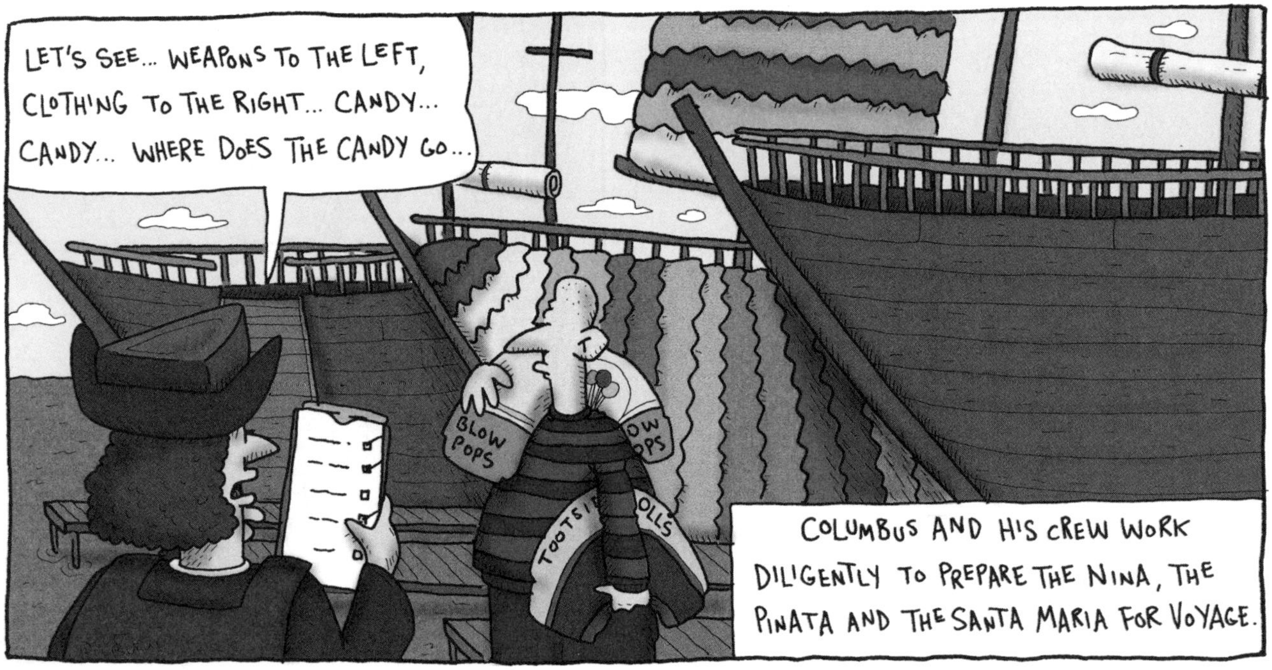
LET'S SEE... WEAPONS TO THE LEFT, CLOTHING TO THE RIGHT... CANDY... CANDY... WHERE DOES THE CANDY GO...
BLOW POPS
OW OPS
TOOTSIE ROLLS
COLUMBUS AND HIS CREW WORK DILIGENTLY TO PREPARE THE NINA, THE PINATA AND THE SANTA MARIA FOR VOYAGE.

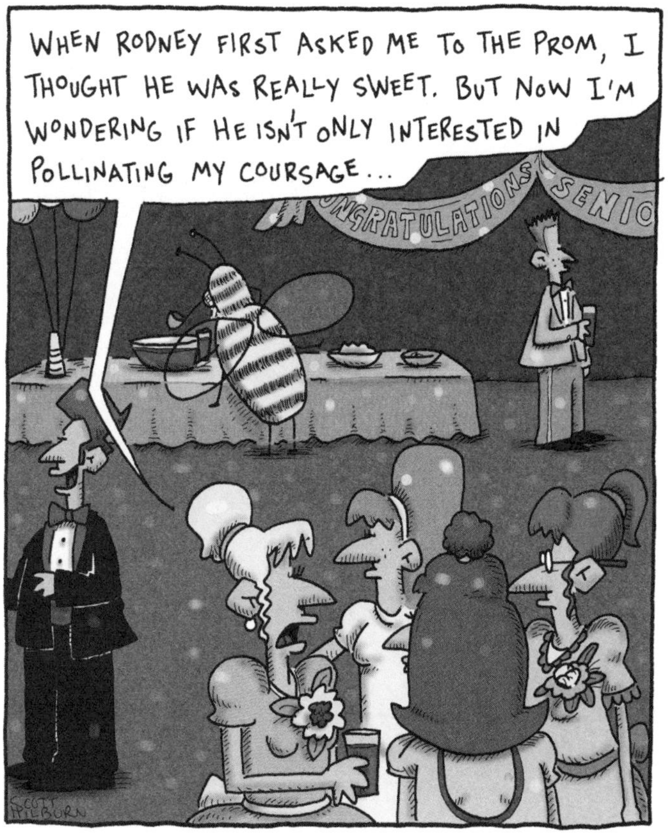
WHEN RODNEY FIRST ASKED ME TO THE PROM, I THOUGHT HE WAS REALLY SWEET. BUT NOW I'M WONDERING IF HE ISN'T ONLY INTERESTED IN POLLINATING MY COURSAGE...
CONGRATULATIONS SENIO
SCOTT HILBURN

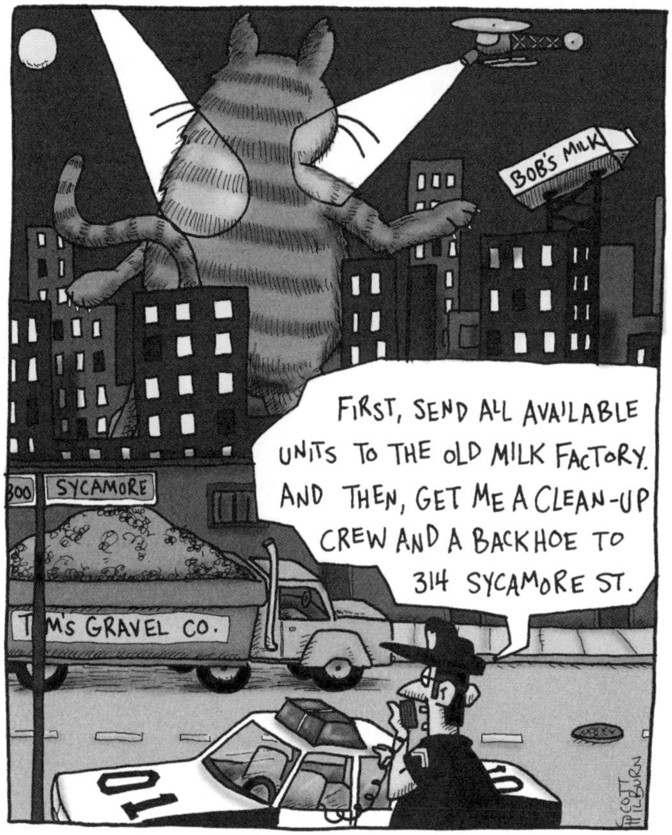
BOB'S MILK
300 SYCAMORE
T M'S GRAVEL CO.
FIRST, SEND ALL AVAILABLE UNITS TO THE OLD MILK FACTORY. AND THEN, GET ME A CLEAN-UP CREW AND A BACKHOE TO 314 SYCAMORE ST.
SCOTT HILBURN

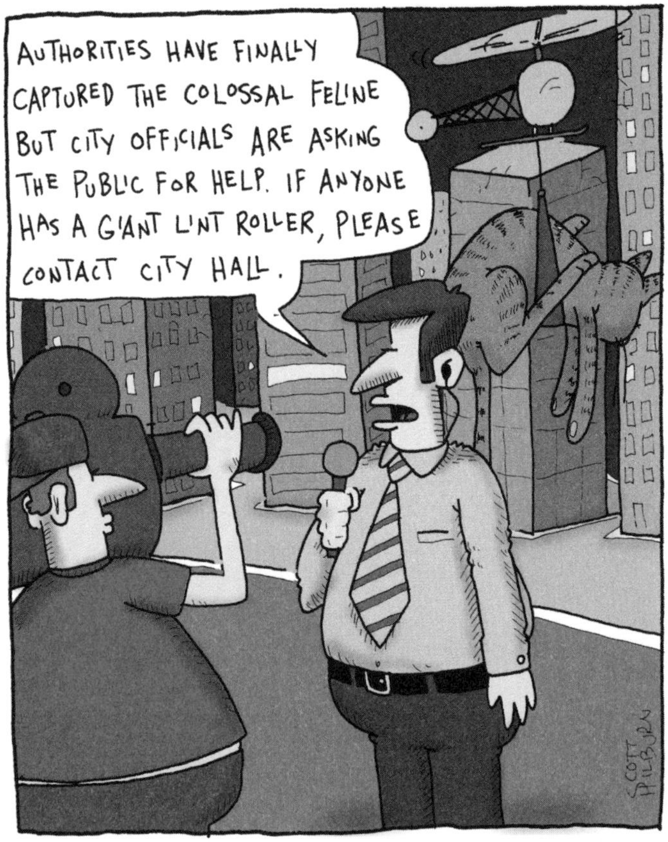
AUTHORITIES HAVE FINALLY CAPTURED THE COLOSSAL FELINE BUT CITY OFFICIALS ARE ASKING THE PUBLIC FOR HELP. IF ANYONE HAS A GIANT LINT ROLLER, PLEASE CONTACT CITY HALL.
SCOTT HILBURN

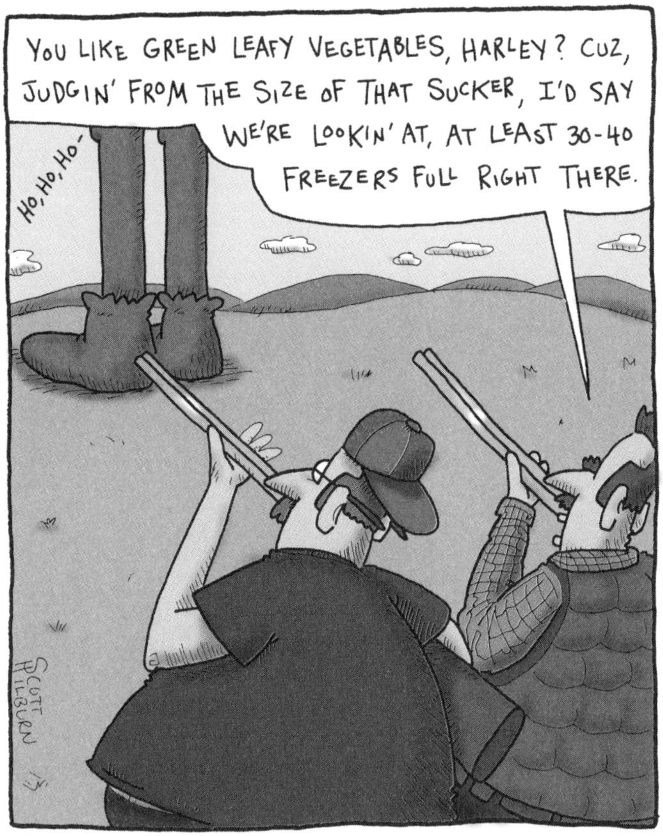
YOU LIKE GREEN LEAFY VEGETABLES, HARLEY? CUZ, JUDGIN' FROM THE SIZE OF THAT SUCKER, I'D SAY WE'RE LOOKIN' AT, AT LEAST 30-40 FREEZERS FULL RIGHT THERE.
HO, HO, HO-
SCOTT HILBURN

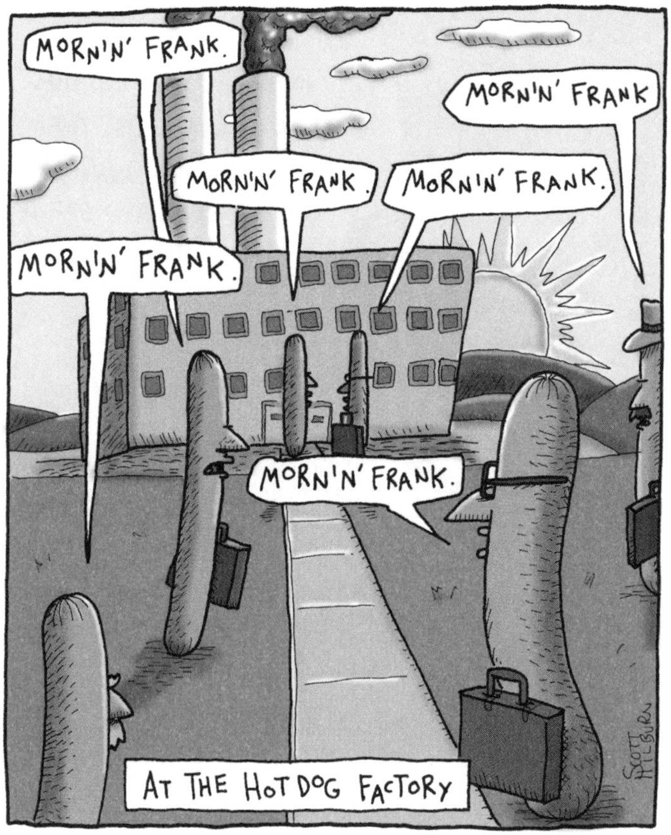
MORN'N' FRANK.
MORN'N' FRANK
MORN'N' FRANK.
MORN'N' FRANK.
MORN'N' FRANK.
MORN'N' FRANK.
AT THE HOT DOG FACTORY
SCOTT HILBURN

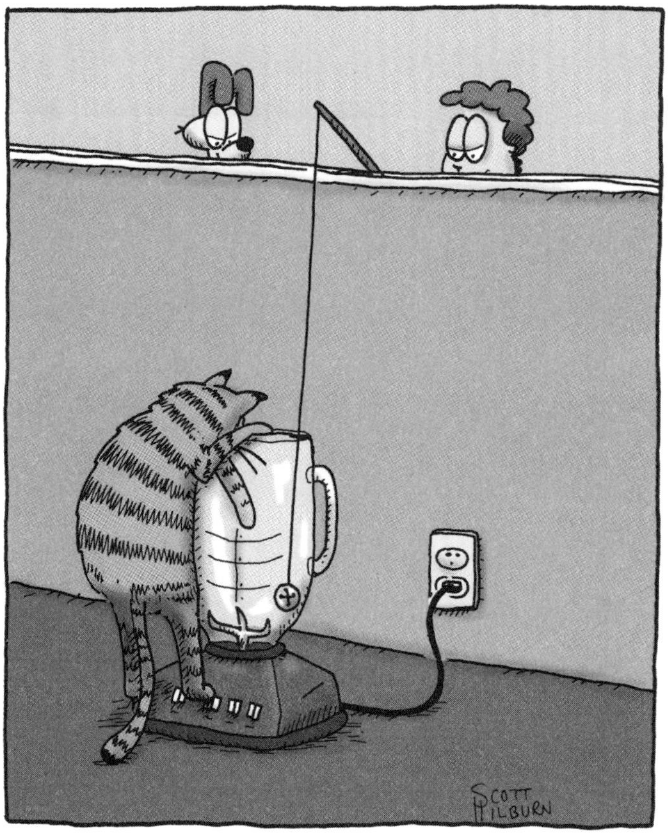
SCOTT HILBURN

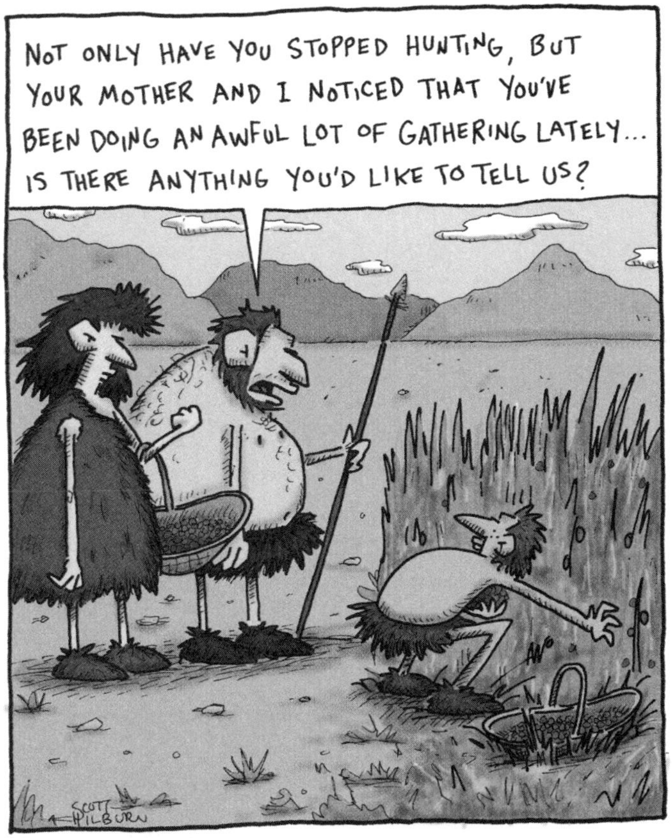
NOT ONLY HAVE YOU STOPPED HUNTING, BUT YOUR MOTHER AND I NOTICED THAT YOU'VE BEEN DOING AN AWFUL LOT OF GATHERING LATELY... IS THERE ANYTHING YOU'D LIKE TO TELL US?
SCOTT HILBURN

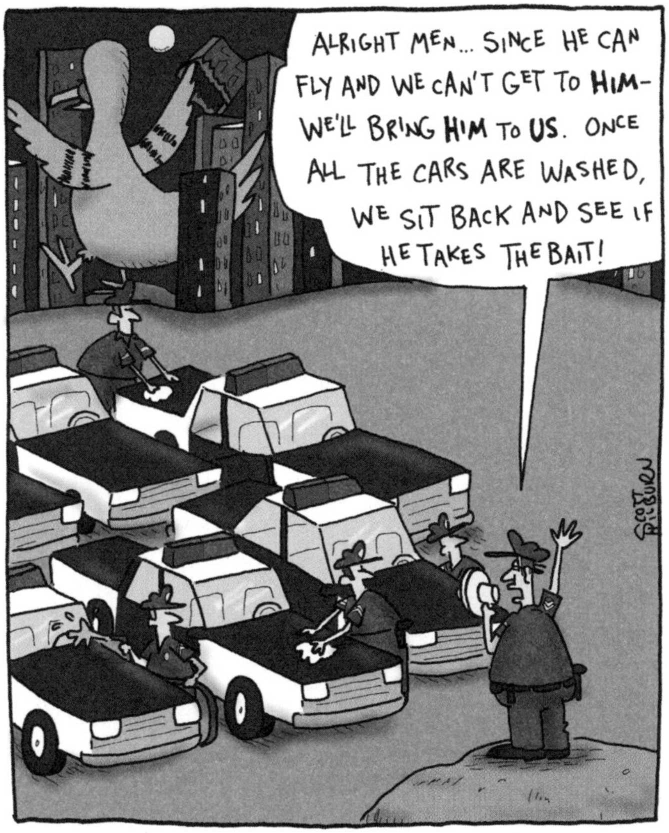
ALRIGHT MEN... SINCE HE CAN FLY AND WE CAN'T GET TO HIM- WE'LL BRING HIM TO US. ONCE ALL THE CARS ARE WASHED, WE SIT BACK AND SEE IF HE TAKES THE BAIT!
SCOTT HILBURN

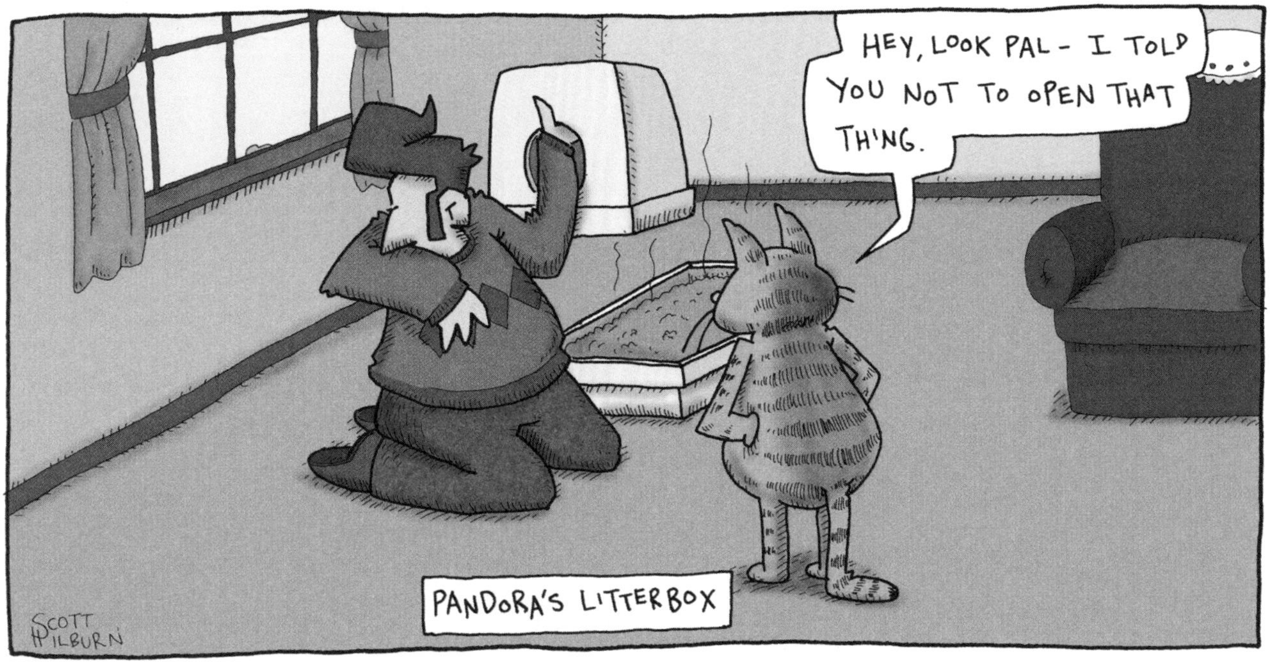
HEY, LOOK PAL - I TOLD YOU NOT TO OPEN THAT THING.
PANDORA'S LITTERBOX
SCOTT HILBURN

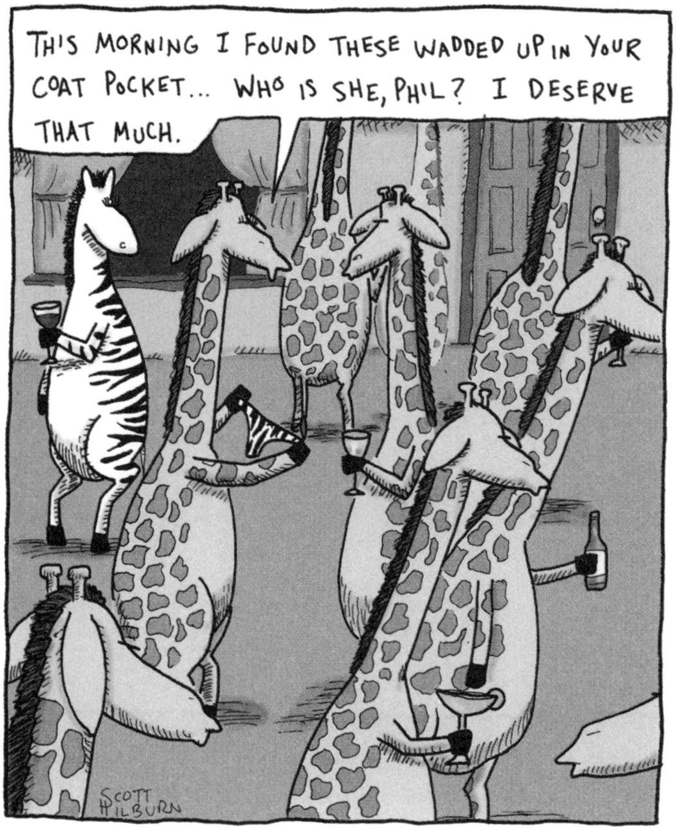
THIS MORNING I FOUND THESE WADDED UP IN YOUR COAT POCKET... WHO IS SHE, PHIL? I DESERVE THAT MUCH.
SCOTT HILBURN

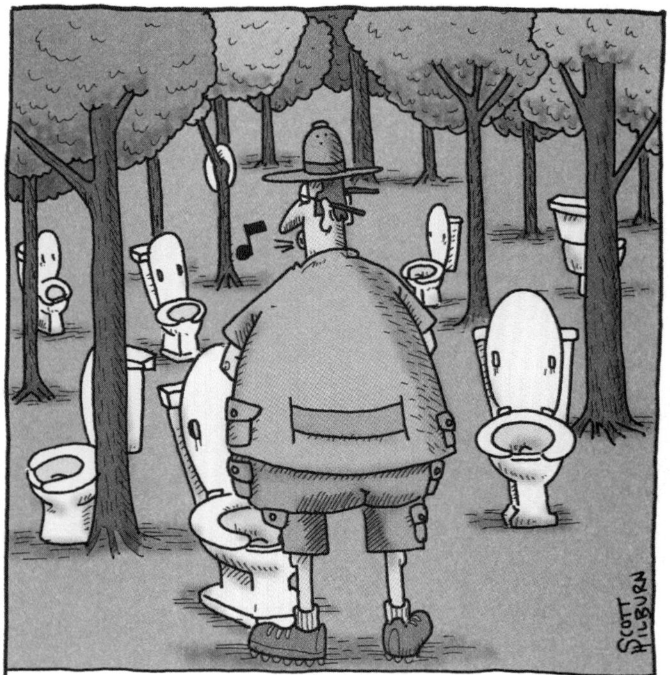
SCOTT HILBURN
UNABLE TO CONTAIN HIMSELF ANY LONGER, PROFESSOR WALTHORPE ACCIDENTALLY AND UNWITTINGLY DESECRATES THE SECRET GOLDFISH BURIAL GROUNDS.

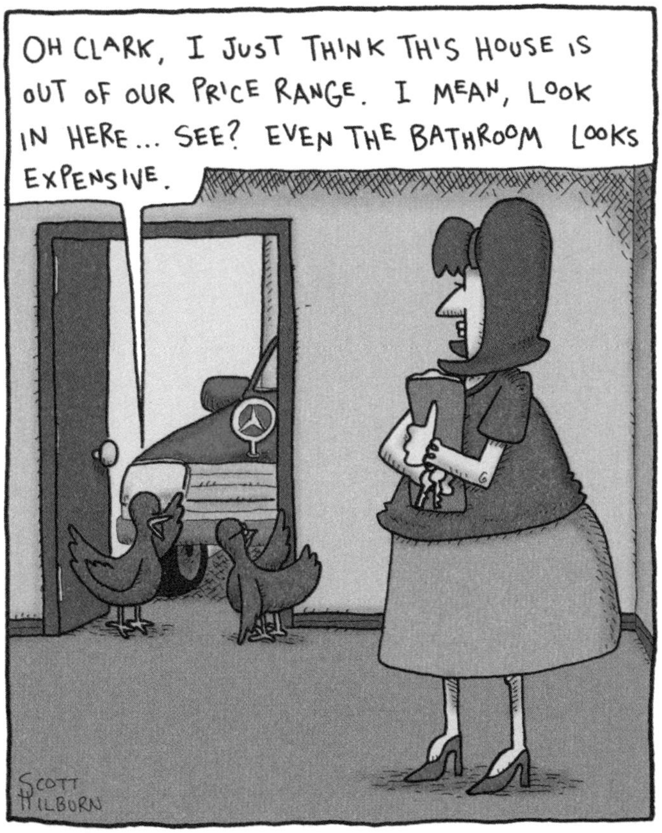
OH CLARK, I JUST THINK THIS HOUSE IS OUT OF OUR PRICE RANGE. I MEAN, LOOK IN HERE... SEE? EVEN THE BATHROOM LOOKS EXPENSIVE.
SCOTT HILBURN

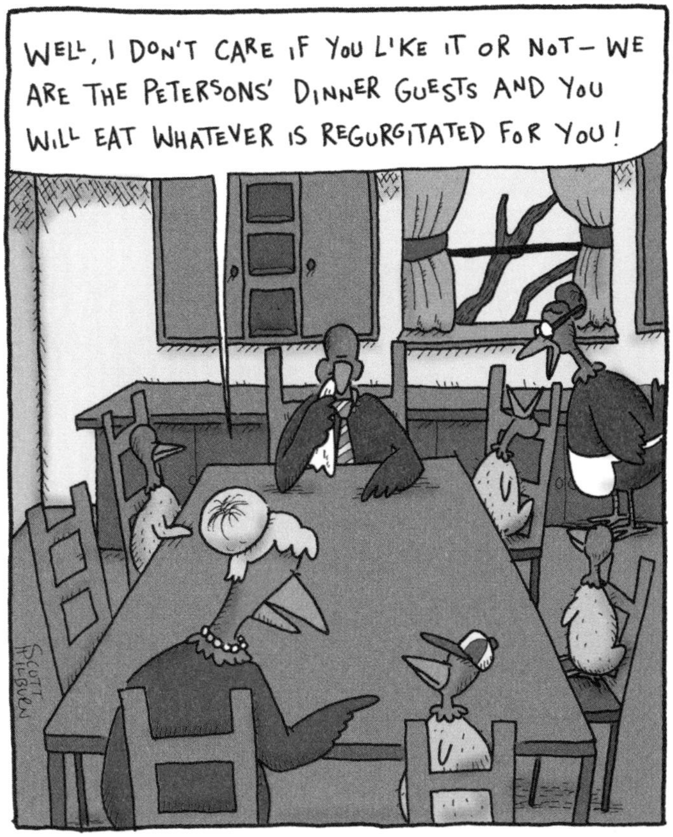
WELL, I DON'T CARE IF YOU LIKE IT OR NOT— WE ARE THE PETERSONS' DINNER GUESTS AND YOU WILL EAT WHATEVER IS REGURGITATED FOR YOU!
SCOTT HILBURN

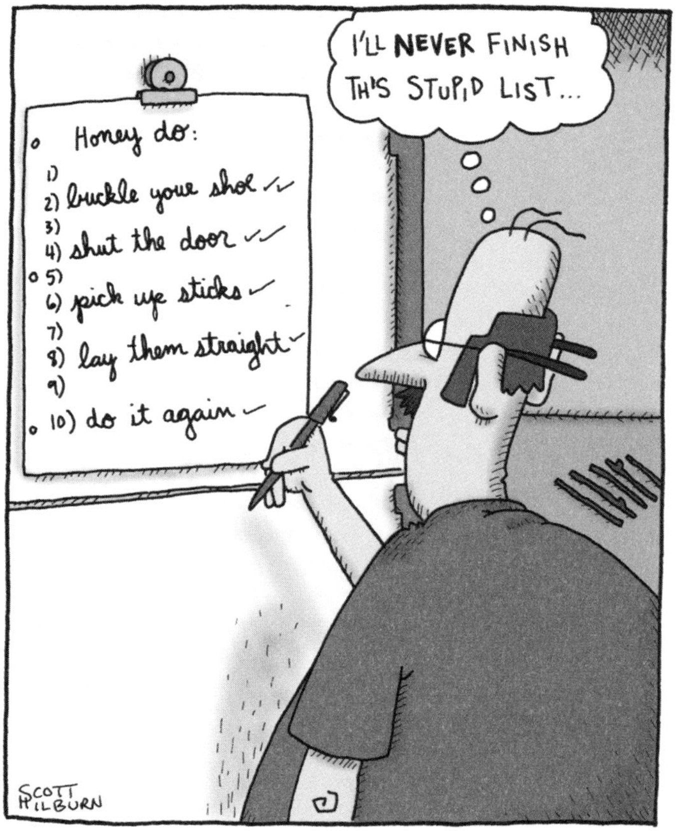
Honey do:
1)
2) buckle your shoe
3)
4) shut the door
5)
6) pick up sticks
7)
8) lay them straight
9)
10) do it again
I'LL NEVER FINISH THIS STUPID LIST...
SCOTT HILBURN

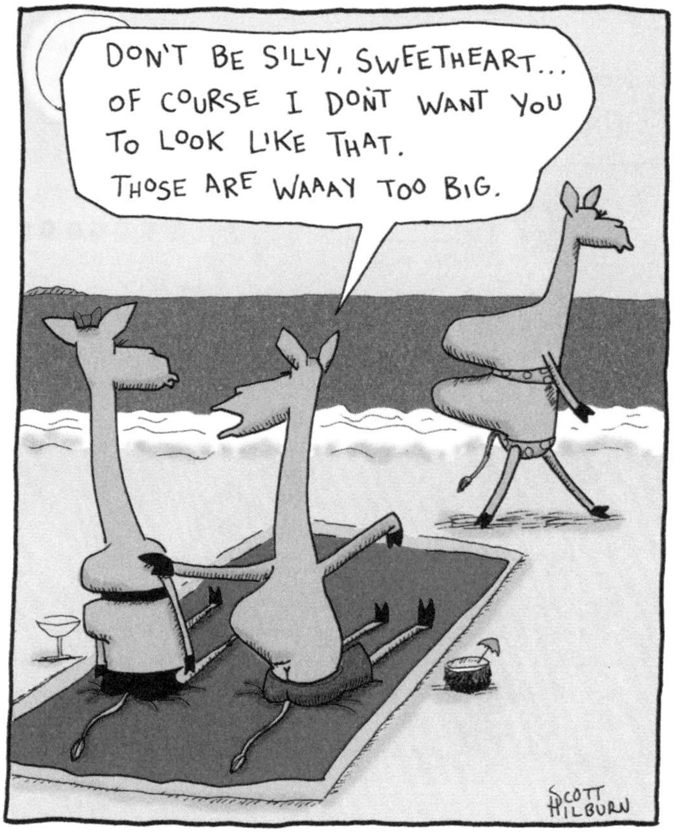
DON'T BE SILLY, SWEETHEART... OF COURSE I DON'T WANT YOU TO LOOK LIKE THAT. THOSE ARE WAAAY TOO BIG.
SCOTT HILBURN

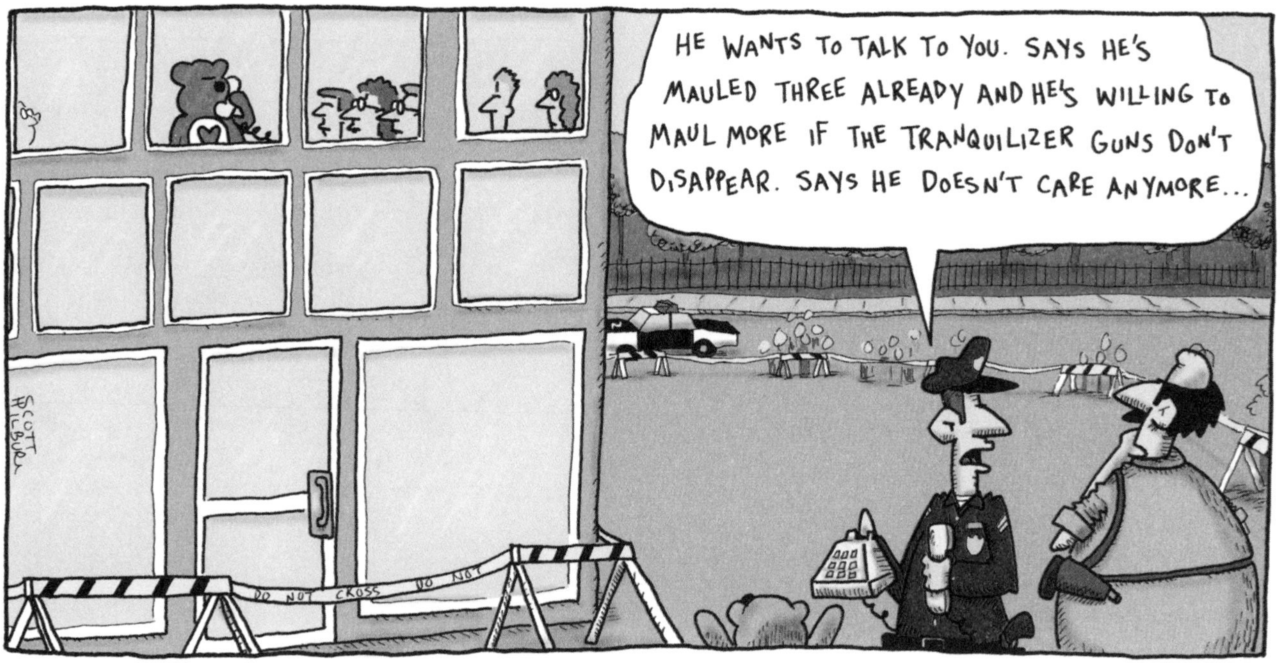
HE WANTS TO TALK TO YOU. SAYS HE'S MAULED THREE ALREADY AND HE'S WILLING TO MAUL MORE IF THE TRANQUILIZER GUNS DON'T DISAPPEAR. SAYS HE DOESN'T CARE ANYMORE...
DO NOT CROSS DO NOT
SCOTT HILBURN

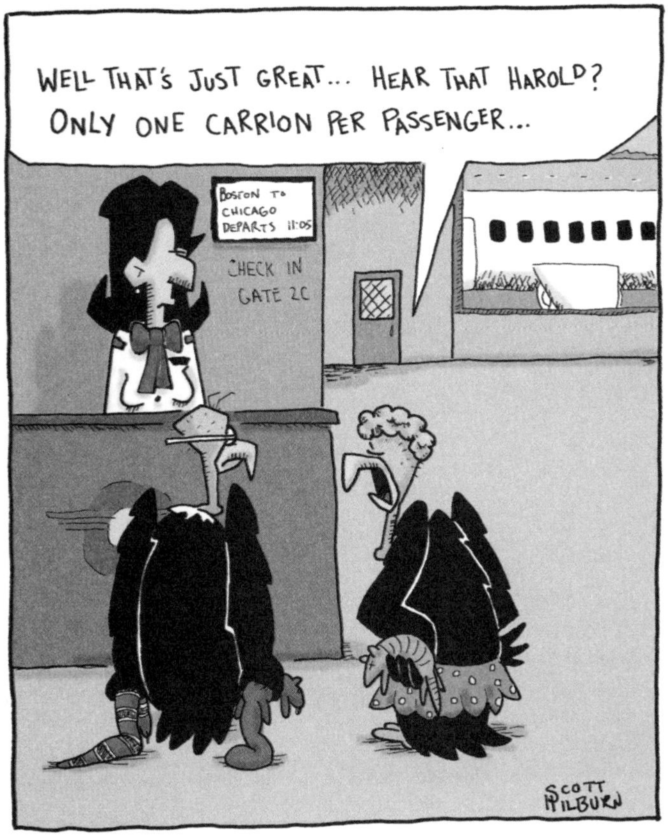
WELL THAT'S JUST GREAT... HEAR THAT HAROLD? ONLY ONE CARRION PER PASSENGER...
BOSTON TO CHICAGO DEPARTS 11:05
CHECK IN GATE 2C
SCOTT HILBURN

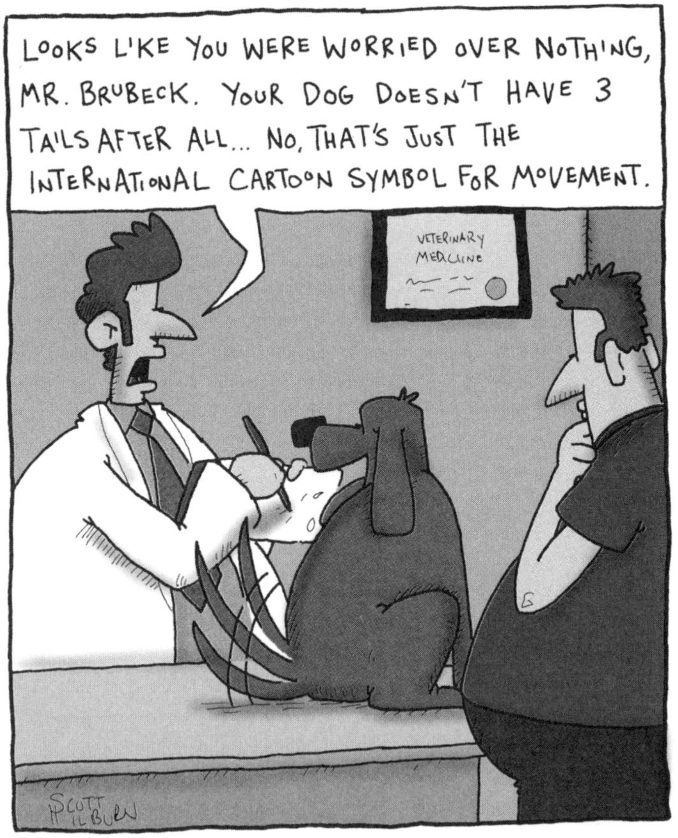
LOOKS LIKE YOU WERE WORRIED OVER NOTHING, MR. BRUBECK. YOUR DOG DOESN'T HAVE 3 TAILS AFTER ALL... NO, THAT'S JUST THE INTERNATIONAL CARTOON SYMBOL FOR MOVEMENT.
VETERINARY MEDICINE
SCOTT HILBURN

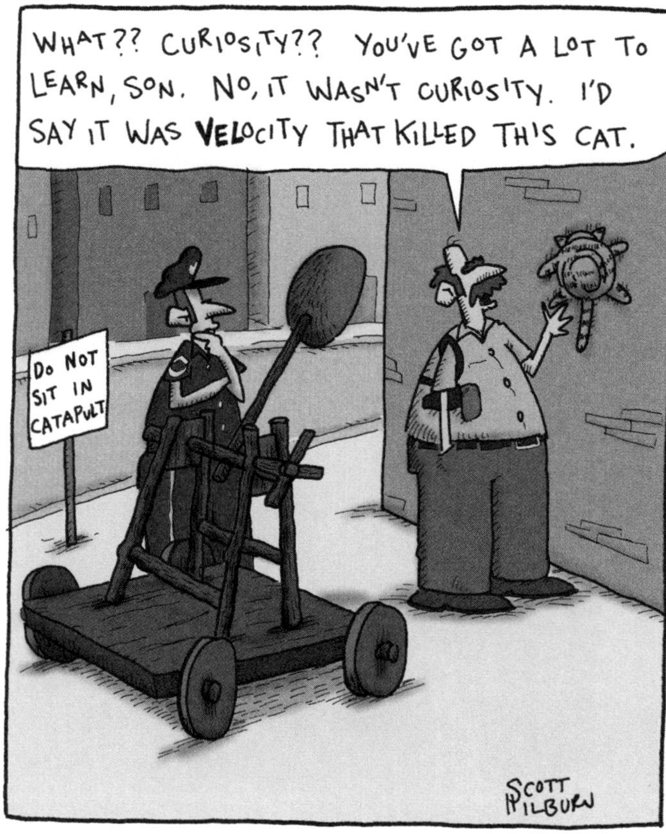
WHAT?? CURIOSITY?? YOU'VE GOT A LOT TO LEARN, SON. NO, IT WASN'T CURIOSITY. I'D SAY IT WAS **VELOCITY** THAT KILLED THIS CAT.
DO NOT SIT IN CATAPULT
SCOTT HILBURN

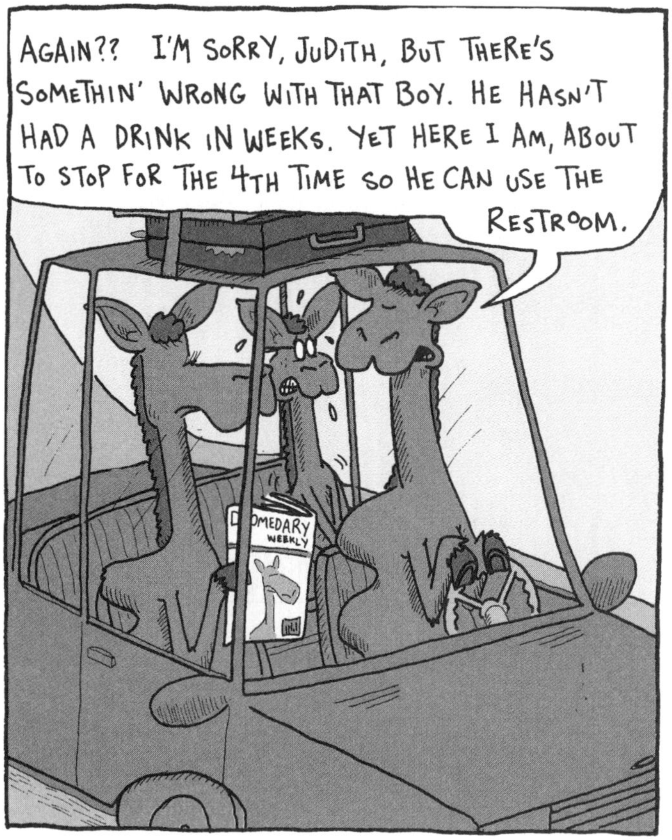
AGAIN?? I'M SORRY, JUDITH, BUT THERE'S SOMETHIN' WRONG WITH THAT BOY. HE HASN'T HAD A DRINK IN WEEKS. YET HERE I AM, ABOUT TO STOP FOR THE 4TH TIME SO HE CAN USE THE RESTROOM.
OMEDARY
WEEKLY

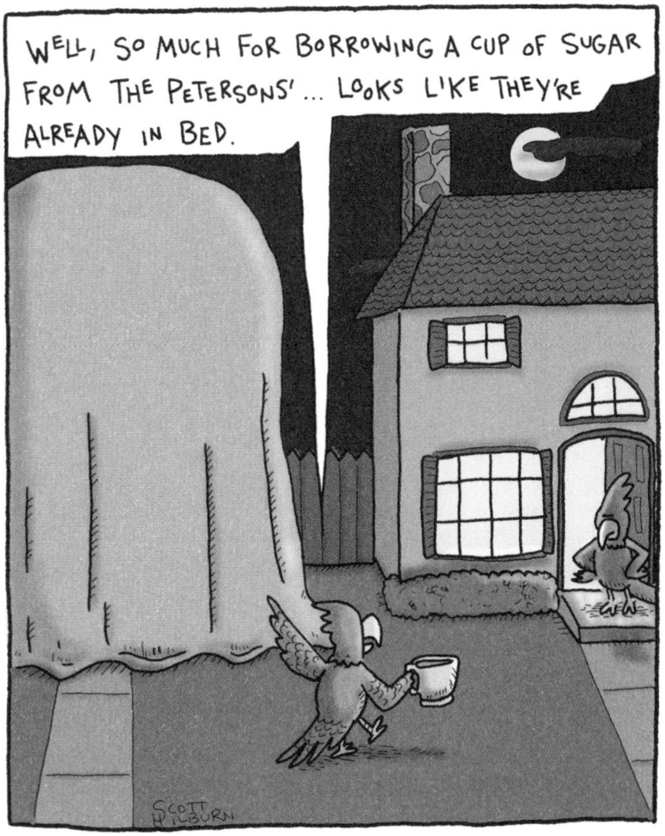
WELL, SO MUCH FOR BORROWING A CUP OF SUGAR FROM THE PETERSONS'... LOOKS LIKE THEY'RE ALREADY IN BED.
SCOTT HILBURN

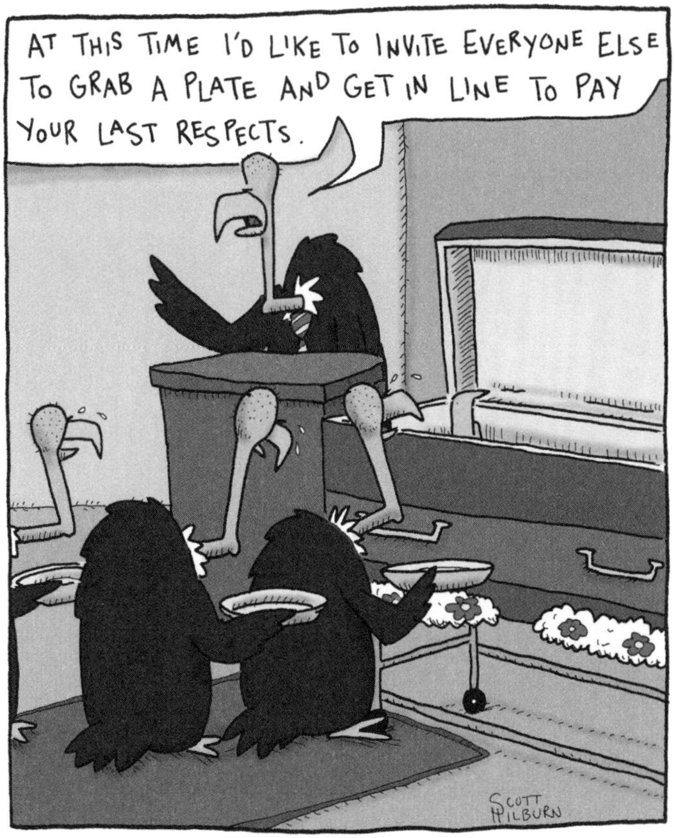
AT THIS TIME I'D LIKE TO INVITE EVERYONE ELSE TO GRAB A PLATE AND GET IN LINE TO PAY YOUR LAST RESPECTS.
SCOTT HILBURN

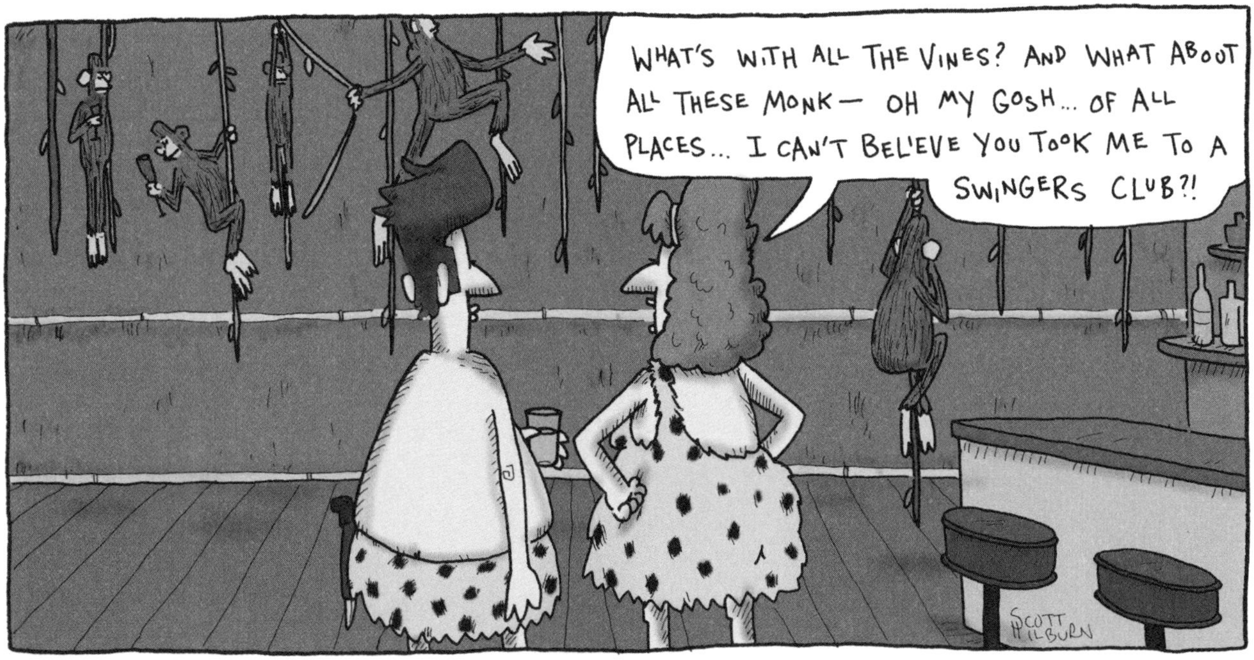
WHAT'S WITH ALL THE VINES? AND WHAT ABOUT ALL THESE MONK— OH MY GOSH... OF ALL PLACES... I CAN'T BELIEVE YOU TOOK ME TO A SWINGERS CLUB?!
SCOTT HILBURN

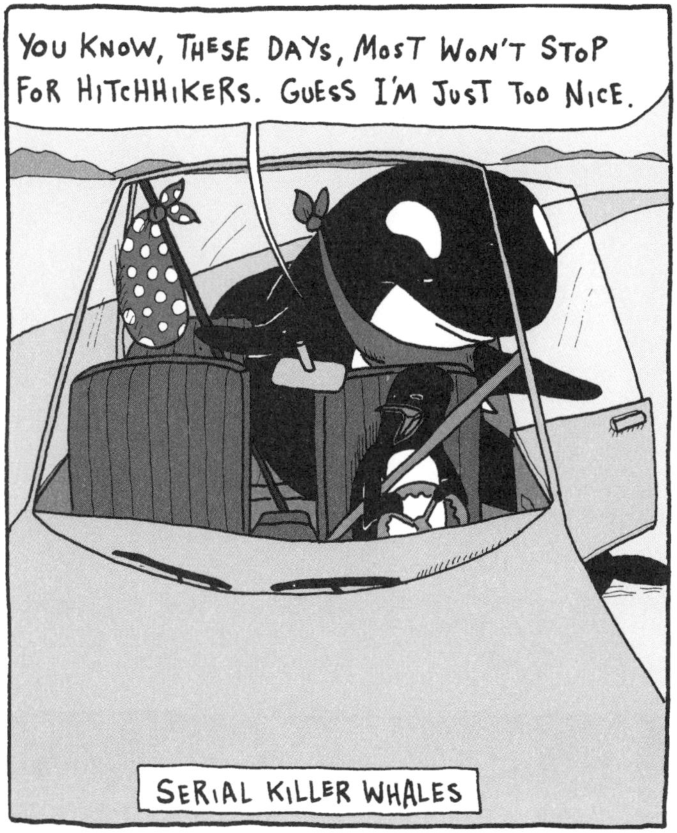
YOU KNOW, THESE DAYS, MOST WON'T STOP FOR HITCHHIKERS. GUESS I'M JUST TOO NICE.

SERIAL KILLER WHALES

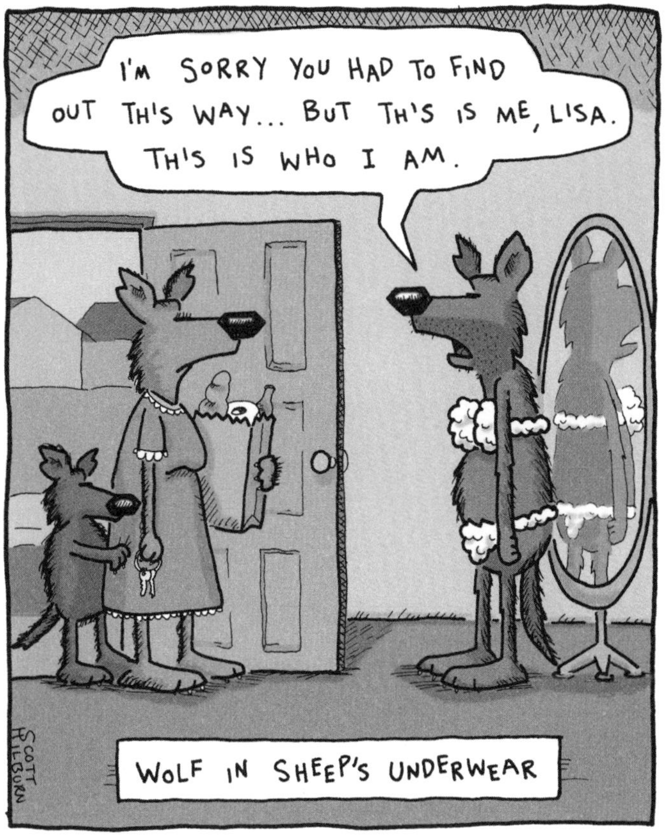
I'M SORRY YOU HAD TO FIND OUT THIS WAY... BUT THIS IS ME, LISA. THIS IS WHO I AM.
SCOTT HILBURN

WOLF IN SHEEP'S UNDERWEAR

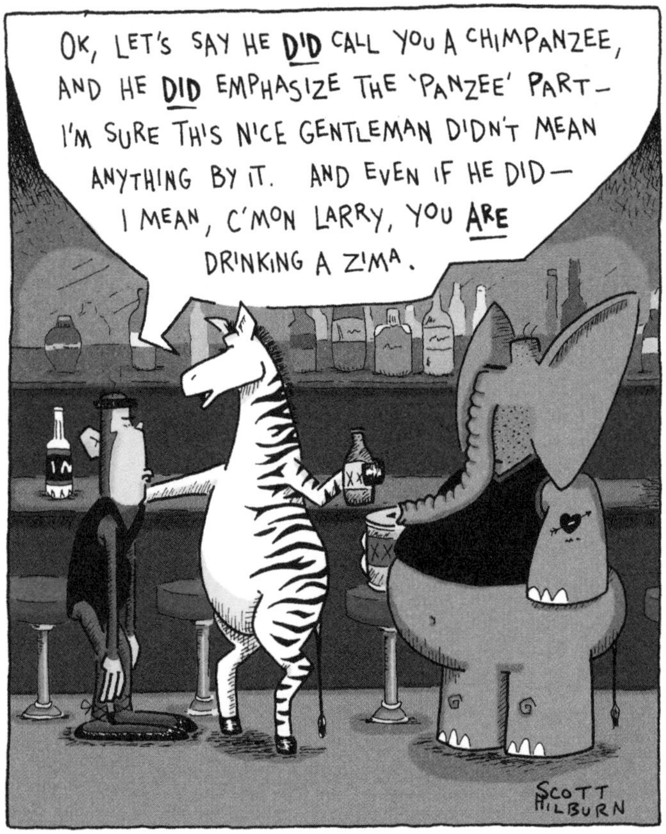
OK, LET'S SAY HE DID CALL YOU A CHIMPANZEE, AND HE DID EMPHASIZE THE 'PANZEE' PART— I'M SURE THIS NICE GENTLEMAN DIDN'T MEAN ANYTHING BY IT. AND EVEN IF HE DID— I MEAN, C'MON LARRY, YOU ARE DRINKING A ZIMA.
SCOTT HILBURN

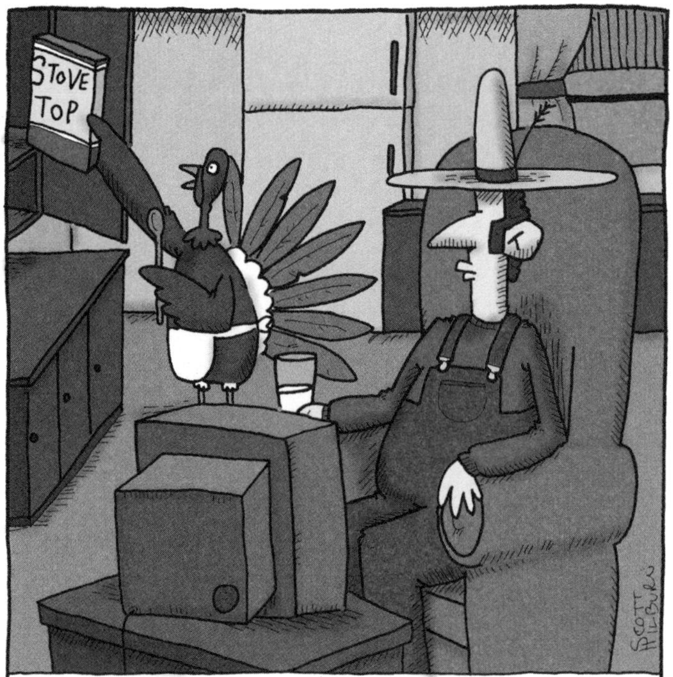
STOVE TOP
SCOTT HILBURN
AS SHE OPENS THE CUPBOARD, LOUISE SUDDENLY REALIZES THAT THEIR ENTIRE RELATIONSHIP WAS A SHAM. FRANK WAS ONLY INTERESTED IN HER FOR HER BODY.

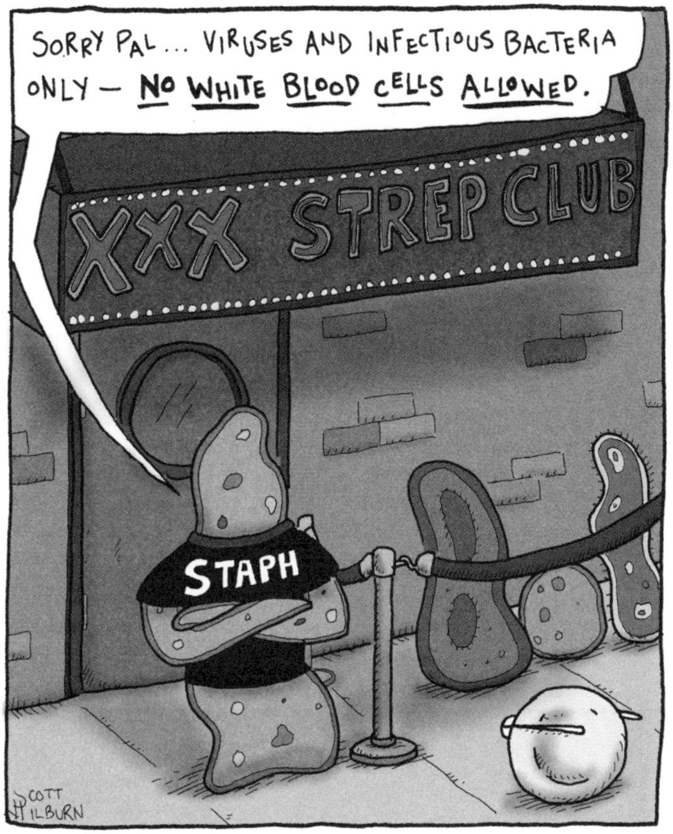
SORRY PAL... VIRUSES AND INFECTIOUS BACTERIA ONLY — NO WHITE BLOOD CELLS ALLOWED.
XXX STREP CLUB
STAPH
SCOTT HILBURN

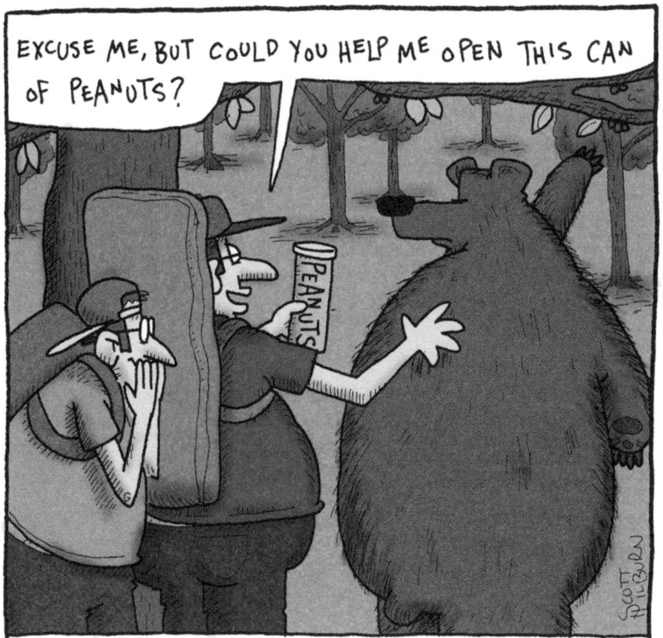
EXCUSE ME, BUT COULD YOU HELP ME OPEN THIS CAN OF PEANUTS?
PEANUTS
SCOTT HILBURN

IN THEIR EAGERNESS TO TRY OUT THEIR NEW PRANK, BILL AND PERCY FORGET THE GOLDEN RULE OF THE OUTDOORS: IF, WHILE HIKING, ONE HAPPENS ACROSS A GRIZZLY BEAR, AT ALL COSTS, TRY NOT TO SURPRISE HIM.

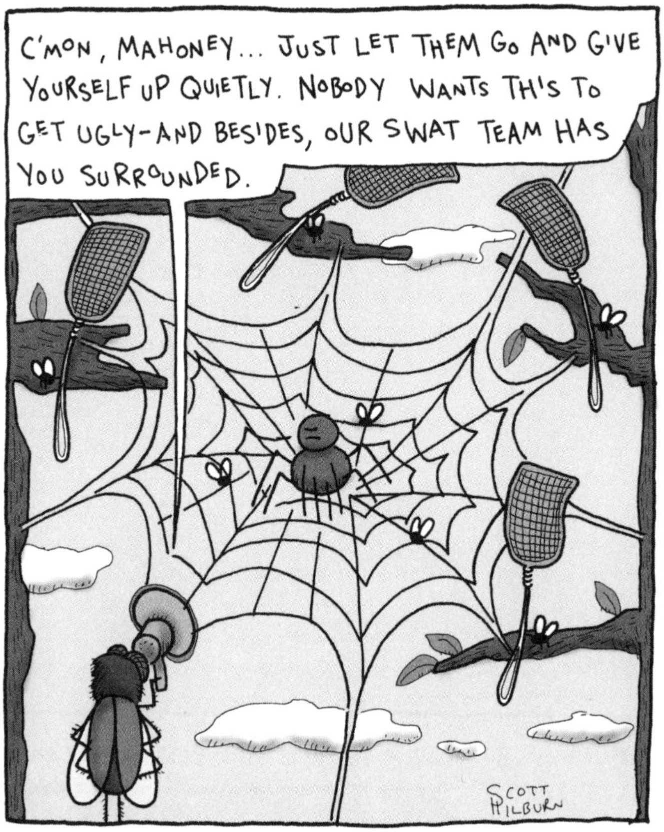
C'MON, MAHONEY... JUST LET THEM GO AND GIVE YOURSELF UP QUIETLY. NOBODY WANTS THIS TO GET UGLY—AND BESIDES, OUR SWAT TEAM HAS YOU SURROUNDED.
SCOTT HILBURN

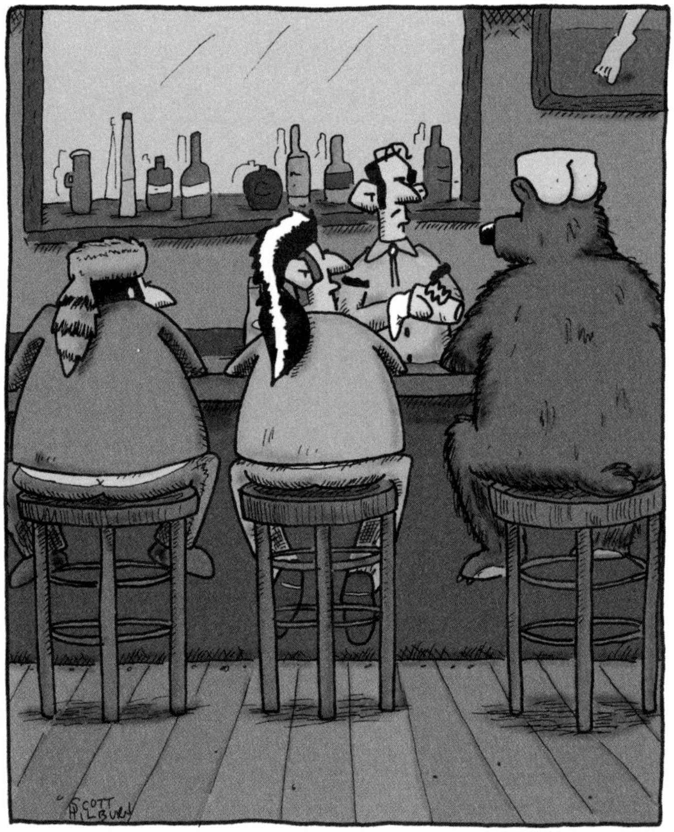
SCOTT HILBURN

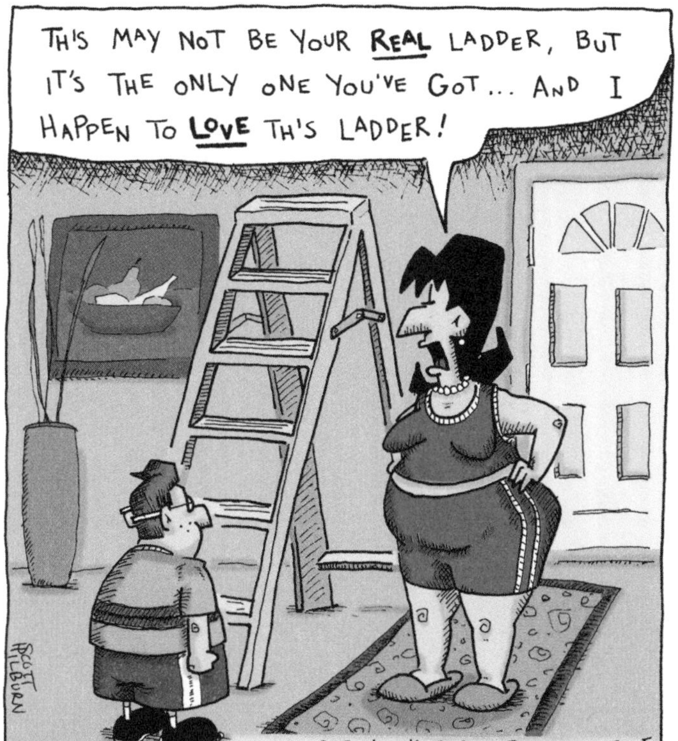
THIS MAY NOT BE YOUR REAL LADDER, BUT IT'S THE ONLY ONE YOU'VE GOT... AND I HAPPEN TO LOVE THIS LADDER!
SCOTT HILBURN
LITTLE STEVIE HAS A DIFFICULT TIME ADJUSTING TO HIS NEW STEP-LADDER.

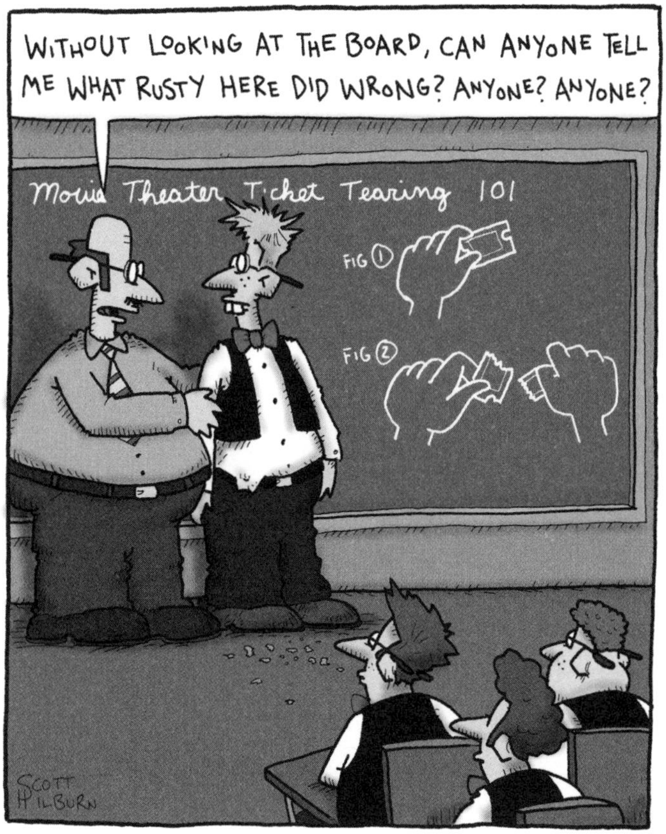
WITHOUT LOOKING AT THE BOARD, CAN ANYONE TELL ME WHAT RUSTY HERE DID WRONG? ANYONE? ANYONE?
Movie Theater Ticket Tearing 101
FIG 1
FIG 2
SCOTT HILBURN

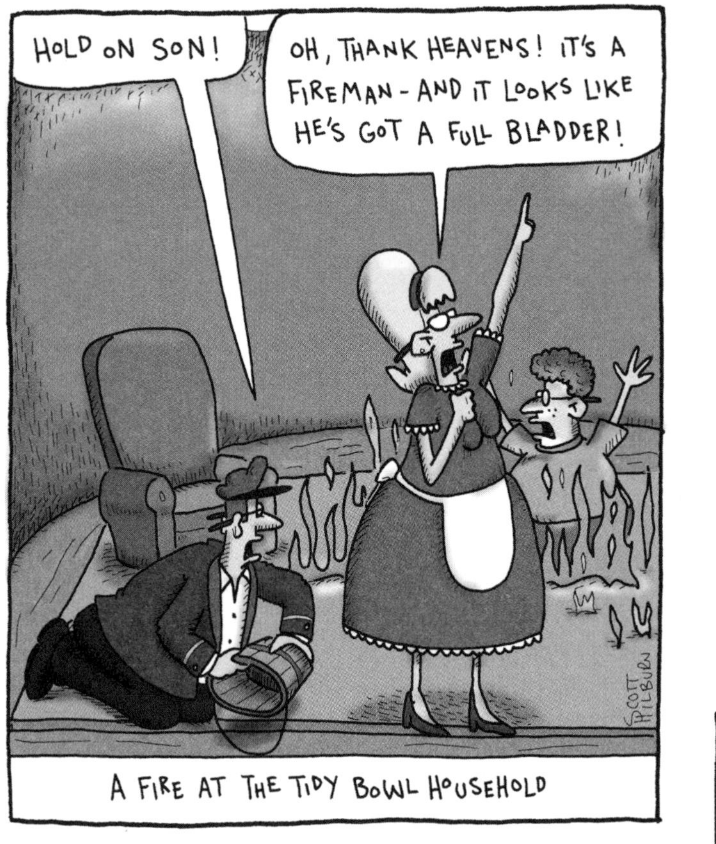
HOLD ON SON!
OH, THANK HEAVENS! IT'S A FIREMAN - AND IT LOOKS LIKE HE'S GOT A FULL BLADDER!
SCOTT HILBURN
A FIRE AT THE TIDY BOWL HOUSEHOLD

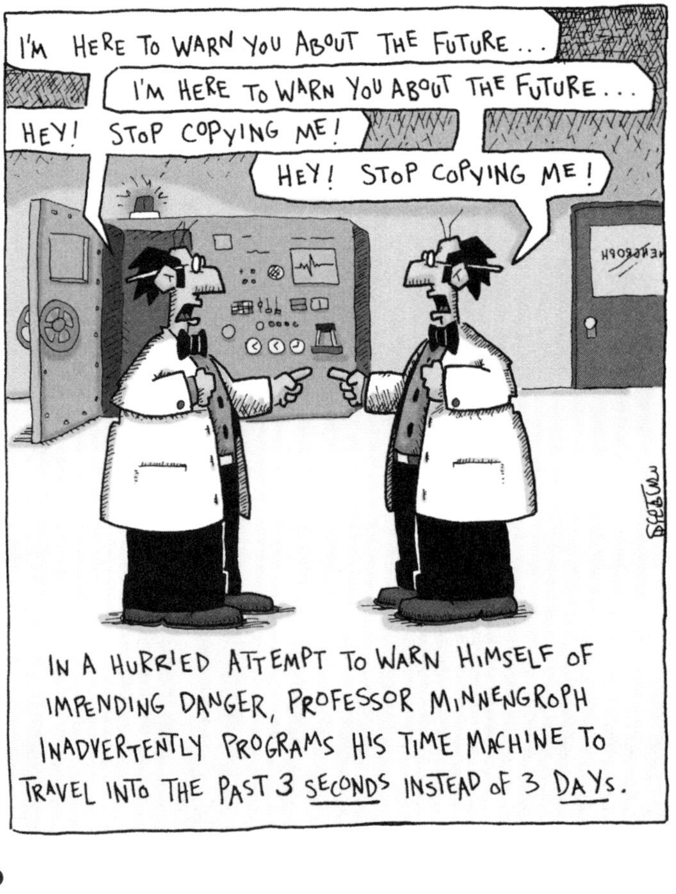
I'M HERE TO WARN YOU ABOUT THE FUTURE...
I'M HERE TO WARN YOU ABOUT THE FUTURE...
HEY! STOP COPYING ME!
HEY! STOP COPYING ME!
IN A HURRIED ATTEMPT TO WARN HIMSELF OF IMPENDING DANGER, PROFESSOR MINNENGROPH INADVERTENTLY PROGRAMS HIS TIME MACHINE TO TRAVEL INTO THE PAST 3 SECONDS INSTEAD OF 3 DAYS.

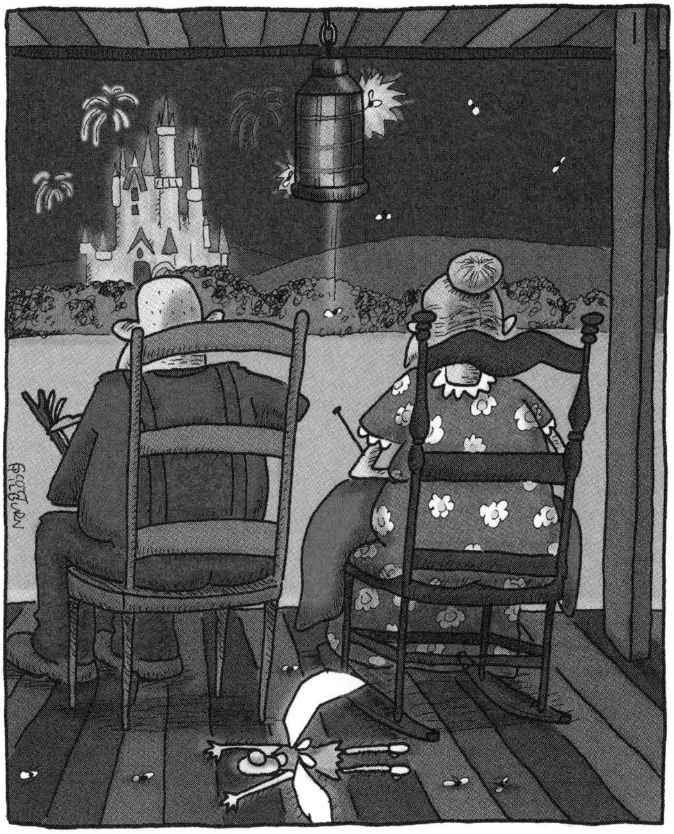

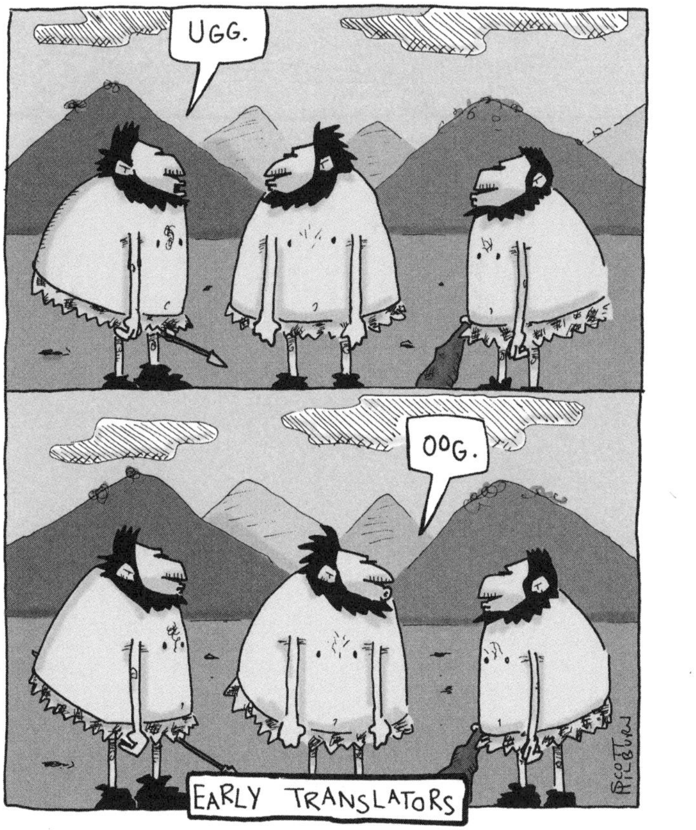
UGG.
OOG.
EARLY TRANSLATORS

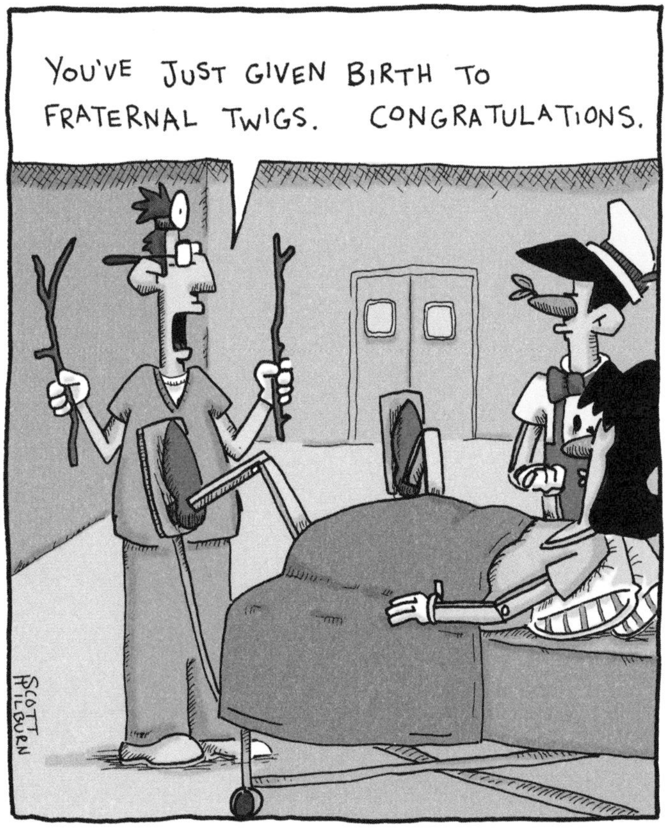
YOU'VE JUST GIVEN BIRTH TO FRATERNAL TWIGS. CONGRATULATIONS.
SCOTT HILBURN

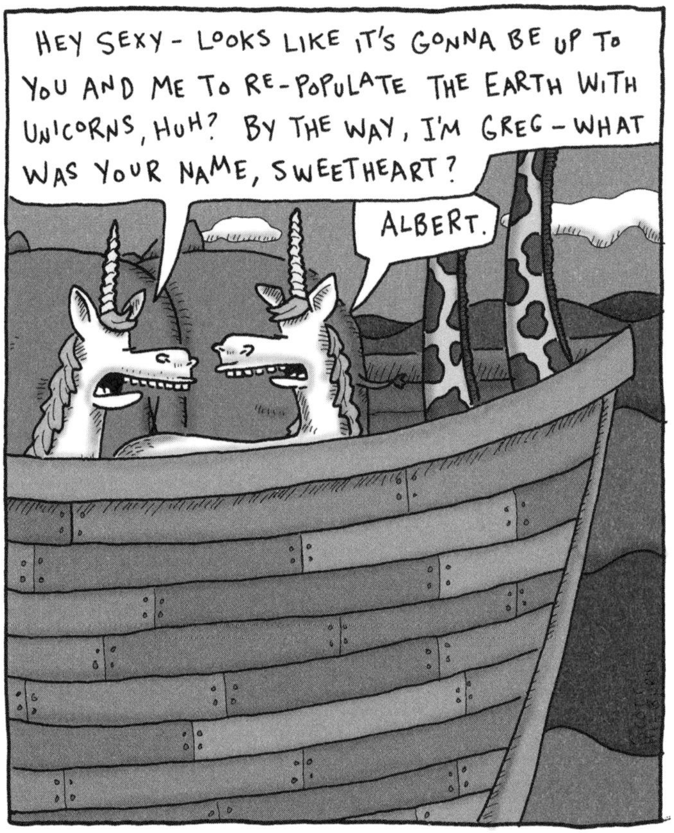
HEY SEXY - LOOKS LIKE IT'S GONNA BE UP TO YOU AND ME TO RE-POPULATE THE EARTH WITH UNICORNS, HUH? BY THE WAY, I'M GREG - WHAT WAS YOUR NAME, SWEETHEART?
ALBERT.

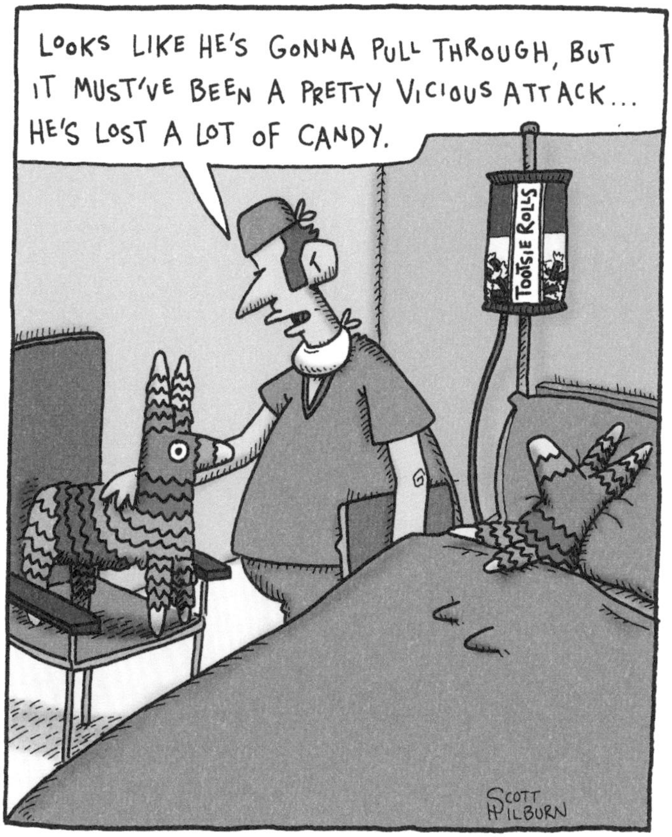
LOOKS LIKE HE'S GONNA PULL THROUGH, BUT IT MUST'VE BEEN A PRETTY VICIOUS ATTACK... HE'S LOST A LOT OF CANDY.
TOOTSIE ROLLS
SCOTT HILBURN

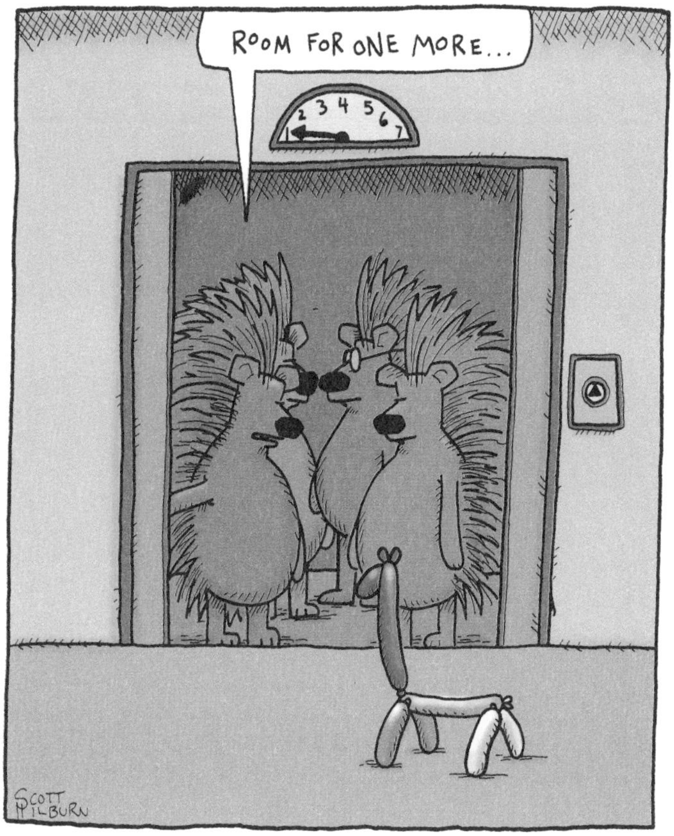
ROOM FOR ONE MORE...
SCOTT HILBURN

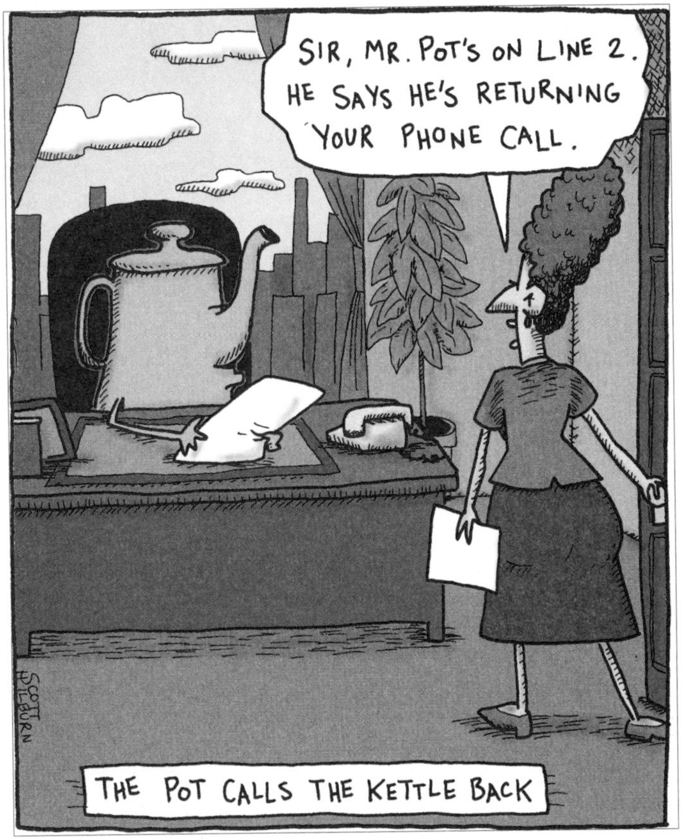
SIR, MR. POT'S ON LINE 2. HE SAYS HE'S RETURNING YOUR PHONE CALL.
SCOTT HILBURN

THE POT CALLS THE KETTLE BACK

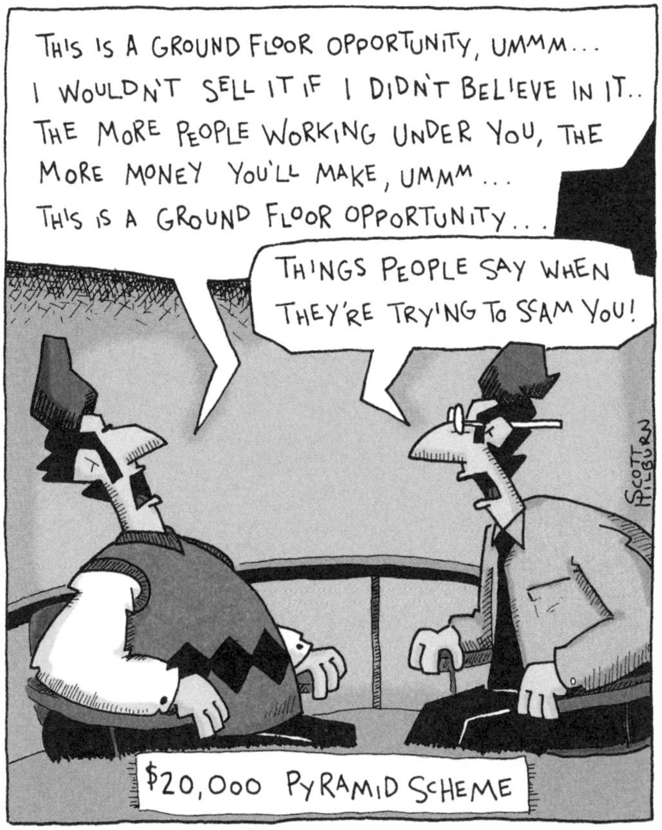
THIS IS A GROUND FLOOR OPPORTUNITY, UMMM... I WOULDN'T SELL IT IF I DIDN'T BELIEVE IN IT.. THE MORE PEOPLE WORKING UNDER YOU, THE MORE MONEY YOU'LL MAKE, UMMM... THIS IS A GROUND FLOOR OPPORTUNITY...
THINGS PEOPLE SAY WHEN THEY'RE TRYING TO SCAM YOU!
SCOTT HILBURN

$20,000 PYRAMID SCHEME

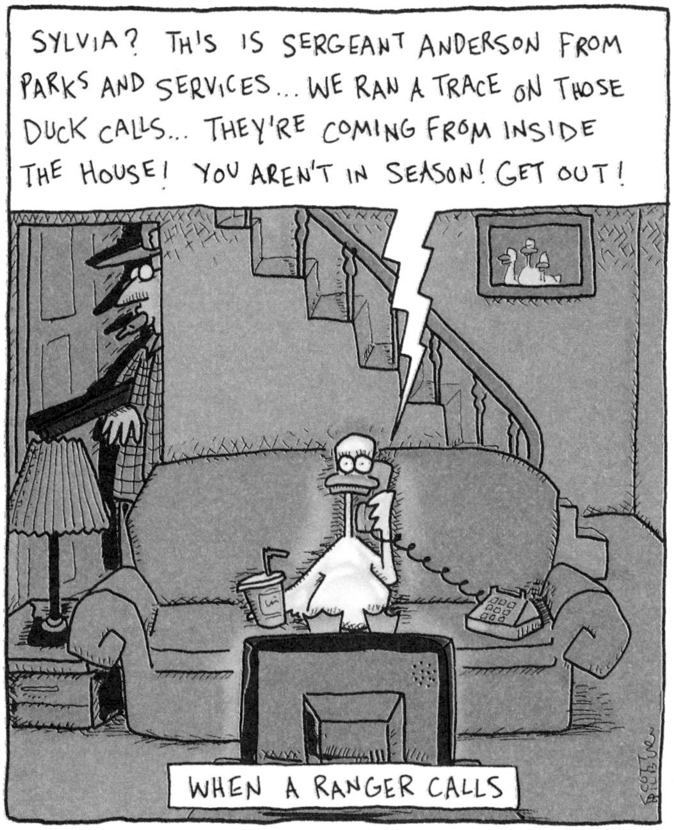
SYLVIA? THIS IS SERGEANT ANDERSON FROM PARKS AND SERVICES... WE RAN A TRACE ON THOSE DUCK CALLS... THEY'RE COMING FROM INSIDE THE HOUSE! YOU AREN'T IN SEASON! GET OUT!
WHEN A RANGER CALLS

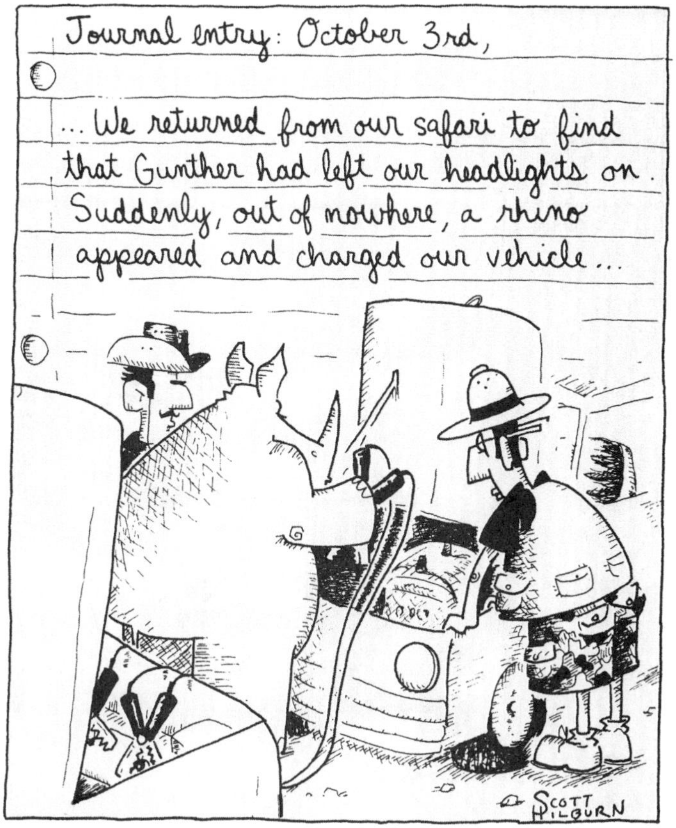
Journal entry: October 3rd,
... We returned from our safari to find that Gunther had left our headlights on. Suddenly, out of nowhere, a rhino appeared and charged our vehicle...
SCOTT HILBURN

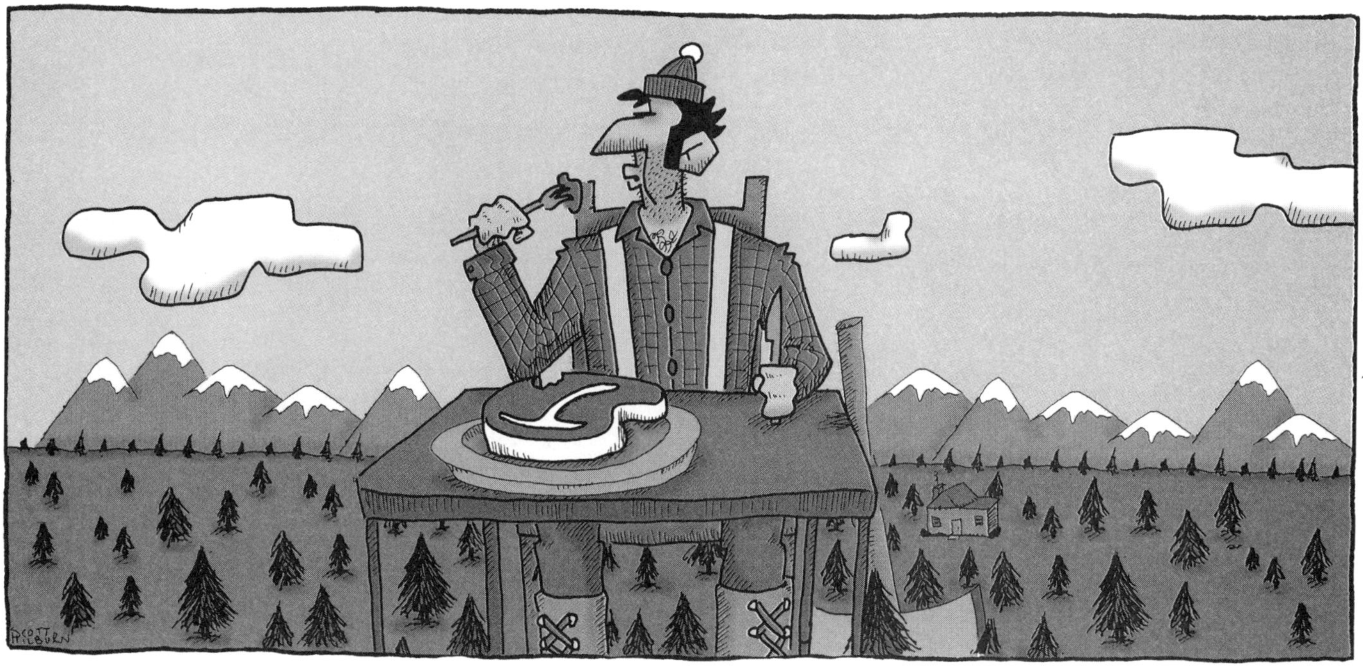
SCOTT HILBURN

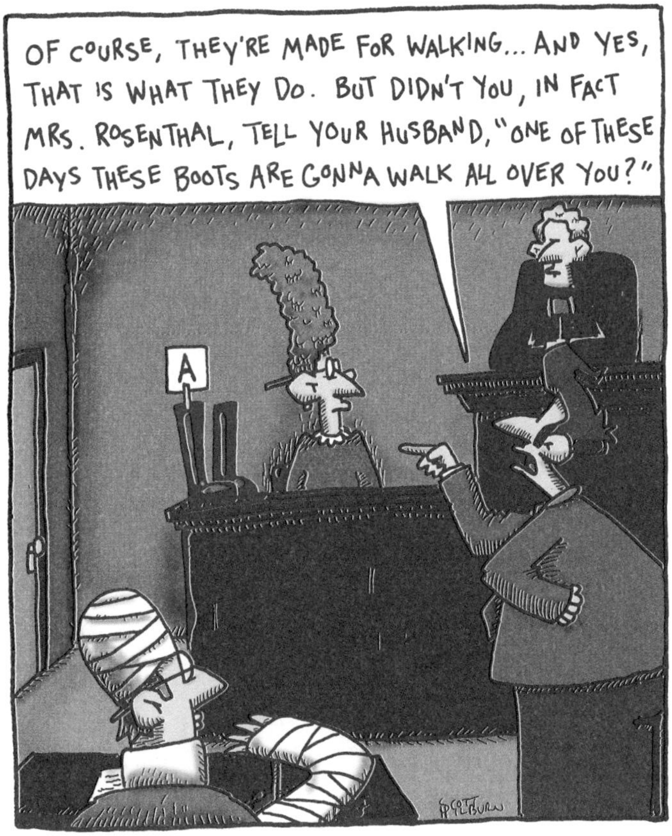
OF COURSE, THEY'RE MADE FOR WALKING... AND YES, THAT IS WHAT THEY DO. BUT DIDN'T YOU, IN FACT MRS. ROSENTHAL, TELL YOUR HUSBAND, "ONE OF THESE DAYS THESE BOOTS ARE GONNA WALK ALL OVER YOU?"
A
SCOTT HILBURN

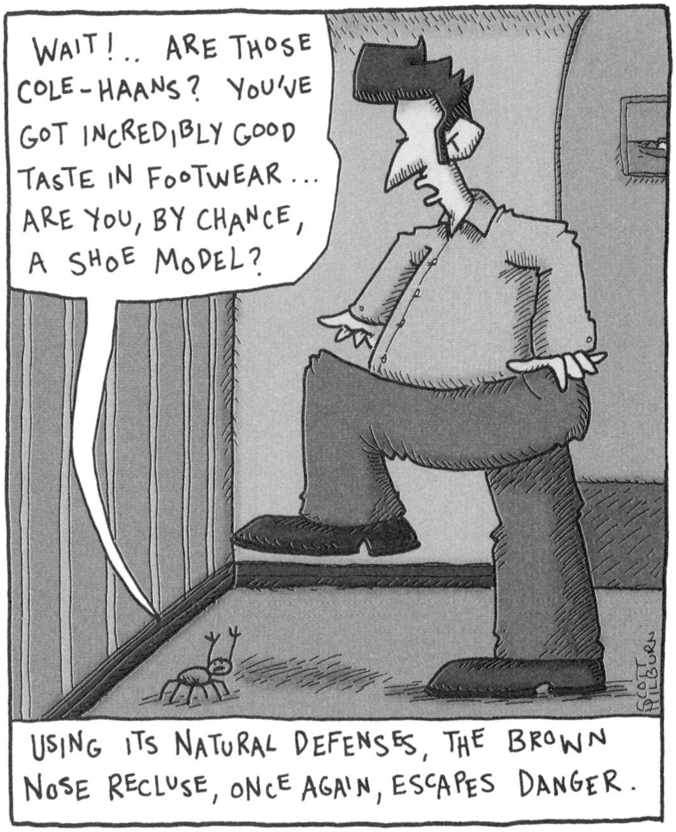
WAIT!.. ARE THOSE COLE-HAANS? YOU'VE GOT INCREDIBLY GOOD TASTE IN FOOTWEAR... ARE YOU, BY CHANCE, A SHOE MODEL?
SCOTT HILBURN
USING ITS NATURAL DEFENSES, THE BROWN NOSE RECLUSE, ONCE AGAIN, ESCAPES DANGER.

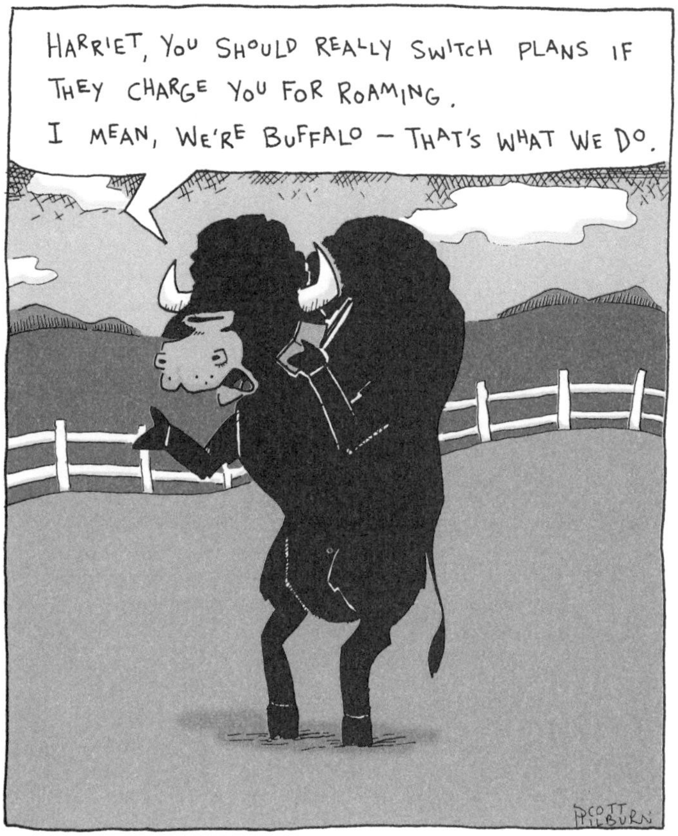
HARRIET, YOU SHOULD REALLY SWITCH PLANS IF THEY CHARGE YOU FOR ROAMING.
I MEAN, WE'RE BUFFALO — THAT'S WHAT WE DO.
SCOTT HILBURN

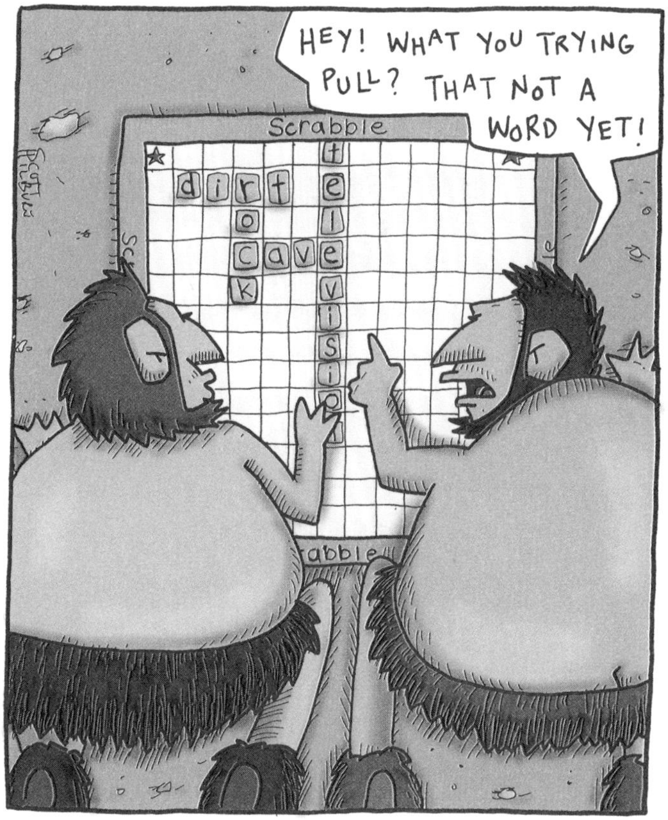
HEY! WHAT YOU TRYING PULL? THAT NOT A WORD YET!
Scrabble
dirt
rock
cave
televisio

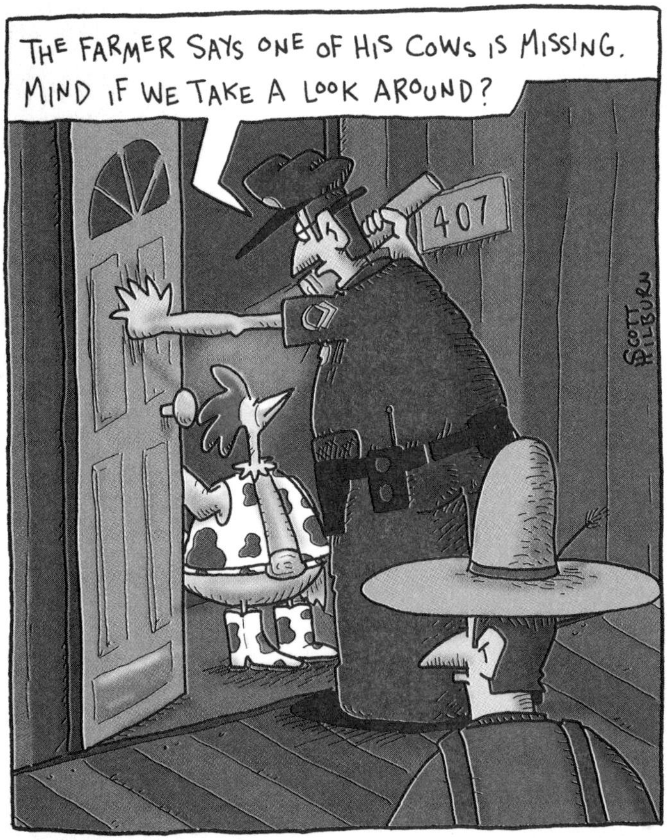
THE FARMER SAYS ONE OF HIS COWS IS MISSING. MIND IF WE TAKE A LOOK AROUND?
407
SCOTT HILBURN

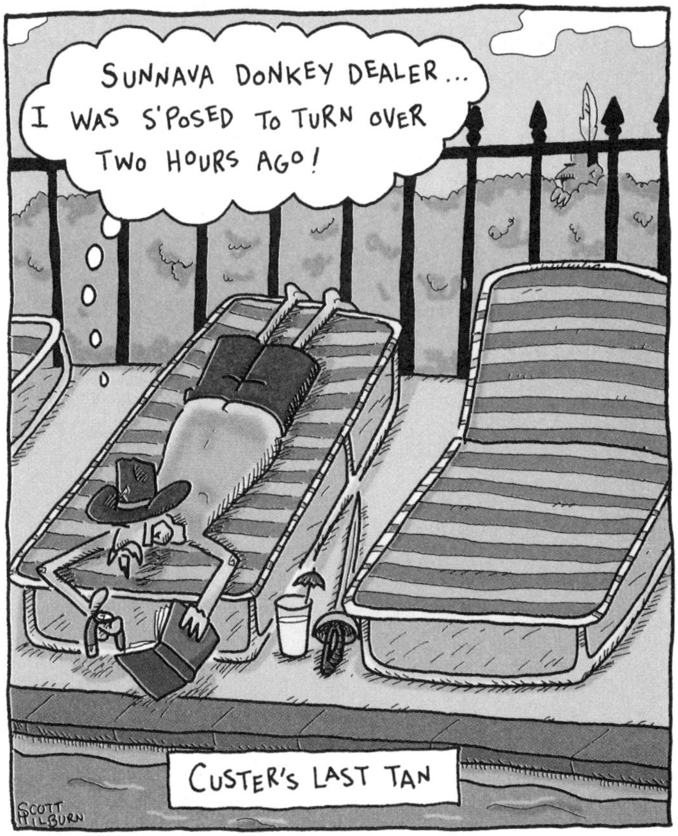
SUNNAVA DONKEY DEALER... I WAS S'POSED TO TURN OVER TWO HOURS AGO!
CUSTER'S LAST TAN
SCOTT HILBURN

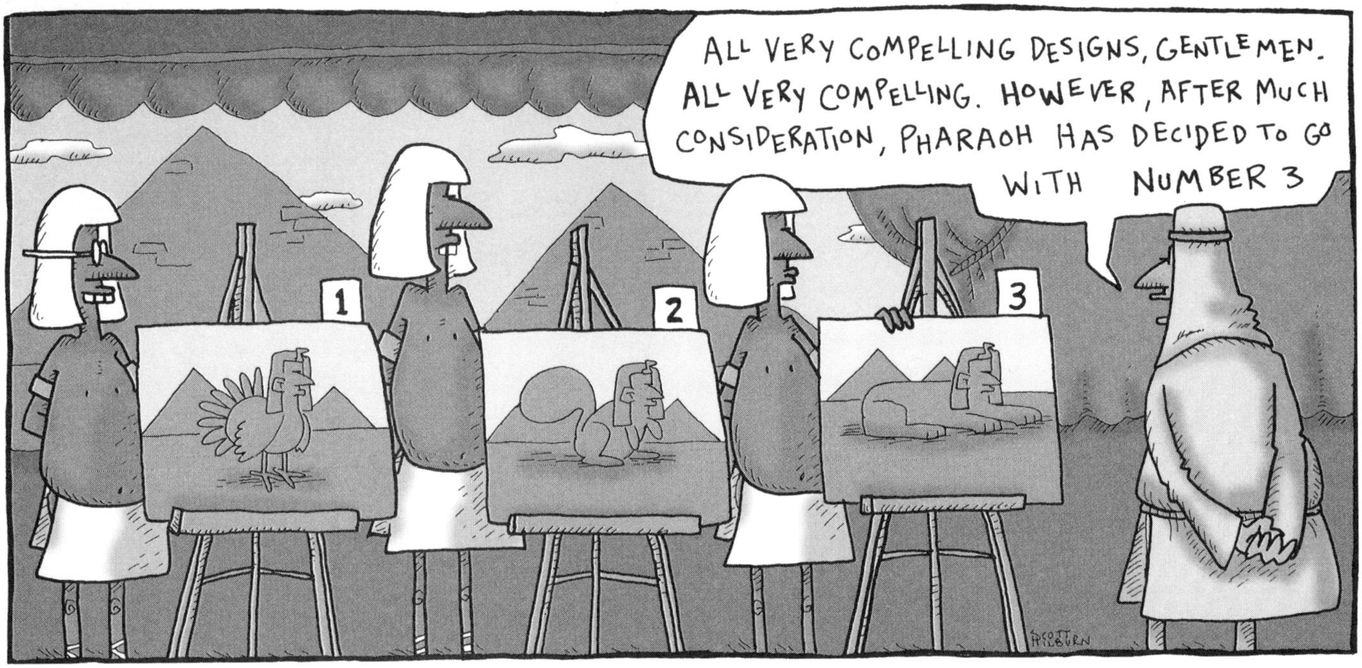
ALL VERY COMPELLING DESIGNS, GENTLEMEN. ALL VERY COMPELLING. HOWEVER, AFTER MUCH CONSIDERATION, PHARAOH HAS DECIDED TO GO WITH NUMBER 3
1
2
3
SCOTT HILBURN

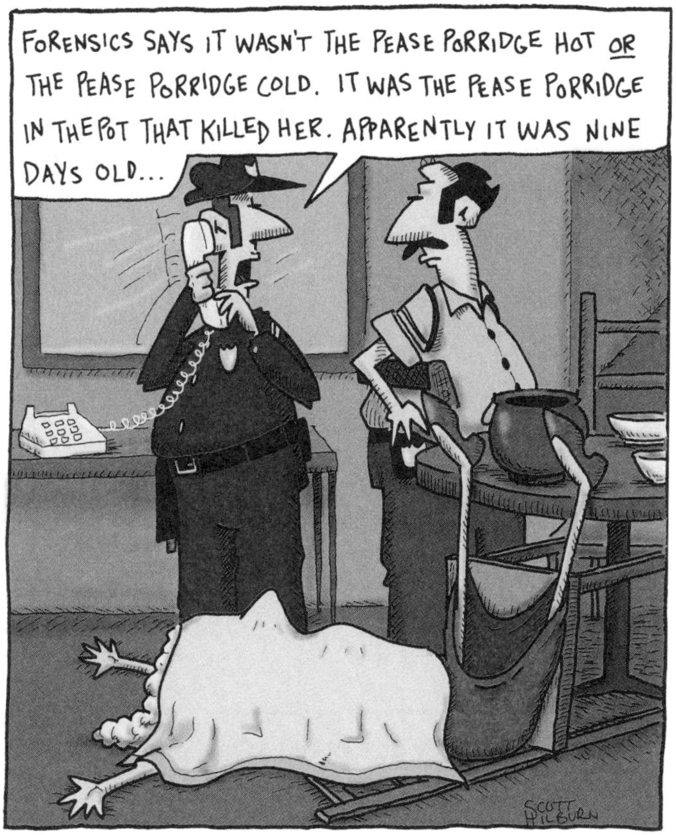
FORENSICS SAYS IT WASN'T THE PEASE PORRIDGE HOT OR THE PEASE PORRIDGE COLD. IT WAS THE PEASE PORRIDGE IN THE POT THAT KILLED HER. APPARENTLY IT WAS NINE DAYS OLD...
SCOTT HILBURN

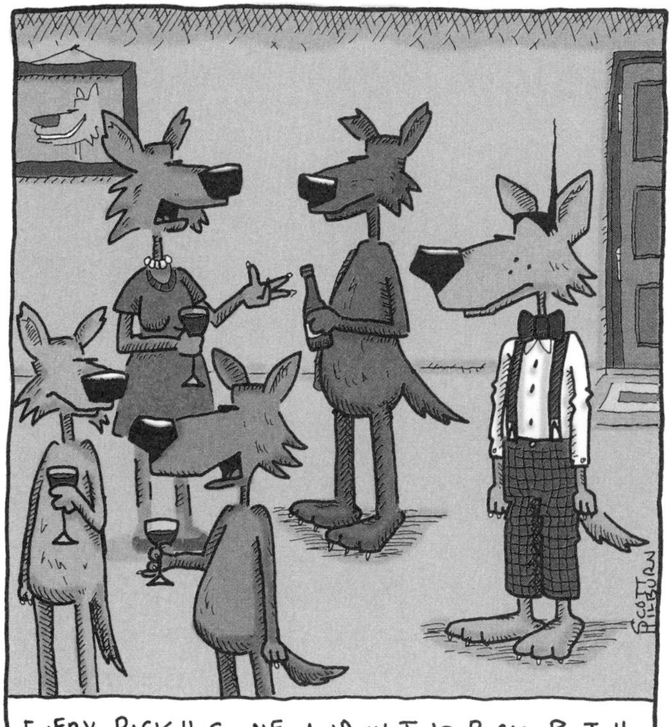
SCOTT HILBURN

EVERY PACK HAS ONE, AND IN THIS PACK, BUTCH WAS, WITHOUT QUESTION, THE ALFALFA MALE.

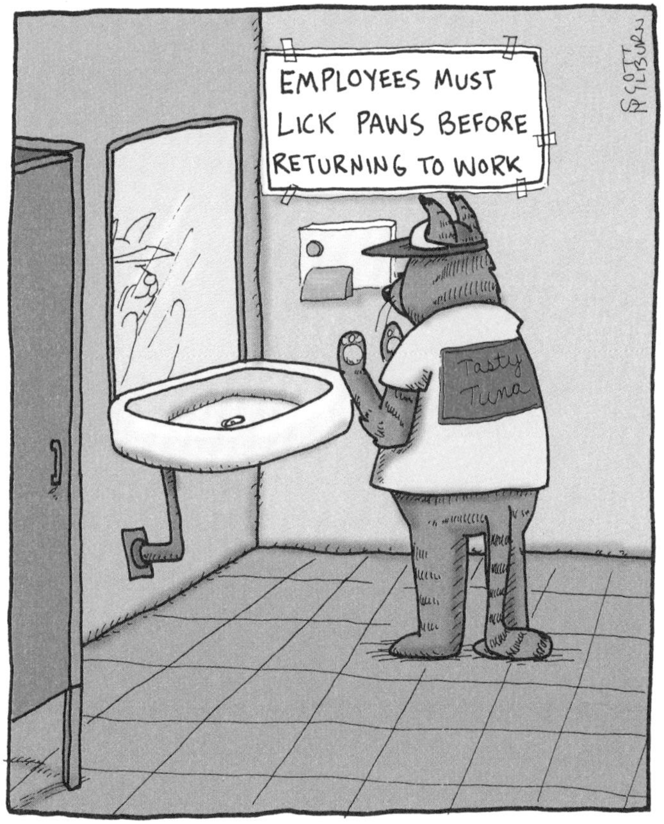
EMPLOYEES MUST LICK PAWS BEFORE RETURNING TO WORK
Tasty Tuna
SCOTT HILBURN

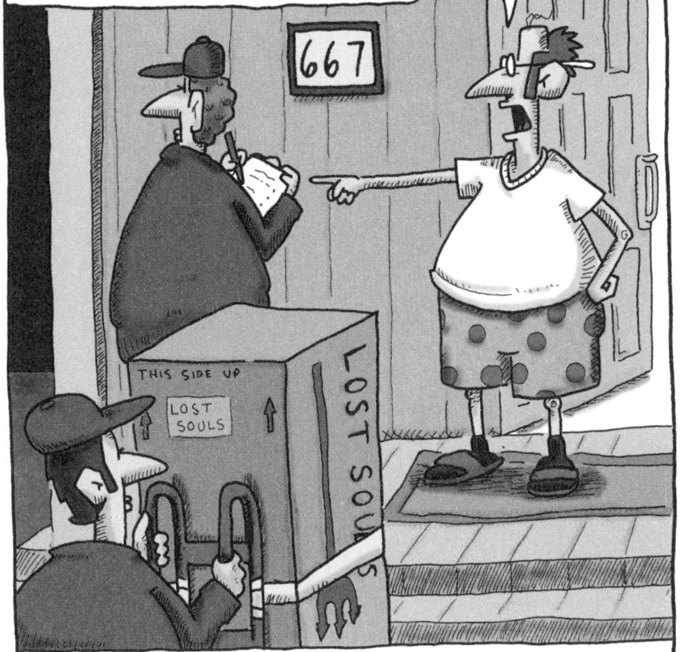
NO, THIS IS 667 ROSEMONT... YOU'RE LOOKING FOR THE HOUSE NEXT DOOR.
667
THIS SIDE UP
LOST SOULS
LOST SOULS

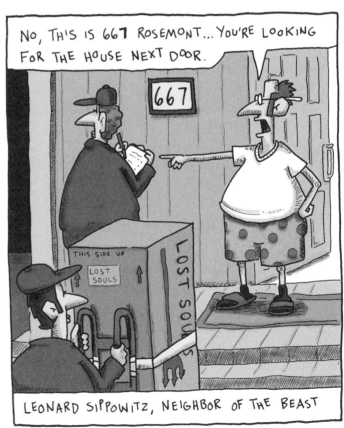

LEONARD SIPPOWITZ, NEIGHBOR OF THE BEAST

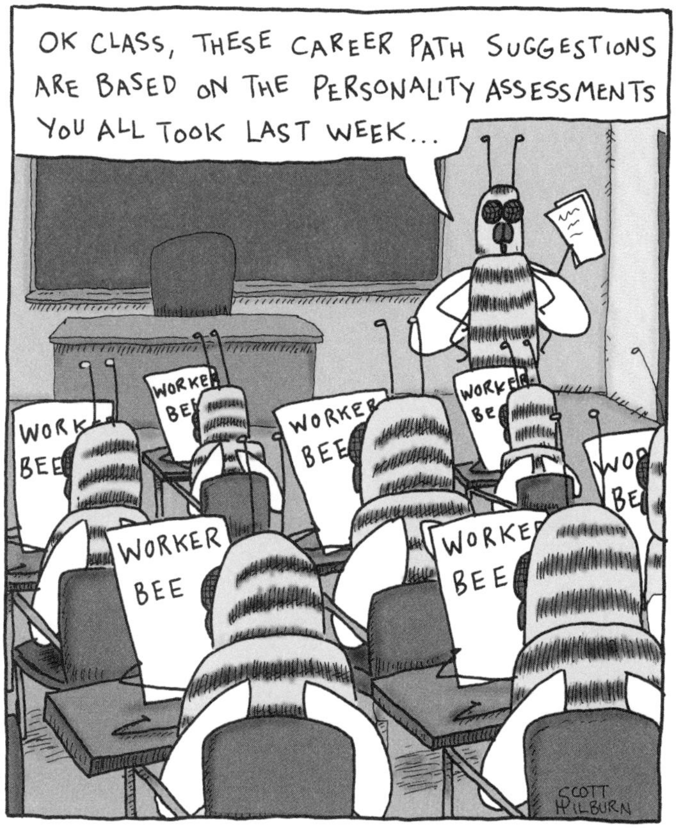
OK CLASS, THESE CAREER PATH SUGGESTIONS ARE BASED ON THE PERSONALITY ASSESSMENTS YOU ALL TOOK LAST WEEK...
WORKER BEE
WORKER BEE
WORKER BEE
WORKER BEE
WORKER BEE
SCOTT HILBURN

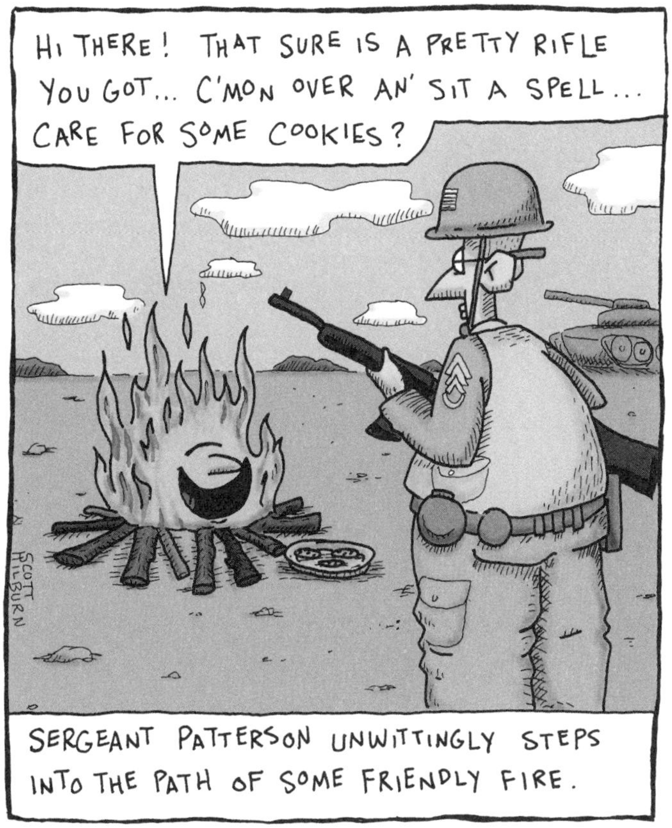
HI THERE! THAT SURE IS A PRETTY RIFLE YOU GOT... C'MON OVER AN' SIT A SPELL... CARE FOR SOME COOKIES?
SCOTT HILBURN
SERGEANT PATTERSON UNWITTINGLY STEPS INTO THE PATH OF SOME FRIENDLY FIRE.

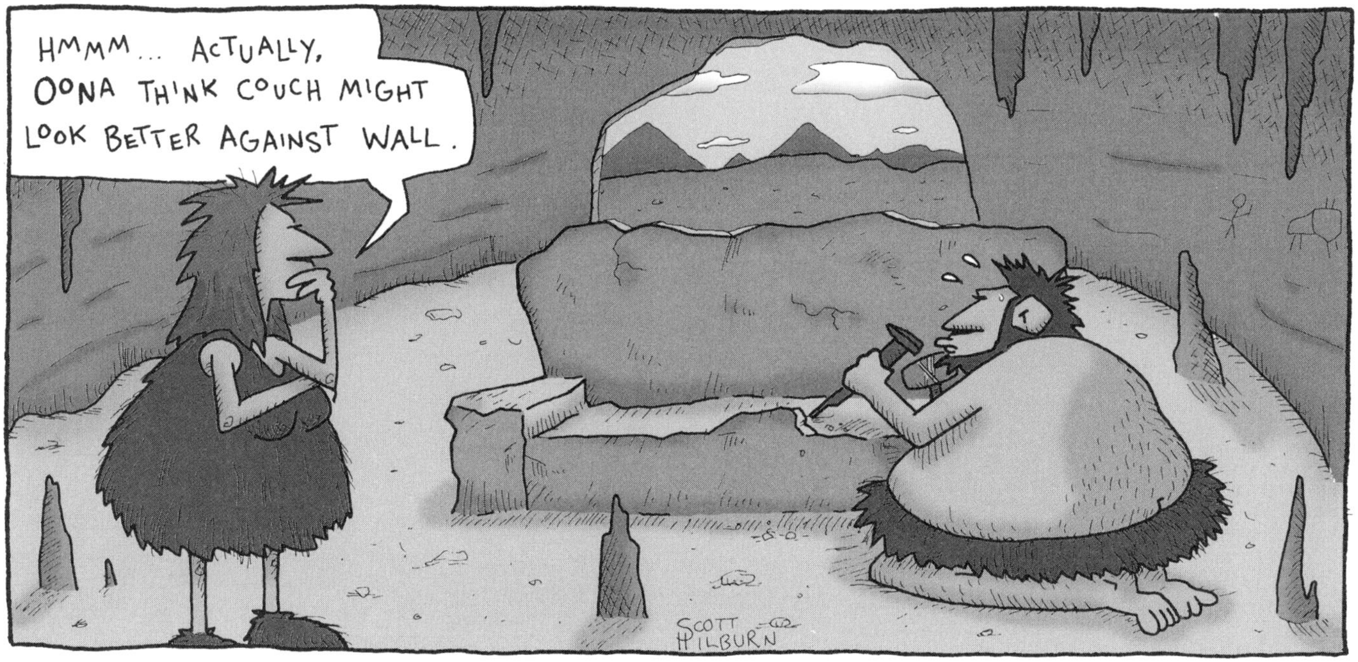
HMMM... ACTUALLY, OONA THINK COUCH MIGHT LOOK BETTER AGAINST WALL.
SCOTT HILBURN

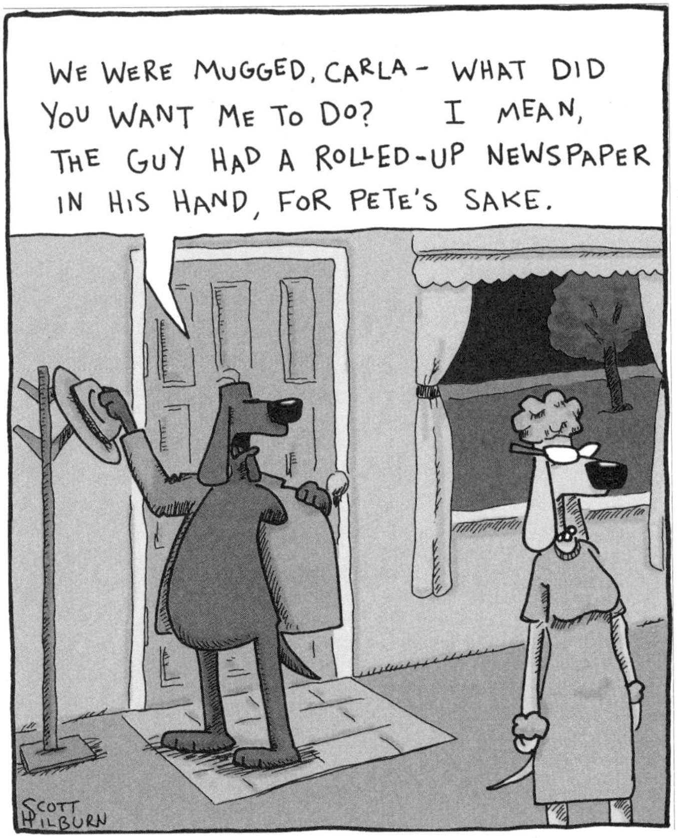
WE WERE MUGGED, CARLA - WHAT DID YOU WANT ME TO DO? I MEAN, THE GUY HAD A ROLLED-UP NEWSPAPER IN HIS HAND, FOR PETE'S SAKE.
SCOTT HILBURN

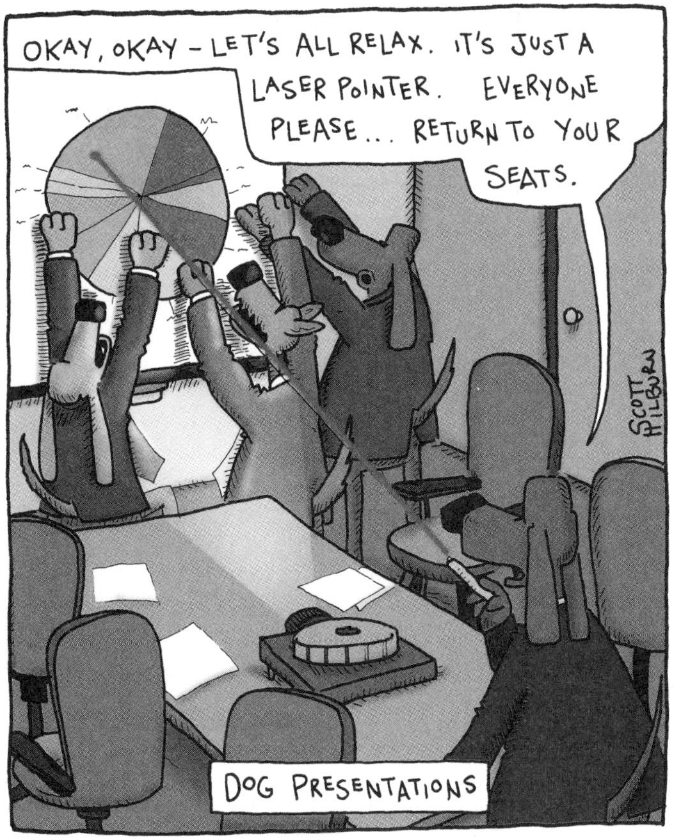
OKAY, OKAY - LET'S ALL RELAX. IT'S JUST A LASER POINTER. EVERYONE PLEASE... RETURN TO YOUR SEATS.
SCOTT HILBURN
DOG PRESENTATIONS

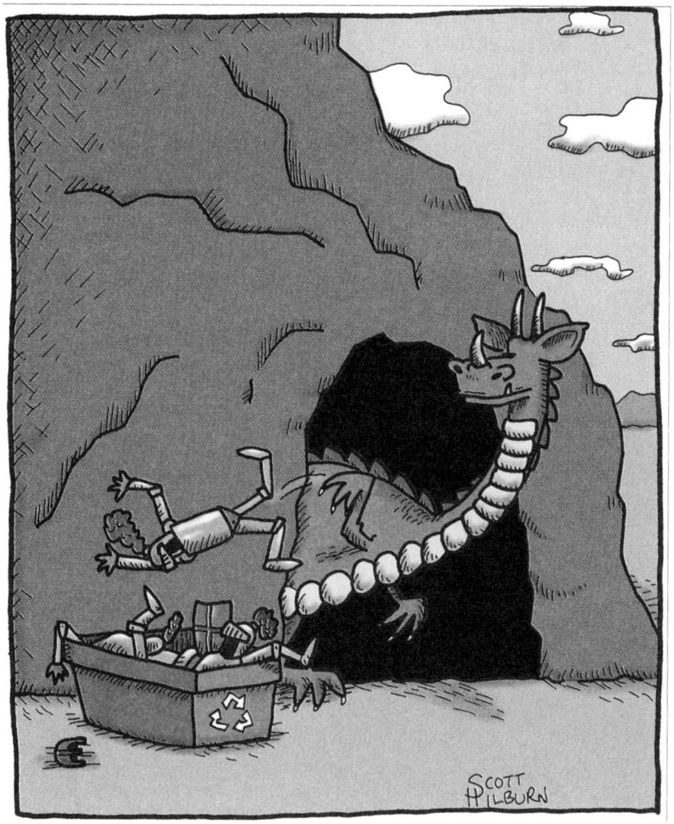
SCOTT HILBURN

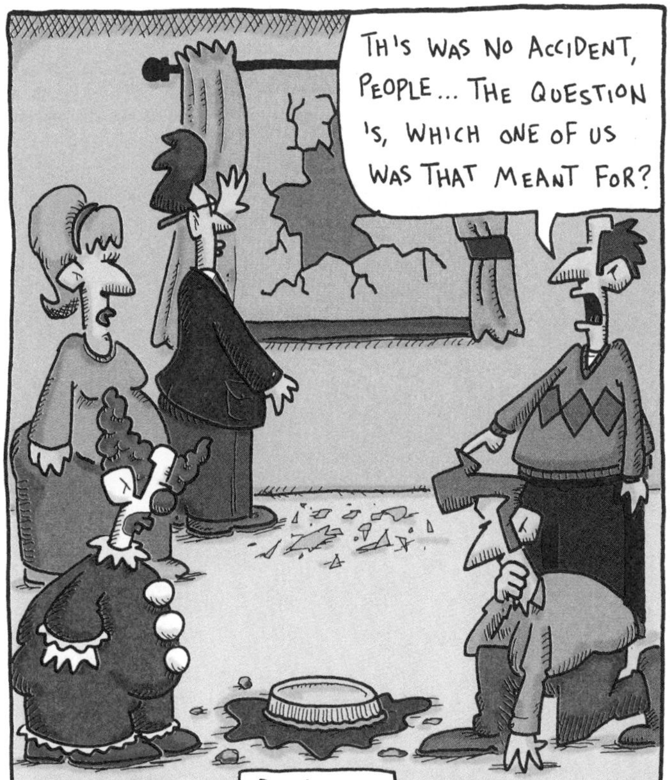
TH'S WAS NO ACCIDENT, PEOPLE... THE QUESTION 'S, WHICH ONE OF US WAS THAT MEANT FOR?
DRIVE-PIE
SCOTT HILBURN

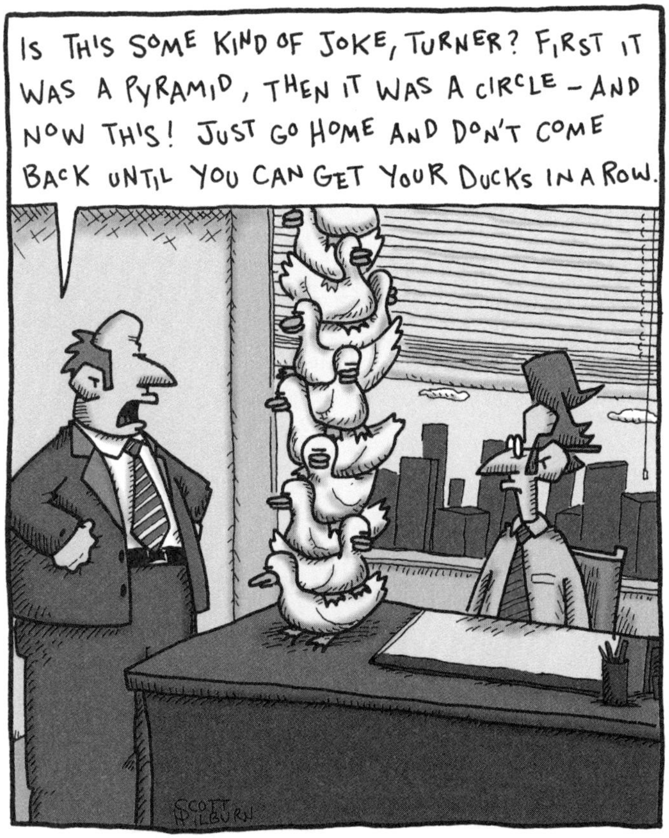
IS THIS SOME KIND OF JOKE, TURNER? FIRST IT WAS A PYRAMID, THEN IT WAS A CIRCLE – AND NOW THIS! JUST GO HOME AND DON'T COME BACK UNTIL YOU CAN GET YOUR DUCKS IN A ROW.
SCOTT HILBURN

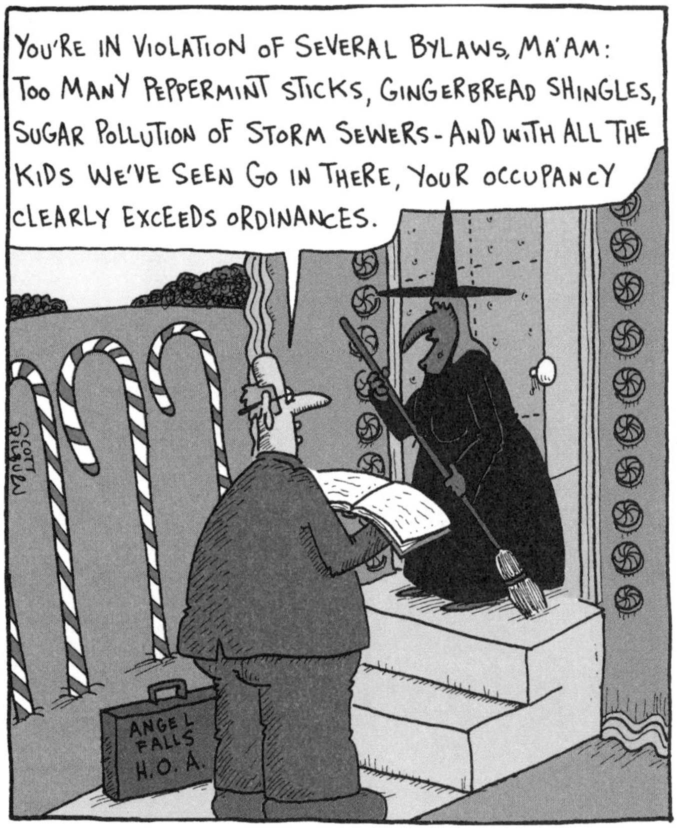
YOU'RE IN VIOLATION OF SEVERAL BYLAWS, MA'AM: TOO MANY PEPPERMINT STICKS, GINGERBREAD SHINGLES, SUGAR POLLUTION OF STORM SEWERS – AND WITH ALL THE KIDS WE'VE SEEN GO IN THERE, YOUR OCCUPANCY CLEARLY EXCEEDS ORDINANCES.
SCOTT HILBURN
ANGEL FALLS H.O.A.

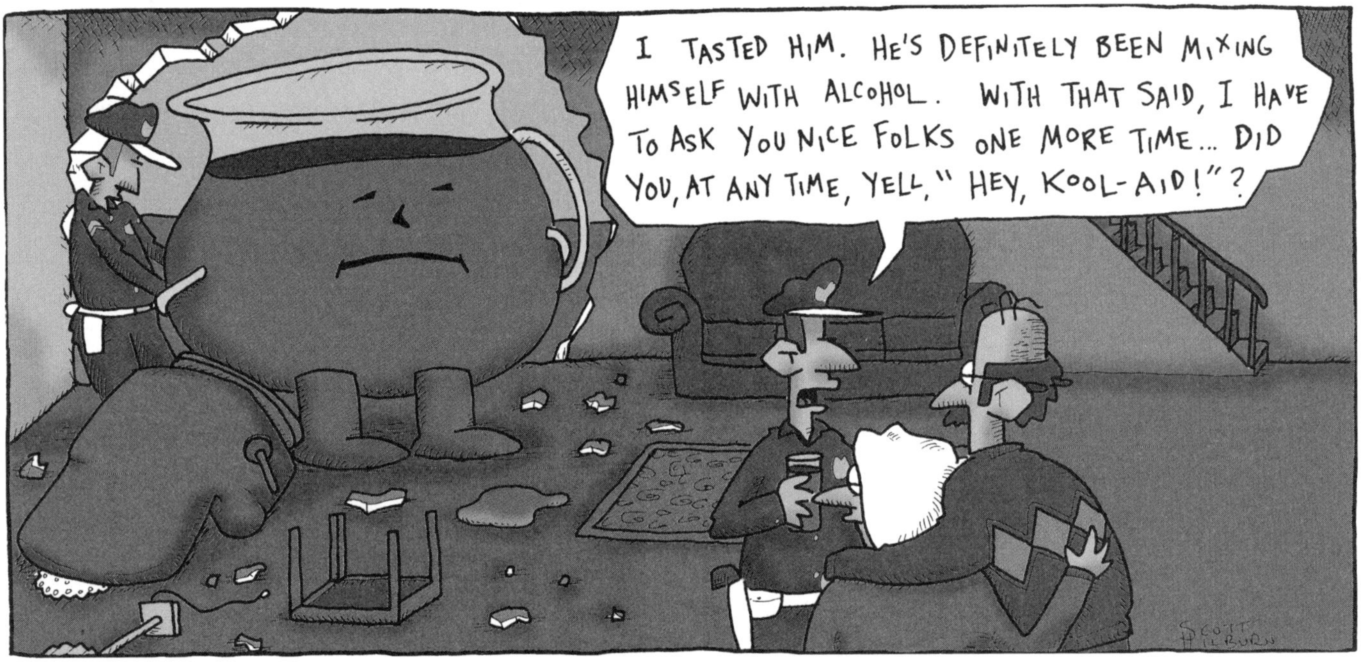
I TASTED HIM. HE'S DEFINITELY BEEN MIXING HIMSELF WITH ALCOHOL. WITH THAT SAID, I HAVE TO ASK YOU NICE FOLKS ONE MORE TIME... DID YOU, AT ANY TIME, YELL, "HEY, KOOL-AID!"?
SCOTT HILBURN

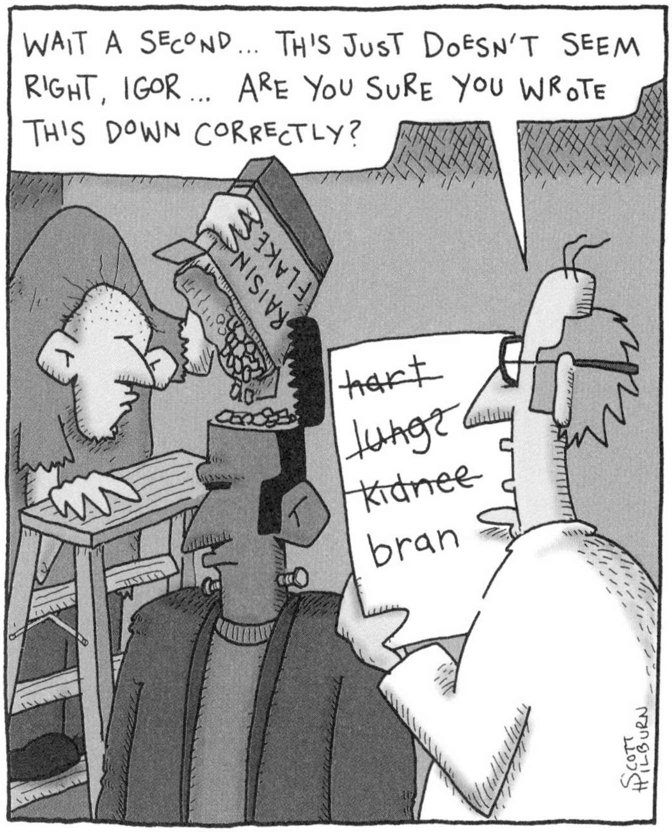
WAIT A SECOND... THIS JUST DOESN'T SEEM RIGHT, IGOR... ARE YOU SURE YOU WROTE THIS DOWN CORRECTLY?
RAISIN FLAKES
hart
lungs
kidnee
bran
SCOTT HILBURN

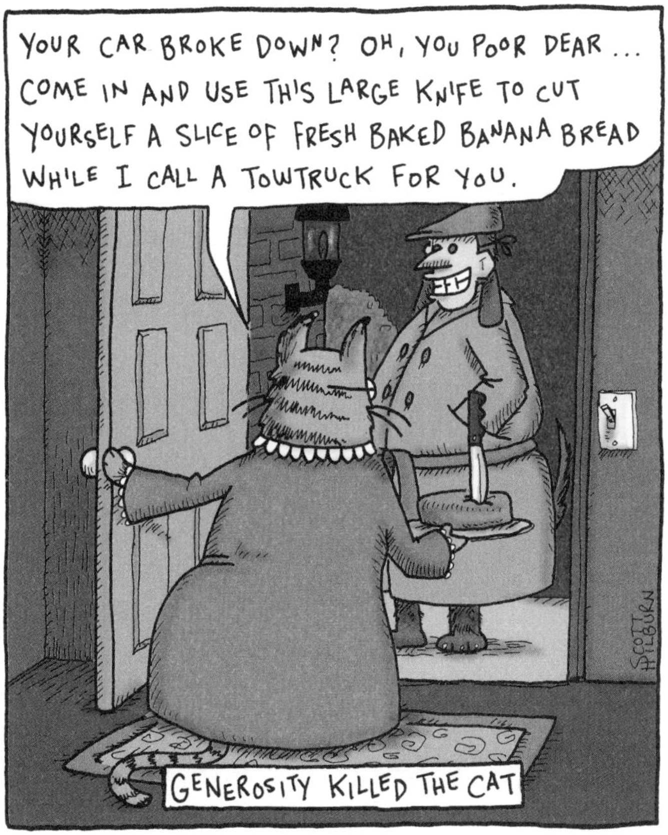
YOUR CAR BROKE DOWN? OH, YOU POOR DEAR... COME IN AND USE THIS LARGE KNIFE TO CUT YOURSELF A SLICE OF FRESH BAKED BANANA BREAD WHILE I CALL A TOWTRUCK FOR YOU.
SCOTT HILBURN
GENEROSITY KILLED THE CAT

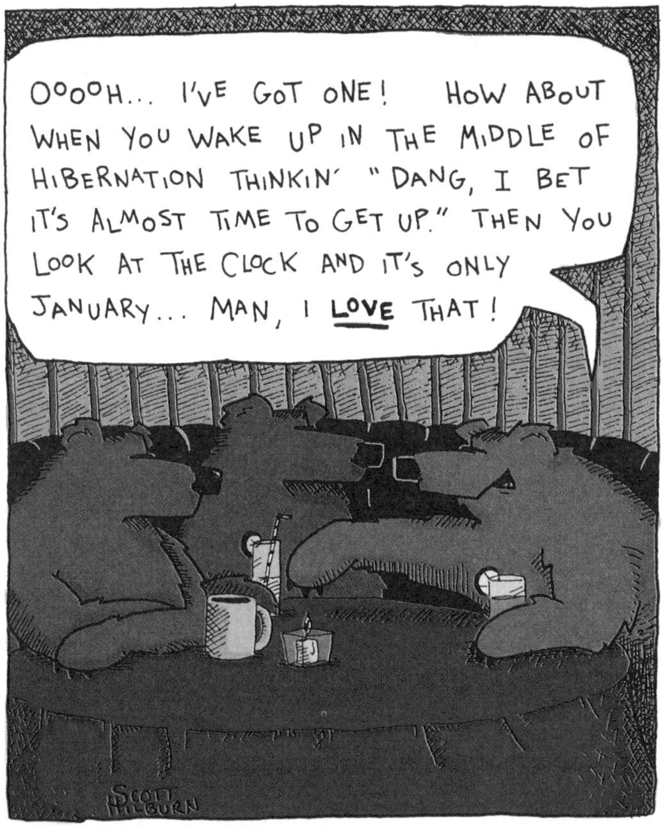
OOOOH... I'VE GOT ONE! HOW ABOUT WHEN YOU WAKE UP IN THE MIDDLE OF HIBERNATION THINKIN' "DANG, I BET IT'S ALMOST TIME TO GET UP." THEN YOU LOOK AT THE CLOCK AND IT'S ONLY JANUARY... MAN, I LOVE THAT!
SCOTT HILBURN

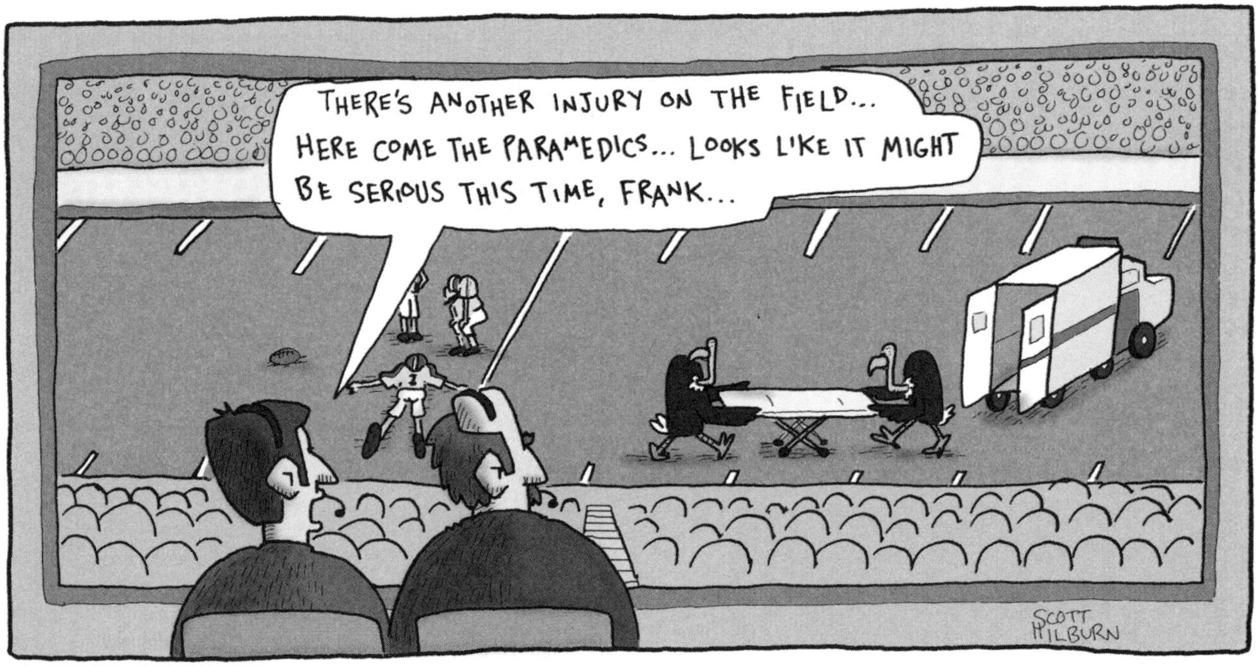
THERE'S ANOTHER INJURY ON THE FIELD... HERE COME THE PARAMEDICS... LOOKS LIKE IT MIGHT BE SERIOUS THIS TIME, FRANK...
SCOTT HILBURN

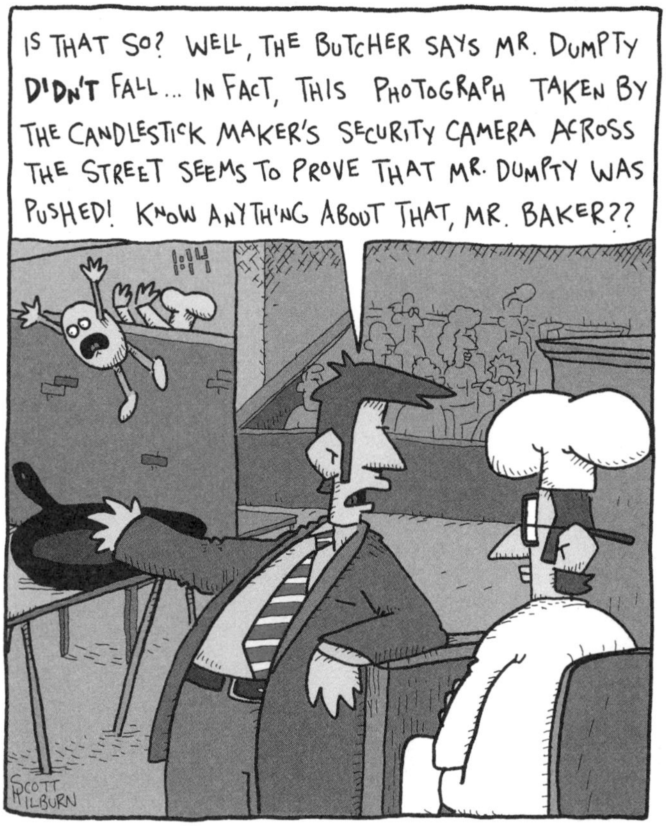
IS THAT SO? WELL, THE BUTCHER SAYS MR. DUMPTY **DIDN'T** FALL... IN FACT, THIS PHOTOGRAPH TAKEN BY THE CANDLESTICK MAKER'S SECURITY CAMERA ACROSS THE STREET SEEMS TO PROVE THAT MR. DUMPTY WAS PUSHED! KNOW ANYTHING ABOUT THAT, MR. BAKER??
SCOTT HILBURN

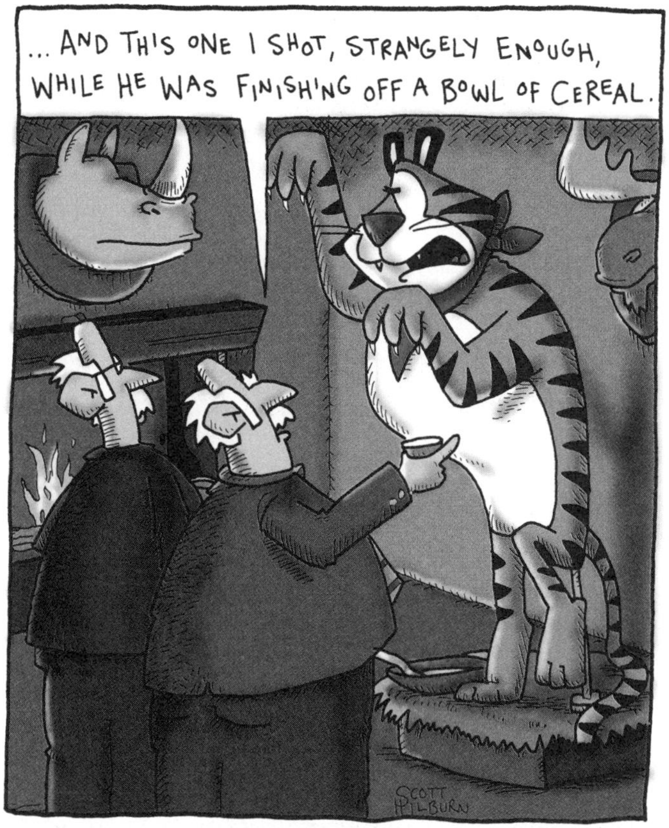
... AND THIS ONE I SHOT, STRANGELY ENOUGH, WHILE HE WAS FINISHING OFF A BOWL OF CEREAL.
SCOTT HILBURN

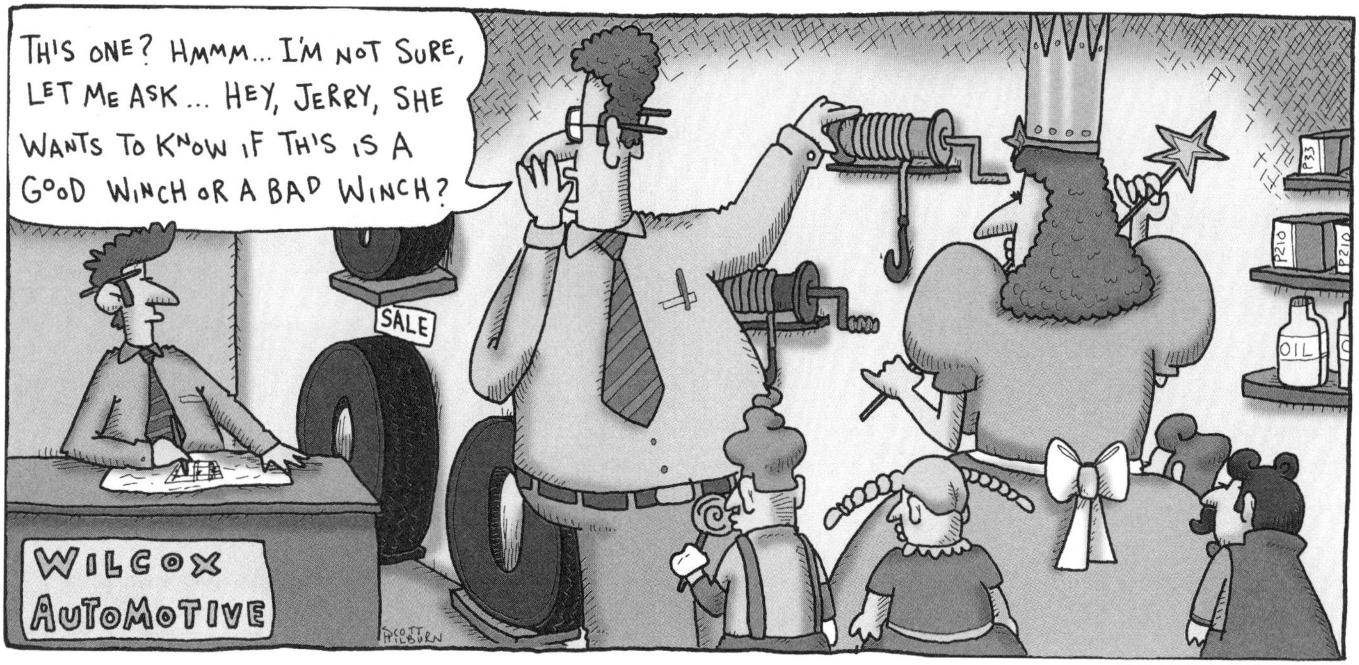
THIS ONE? HMMM... I'M NOT SURE, LET ME ASK... HEY, JERRY, SHE WANTS TO KNOW IF THIS IS A GOOD WINCH OR A BAD WINCH?
SALE
P33
P210
P210
OIL
WILCOX AUTOMOTIVE
SCOTT HILBURN

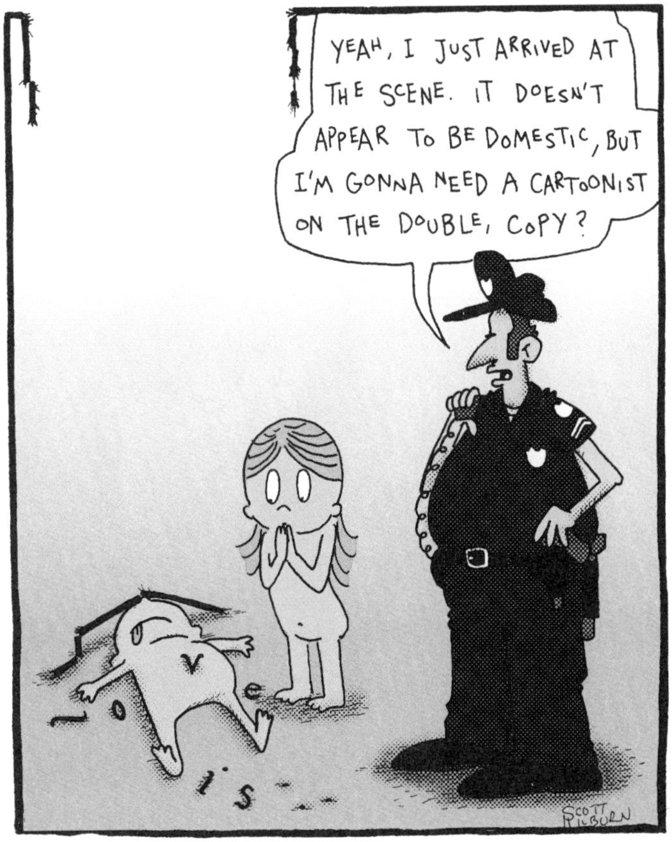
YEAH, I JUST ARRIVED AT THE SCENE. IT DOESN'T APPEAR TO BE DOMESTIC, BUT I'M GONNA NEED A CARTOONIST ON THE DOUBLE, COPY?
l o v e i s
SCOTT HILBURN

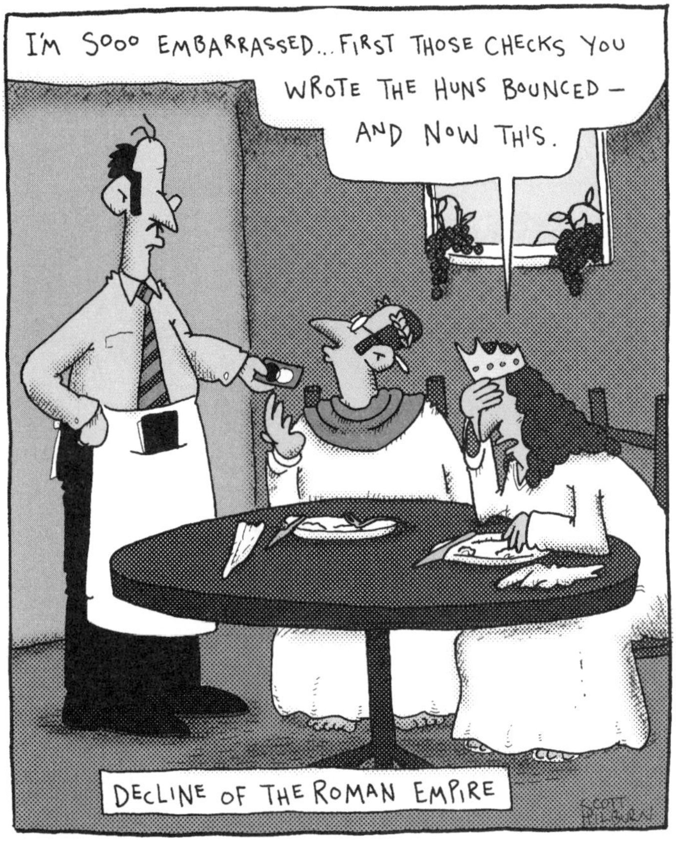
I'M SOOO EMBARRASSED... FIRST THOSE CHECKS YOU WROTE THE HUNS BOUNCED— AND NOW THIS.
DECLINE OF THE ROMAN EMPIRE
SCOTT HILBURN

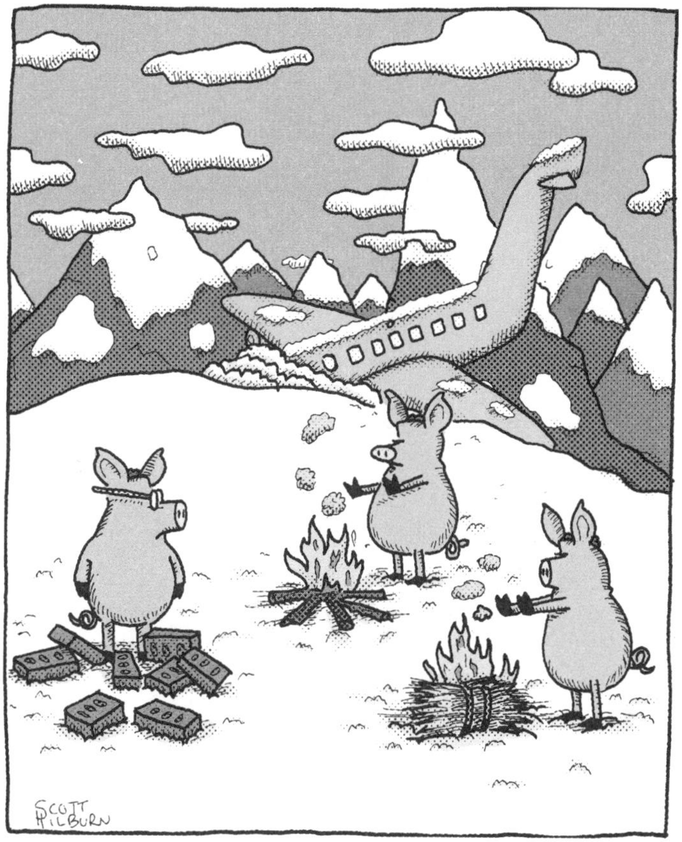

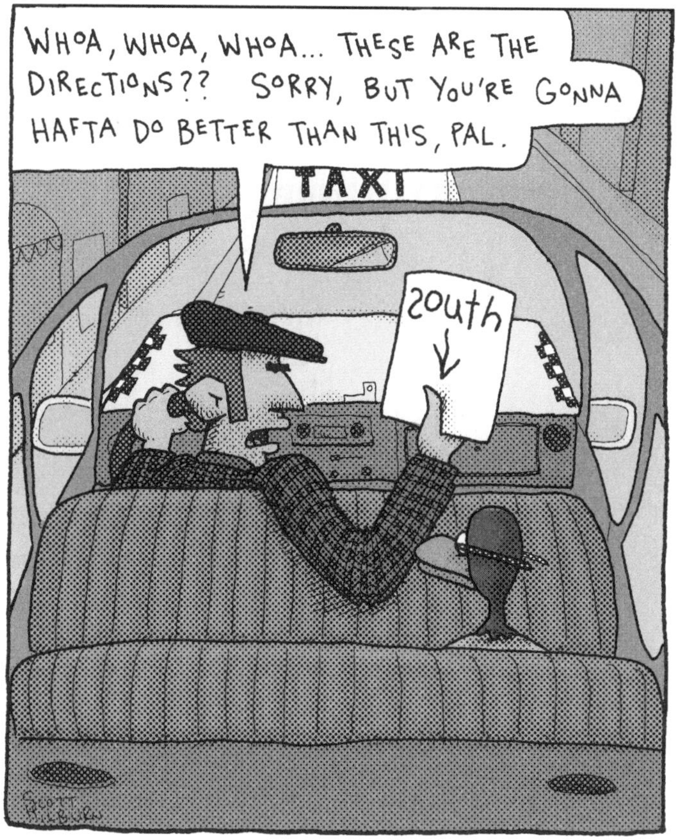
WHOA, WHOA, WHOA... THESE ARE THE DIRECTIONS?? SORRY, BUT YOU'RE GONNA HAFTA DO BETTER THAN THIS, PAL.
TAXI
south

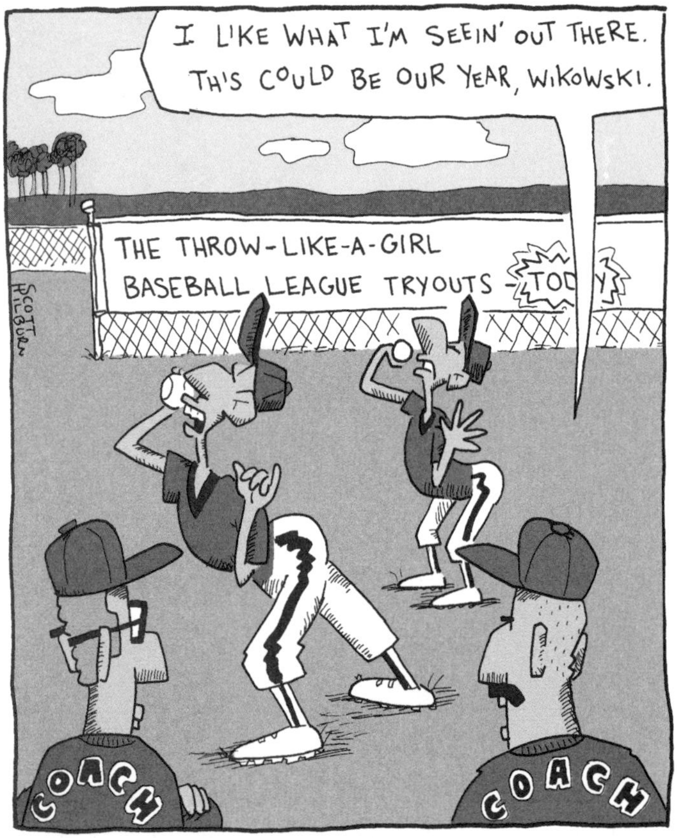
I LIKE WHAT I'M SEEIN' OUT THERE. TH'S COULD BE OUR YEAR, WIKOWSKI.
THE THROW-LIKE-A-GIRL BASEBALL LEAGUE TRYOUTS - TODAY
COACH
COACH
SCOTT HILBURN

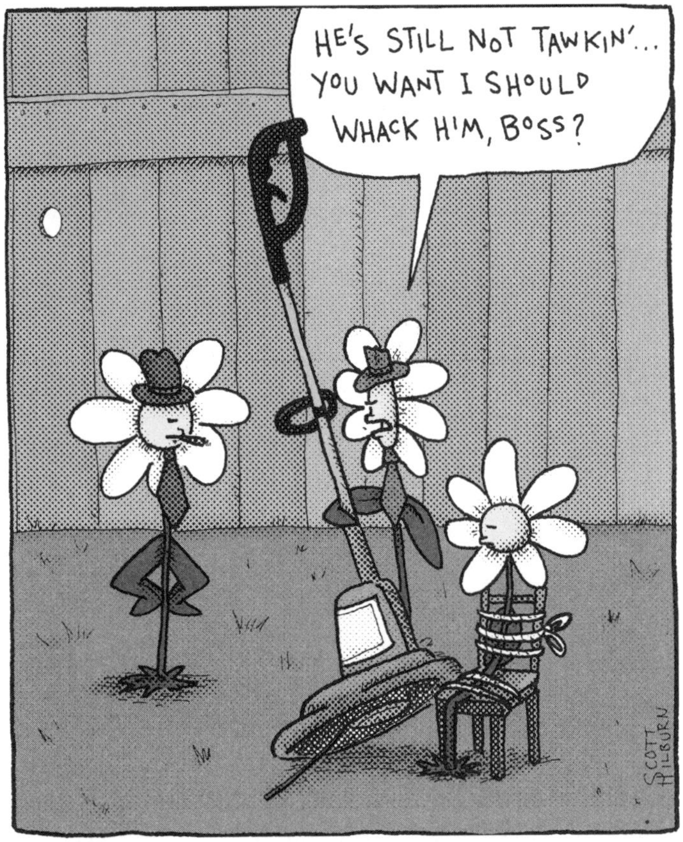
HE'S STILL NOT TAWKIN'... YOU WANT I SHOULD WHACK HIM, BOSS?
SCOTT HILBURN

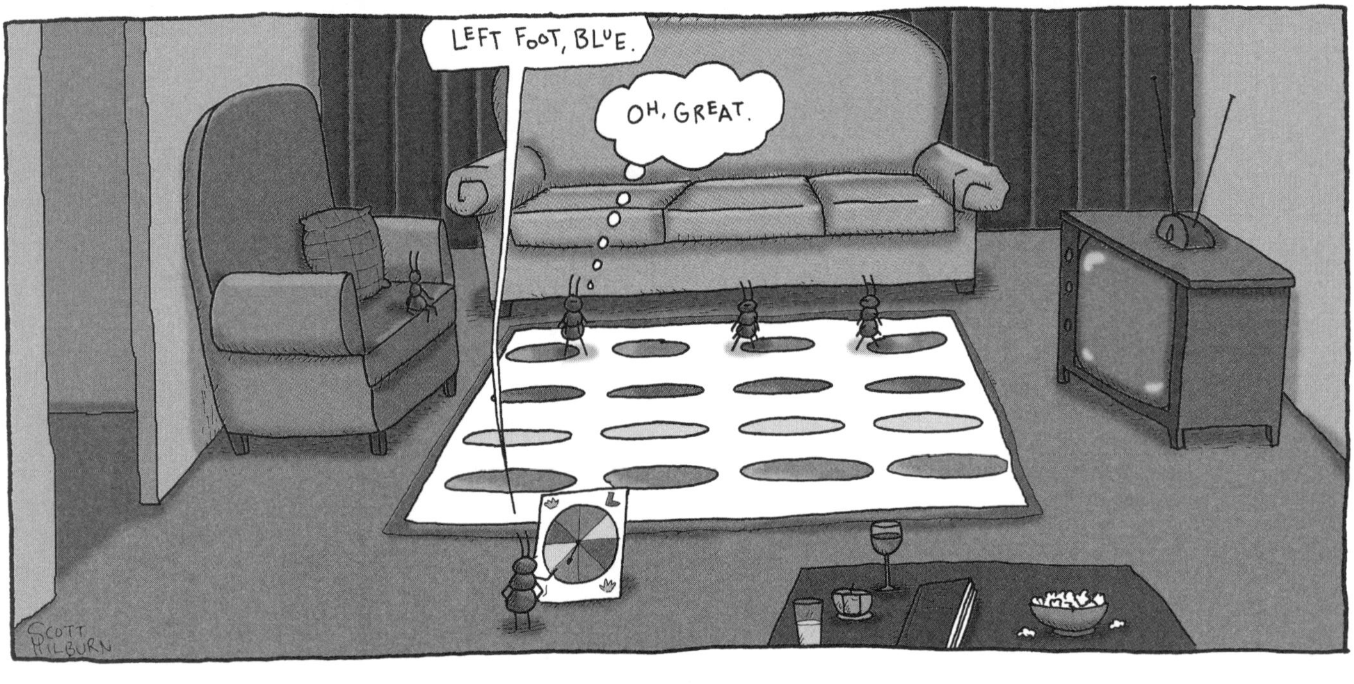
LEFT FOOT, BLUE.
OH, GREAT.
SCOTT HILBURN

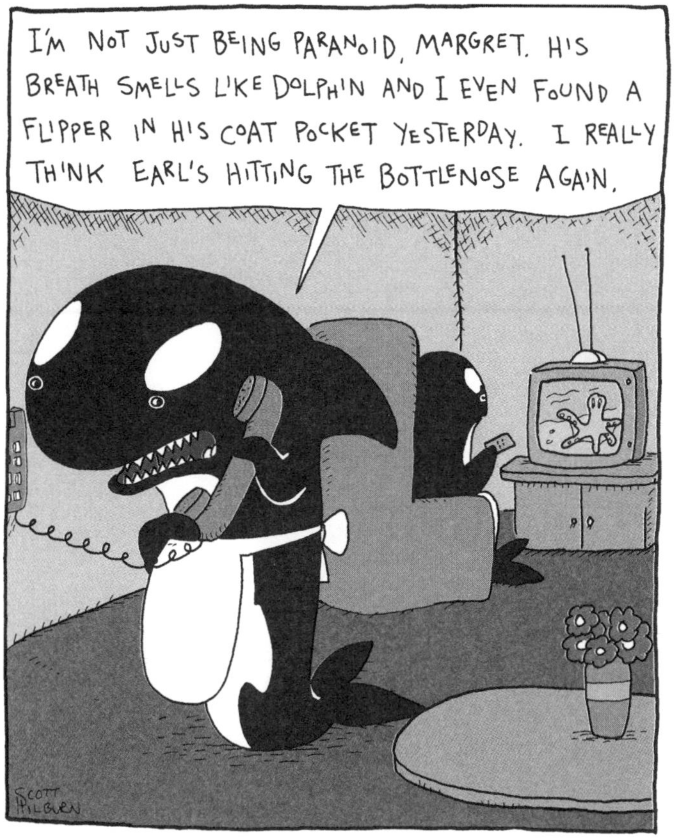
I'M NOT JUST BEING PARANOID, MARGRET. HIS BREATH SMELLS LIKE DOLPHIN AND I EVEN FOUND A FLIPPER IN HIS COAT POCKET YESTERDAY. I REALLY THINK EARL'S HITTING THE BOTTLENOSE AGAIN.
SCOTT HILBURN

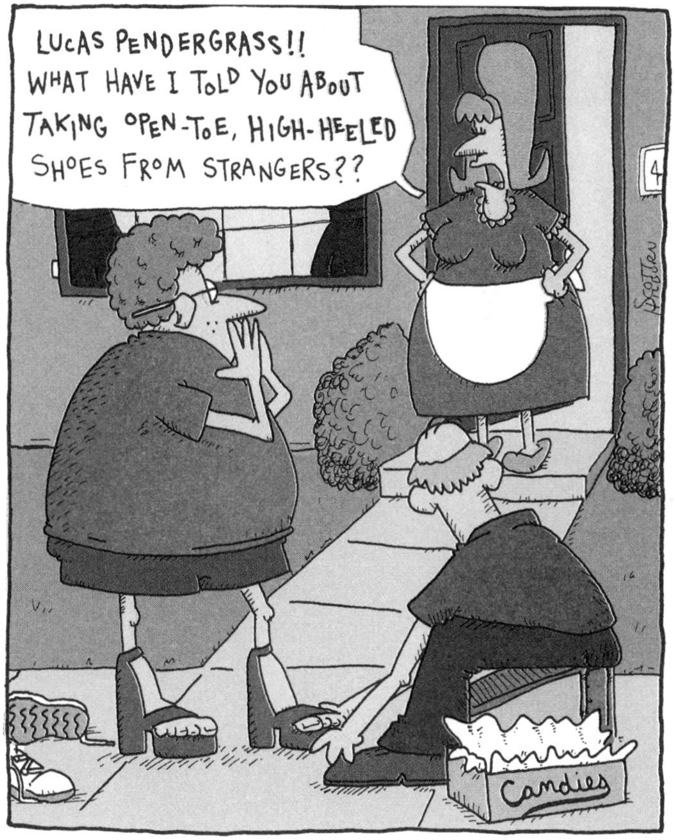
LUCAS PENDERGRASS!! WHAT HAVE I TOLD YOU ABOUT TAKING OPEN-TOE, HIGH-HEELED SHOES FROM STRANGERS??
Candies

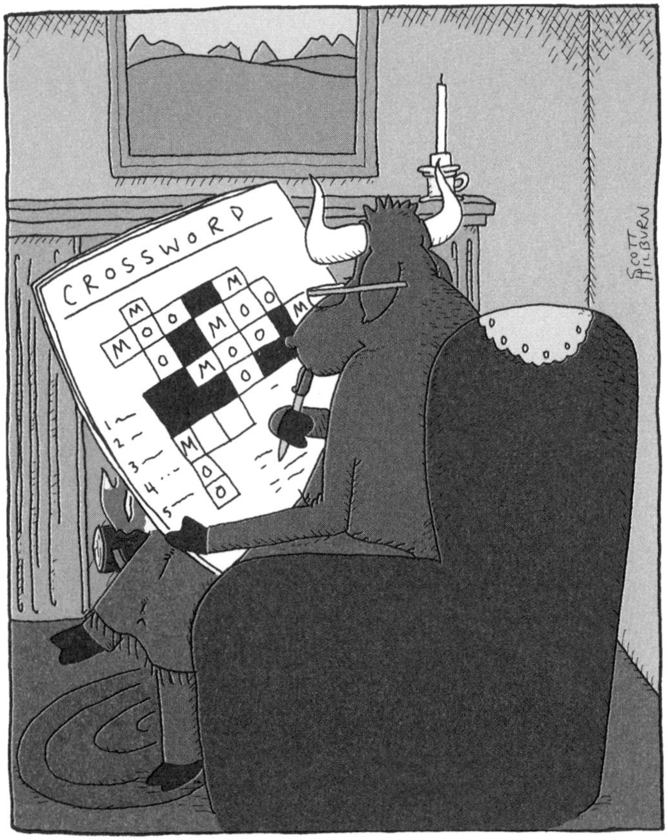
CROSSWORD
SCOTT HILBURN

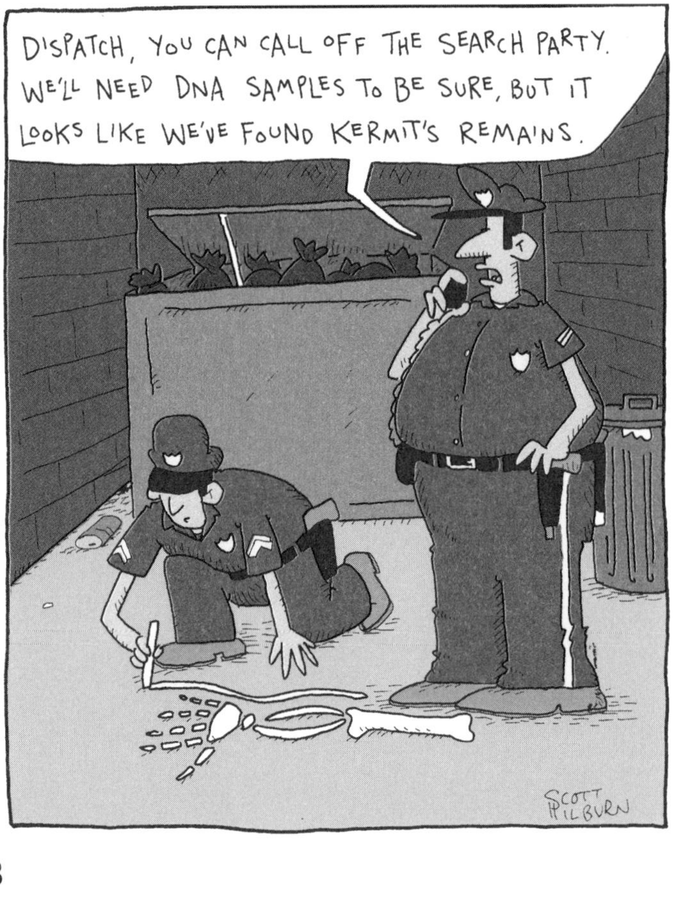
DISPATCH, YOU CAN CALL OFF THE SEARCH PARTY. WE'LL NEED DNA SAMPLES TO BE SURE, BUT IT LOOKS LIKE WE'VE FOUND KERMIT'S REMAINS.
SCOTT HILBURN

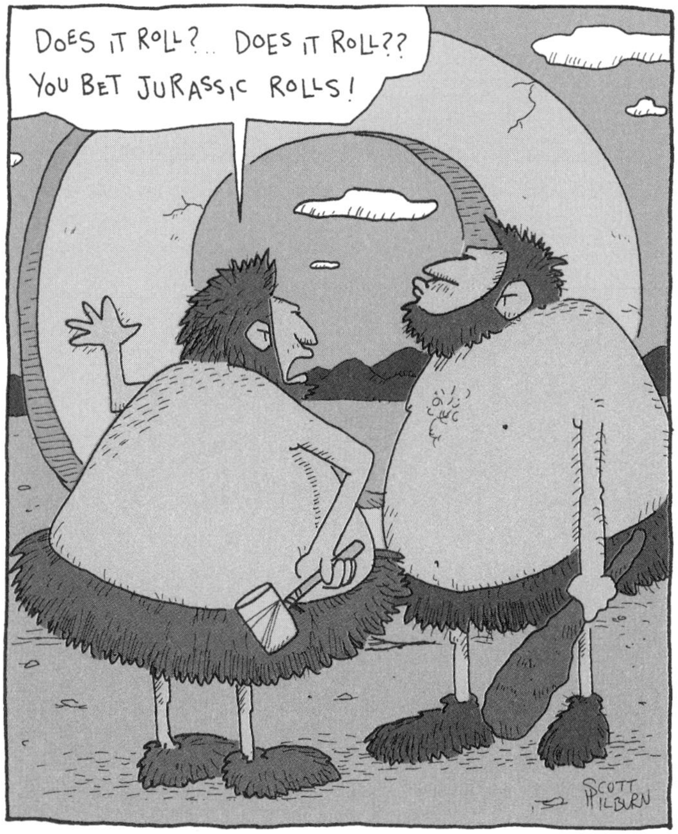
DOES IT ROLL?.. DOES IT ROLL?? YOU BET JURASSIC ROLLS!
SCOTT HILBURN

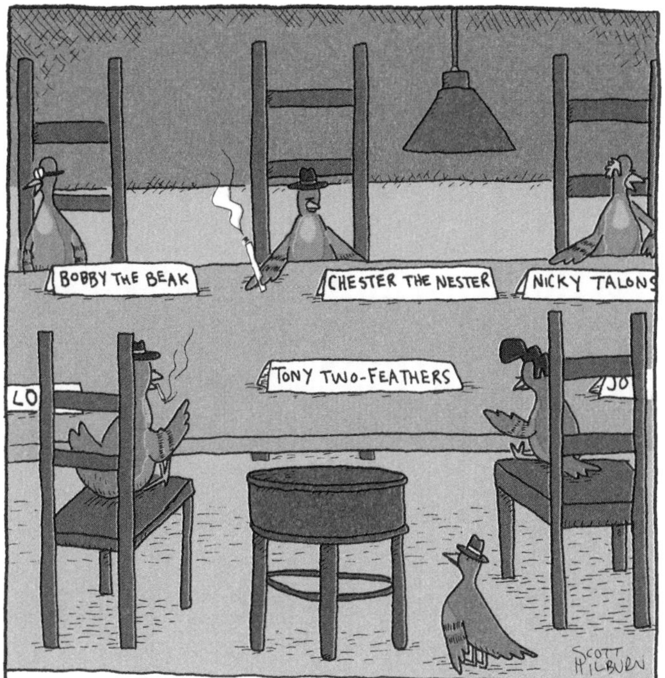
BOBBY THE BEAK
CHESTER THE NESTER
NICKY TALONS
TONY TWO-FEATHERS
SCOTT HILBURN

LAST TO ARRIVE AT THE PIGEON CRIME FAMILY'S WEEKLY MEETING, TONY PONDERS IF THERE'S ANY SIGNIFICANCE TO HIS SEATING ASSIGNMENT OR IF HE'S JUST PARANOID.

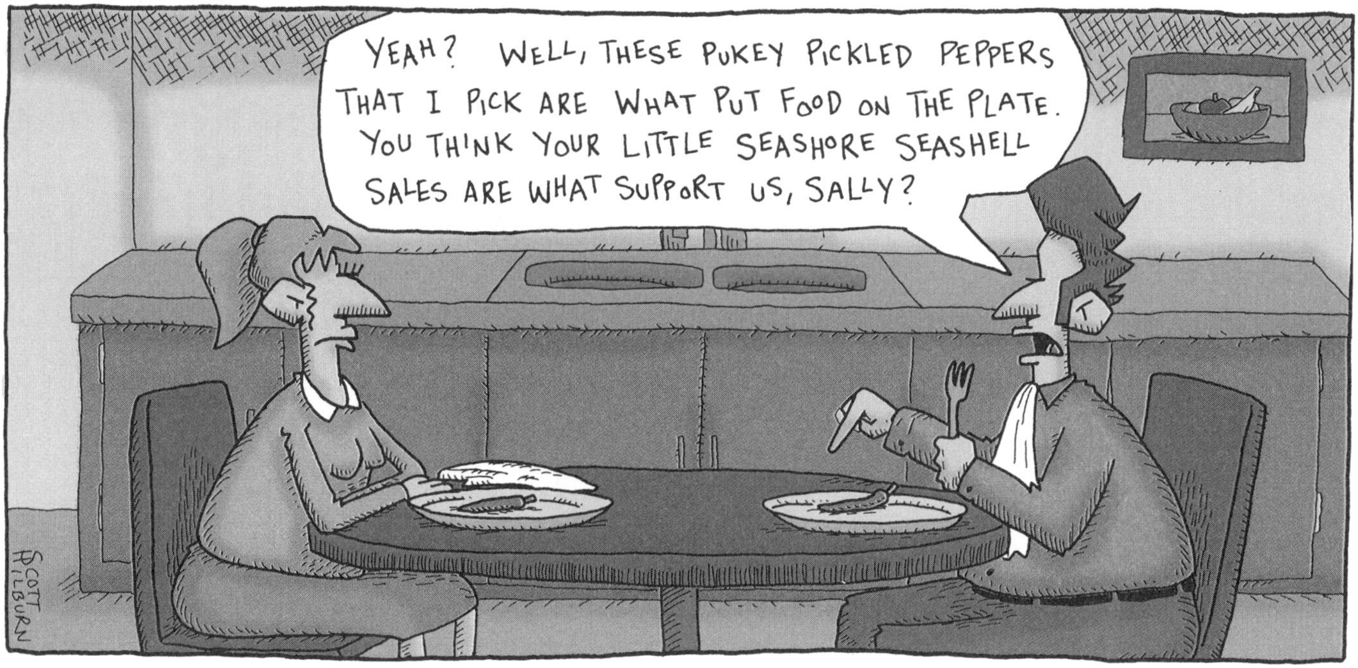
YEAH? WELL, THESE PUKEY PICKLED PEPPERS THAT I PICK ARE WHAT PUT FOOD ON THE PLATE. YOU THINK YOUR LITTLE SEASHORE SEASHELL SALES ARE WHAT SUPPORT US, SALLY?
SCOTT HILBURN

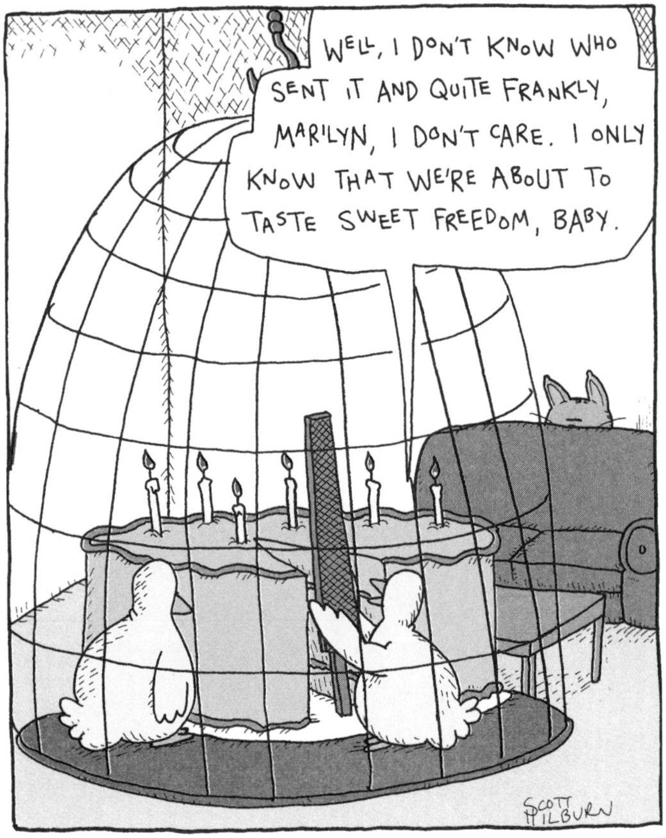
WELL, I DON'T KNOW WHO SENT IT AND QUITE FRANKLY, MARILYN, I DON'T CARE. I ONLY KNOW THAT WE'RE ABOUT TO TASTE SWEET FREEDOM, BABY.
SCOTT HILBURN

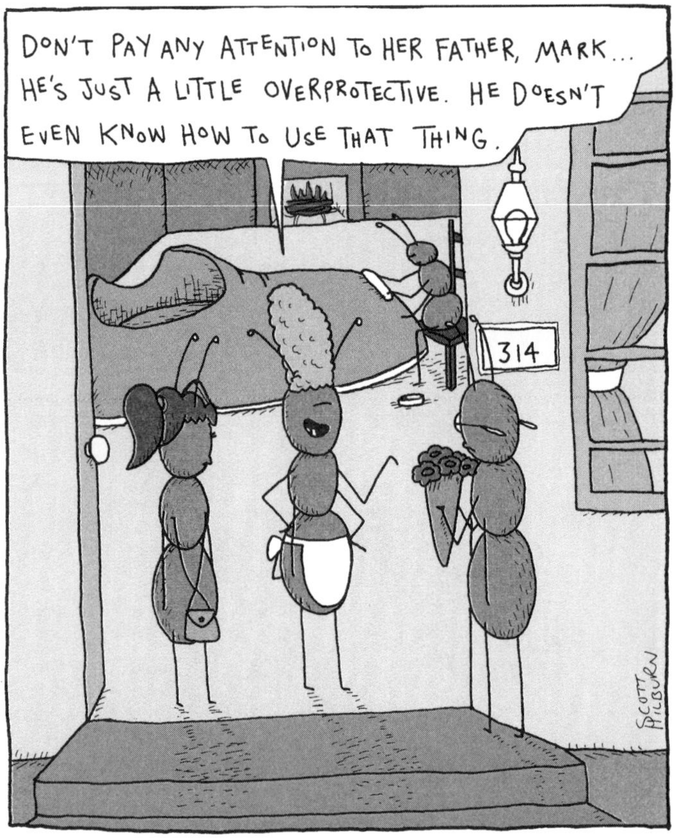
DON'T PAY ANY ATTENTION TO HER FATHER, MARK... HE'S JUST A LITTLE OVERPROTECTIVE. HE DOESN'T EVEN KNOW HOW TO USE THAT THING.
314
SCOTT HILBURN

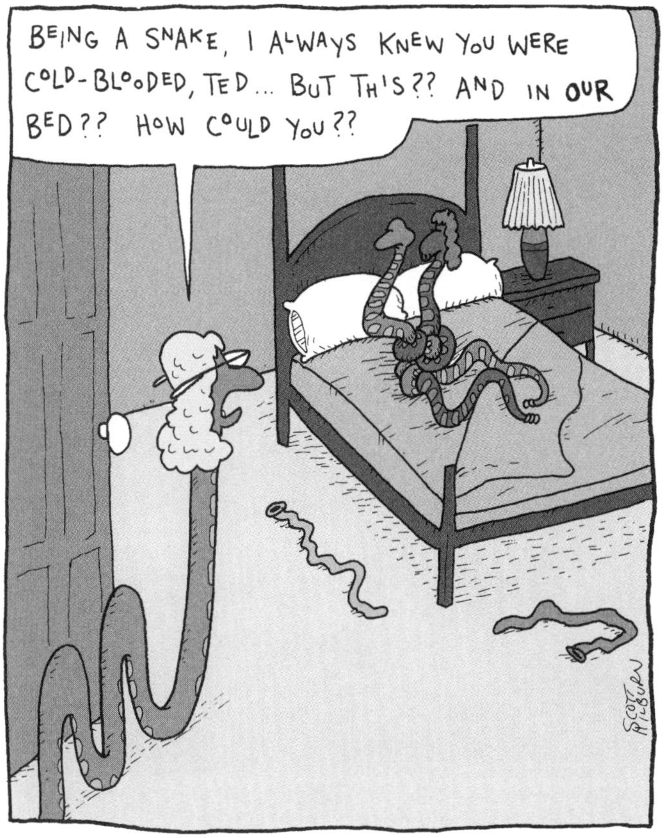
BEING A SNAKE, I ALWAYS KNEW YOU WERE COLD-BLOODED, TED... BUT THIS?? AND IN OUR BED?? HOW COULD YOU??
SCOTT HILBURN

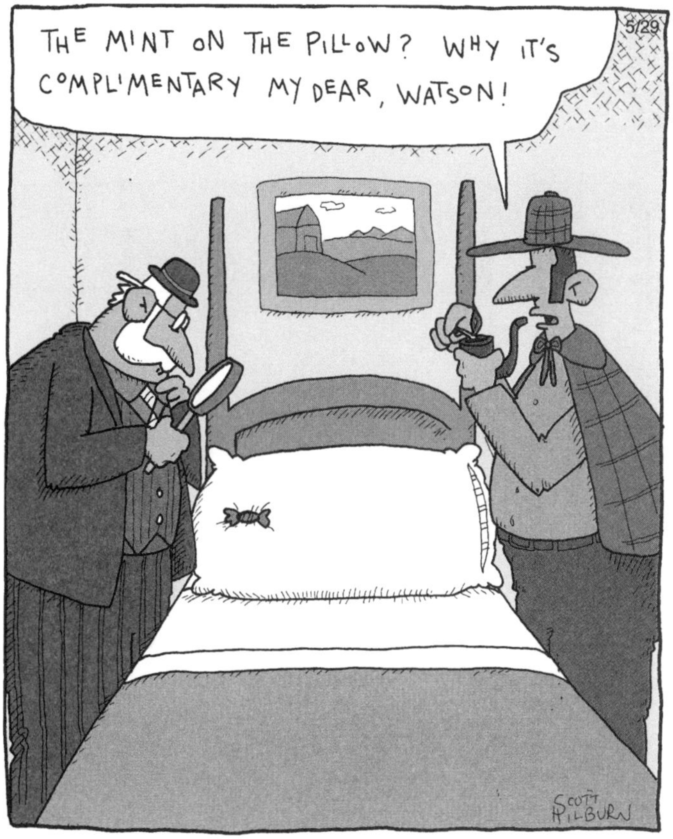
5/29
THE MINT ON THE PILLOW? WHY IT'S COMPLIMENTARY MY DEAR, WATSON!
SCOTT HILBURN

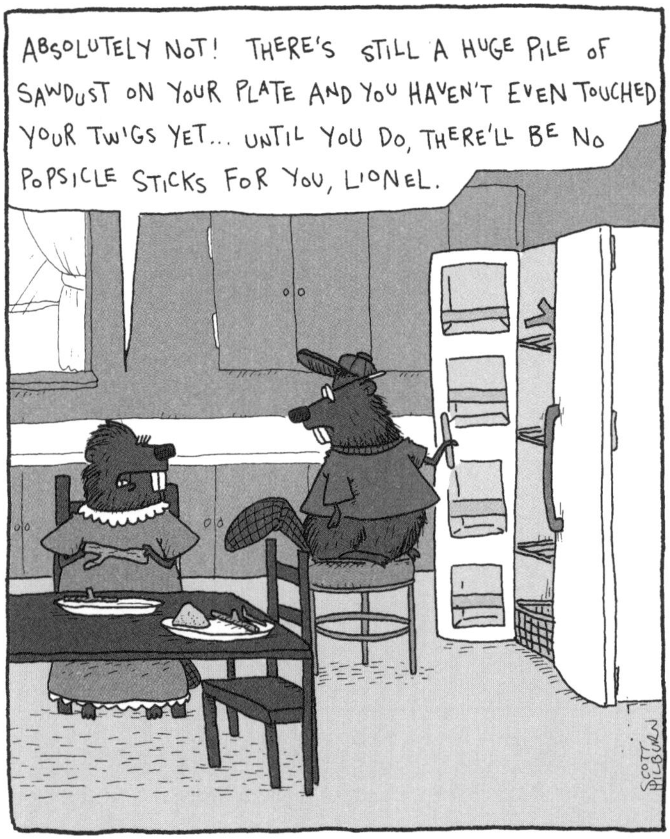
ABSOLUTELY NOT! THERE'S STILL A HUGE PILE OF SAWDUST ON YOUR PLATE AND YOU HAVEN'T EVEN TOUCHED YOUR TWIGS YET... UNTIL YOU DO, THERE'LL BE NO POPSICLE STICKS FOR YOU, LIONEL.
SCOTT HILBURN

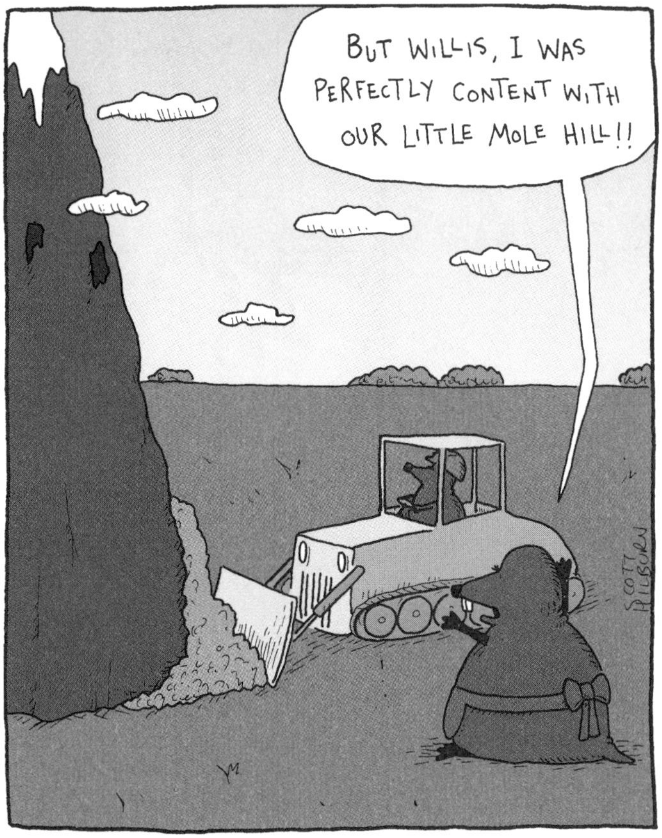
BUT WILLIS, I WAS PERFECTLY CONTENT WITH OUR LITTLE MOLE HILL!!
SCOTT HILBURN

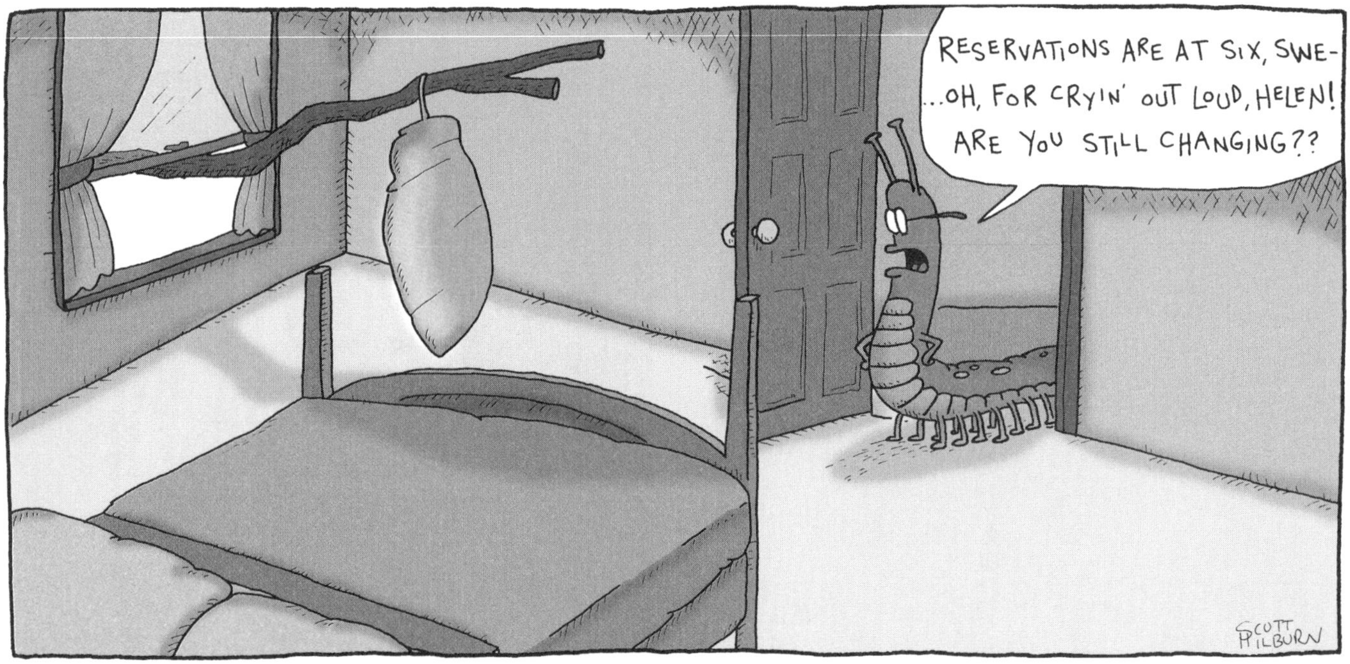
RESERVATIONS ARE AT SIX, SWE- ...OH, FOR CRYIN' OUT LOUD, HELEN! ARE YOU STILL CHANGING??
SCOTT HILBURN

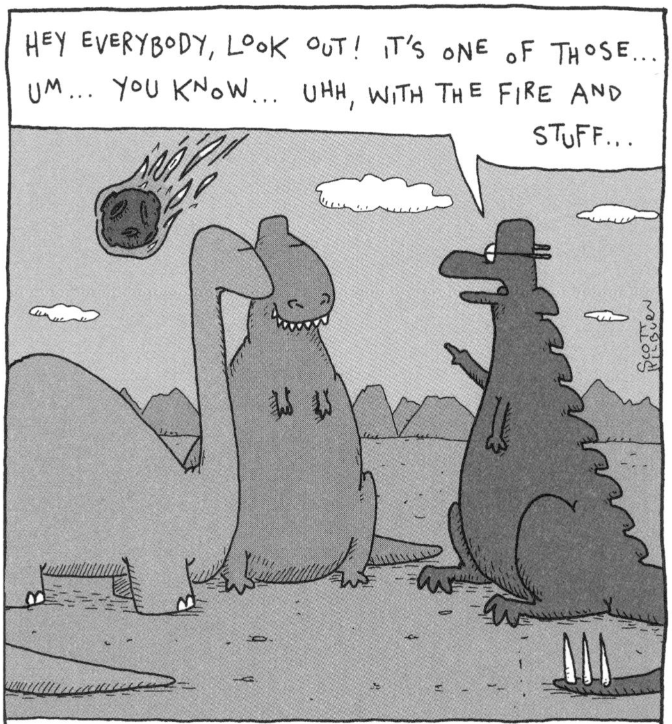
HEY EVERYBODY, LOOK OUT! IT'S ONE OF THOSE... UM... YOU KNOW... UHH, WITH THE FIRE AND STUFF...
SCOTT HILBURN

DESPITE ITS NAME, THE THESAURUS WAS QUITE OFTEN AT A LOSS FOR WORDS.

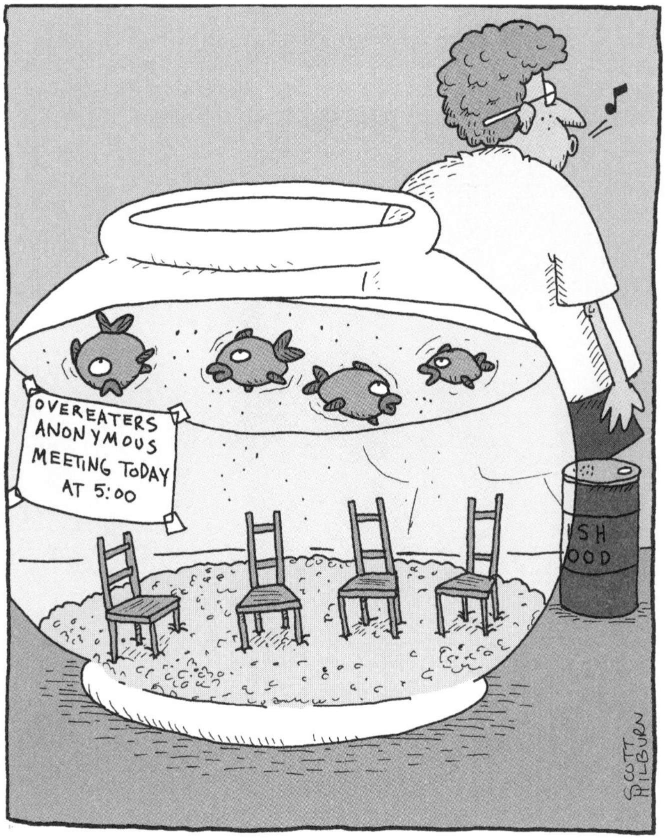
OVEREATERS ANONYMOUS MEETING TODAY AT 5:00
ISH
OOD
SCOTT HILBURN

ILLITERATE GEESE

MEALS ON HEELS, MA'AM.

BEFORE THE WHEEL

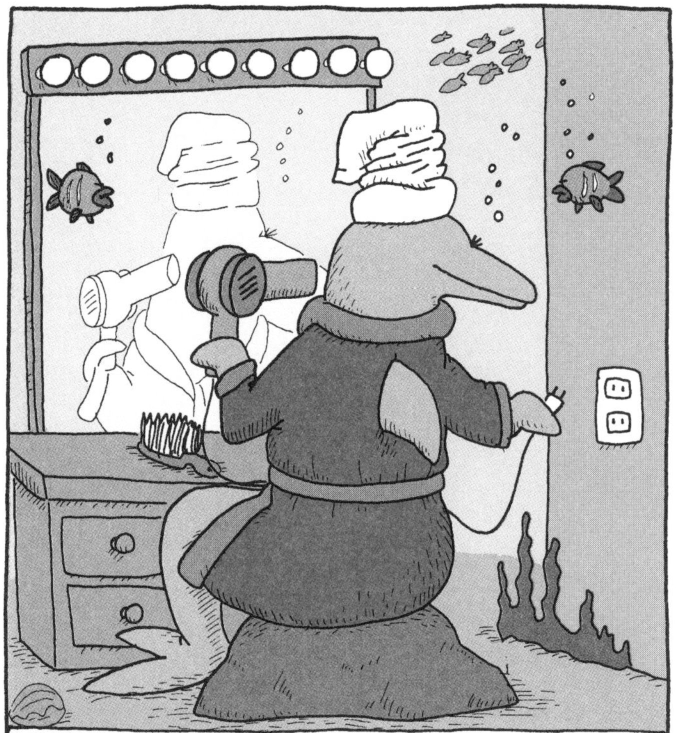

THE REASON DOLPHINS HAVE BECOME AN ENDANGERED SPECIES.

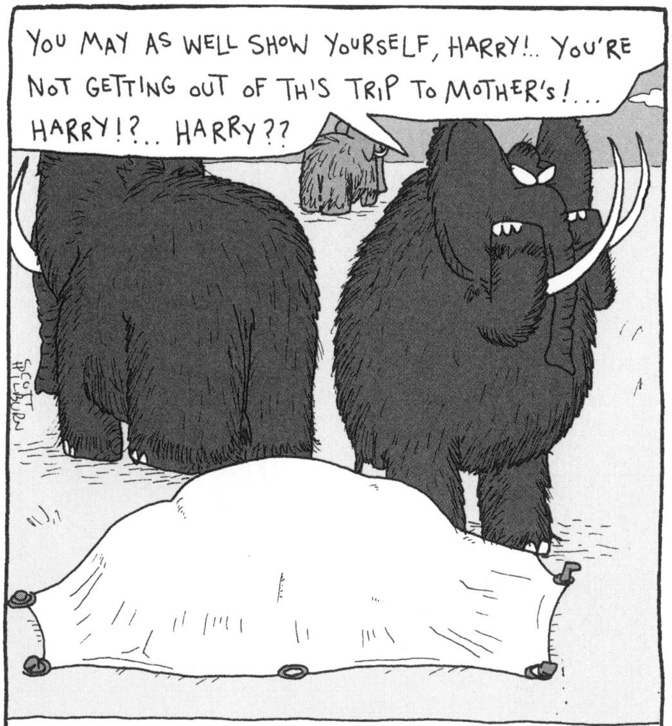
YOU MAY AS WELL SHOW YOURSELF, HARRY!.. YOU'RE NOT GETTING OUT OF THIS TRIP TO MOTHER'S!... HARRY!?.. HARRY??

YET ANOTHER PREHISTORIC MAMMAL IS COVERED UP BY THE LA BREA TARP - NEVER TO BE SEEN AGAIN.

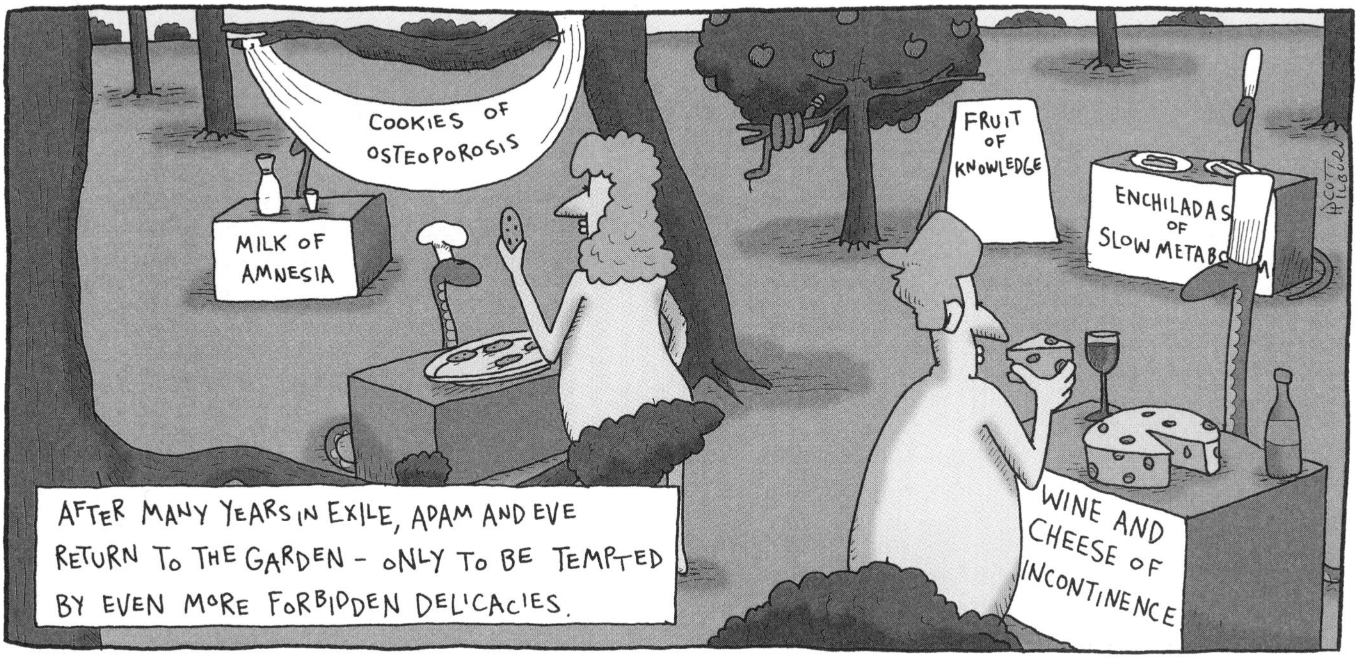
COOKIES OF OSTEOPOROSIS
FRUIT OF KNOWLEDGE
MILK OF AMNESIA
ENCHILADAS OF SLOW METAB
WINE AND CHEESE OF INCONTINENCE

AFTER MANY YEARS IN EXILE, ADAM AND EVE RETURN TO THE GARDEN - ONLY TO BE TEMPTED BY EVEN MORE FORBIDDEN DELICACIES.

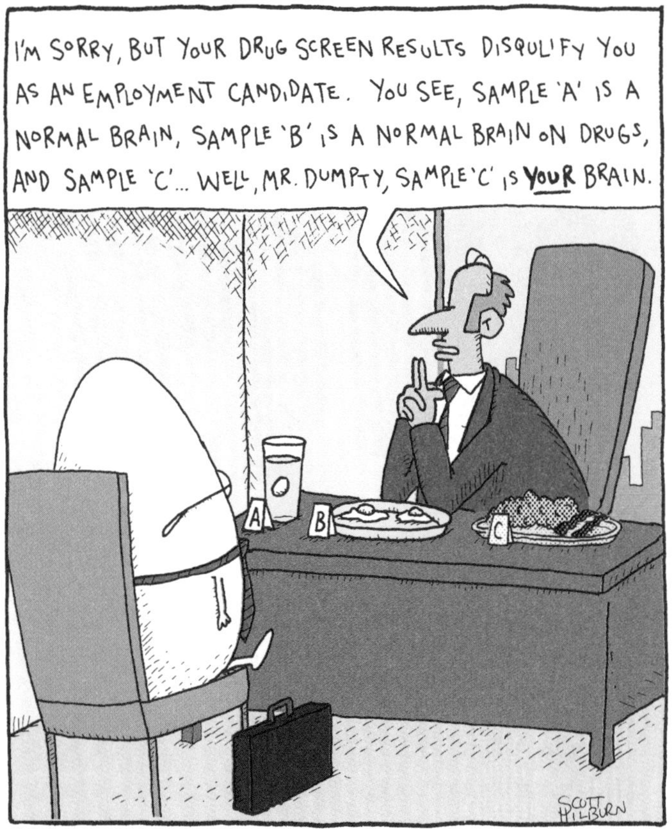
I'M SORRY, BUT YOUR DRUG SCREEN RESULTS DISQULIFY YOU AS AN EMPLOYMENT CANDIDATE. YOU SEE, SAMPLE 'A' IS A NORMAL BRAIN, SAMPLE 'B' IS A NORMAL BRAIN ON DRUGS, AND SAMPLE 'C'... WELL, MR. DUMPTY, SAMPLE 'C' IS **YOUR** BRAIN.
A
B
C
SCOTT HILBURN

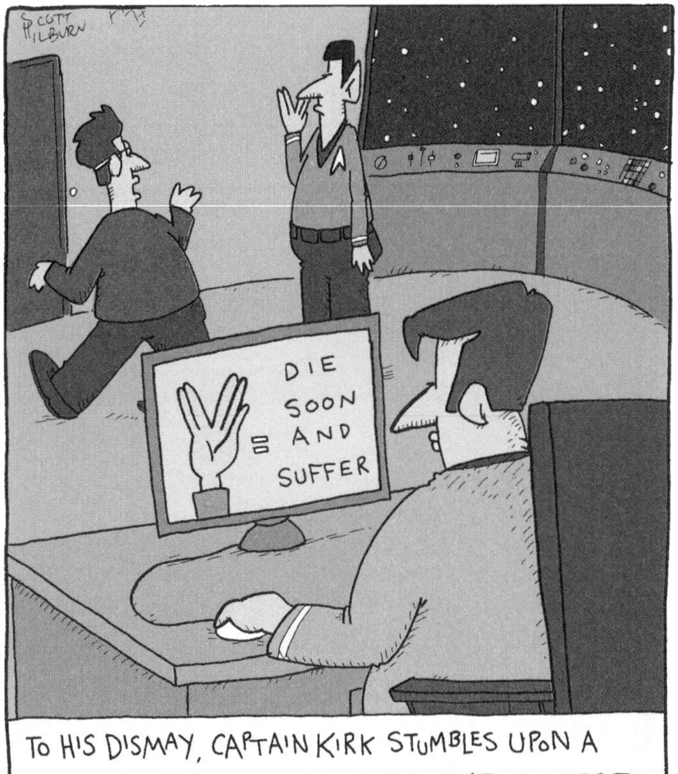
SCOTT HILBURN
DIE
SOON
AND
SUFFER

TO HIS DISMAY, CAPTAIN KIRK STUMBLES UPON A VULCAN HANDSIGN-TO-ENGLISH TRANSLATION WEBSITE.

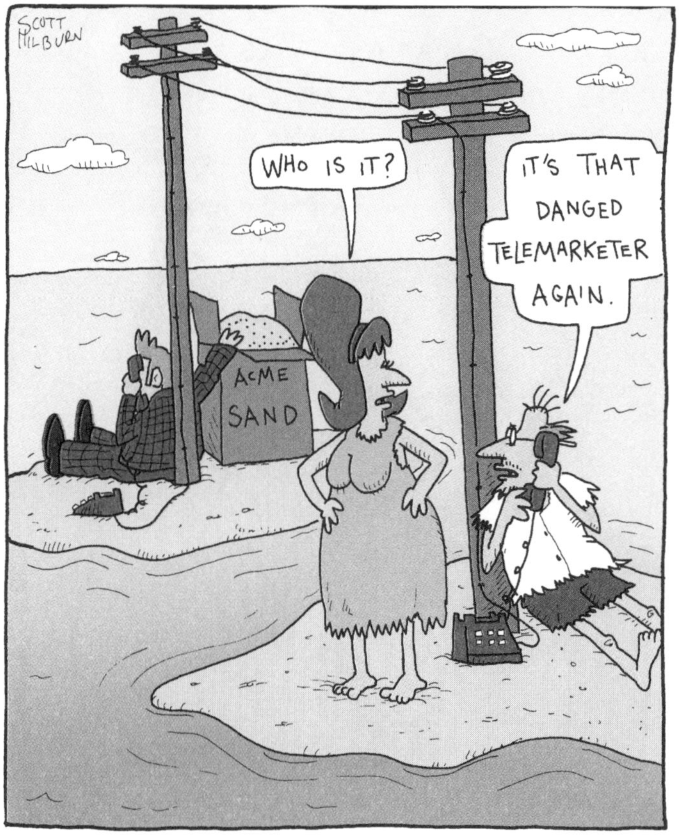
SCOTT MILBURN
WHO IS IT?
IT'S THAT DANGED TELEMARKETER AGAIN.
ACME SAND

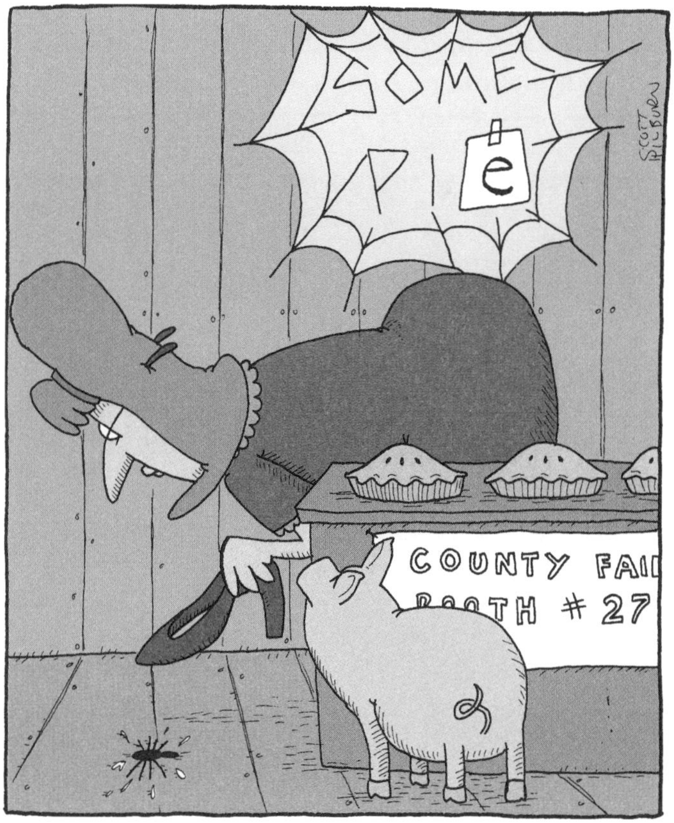
SOME PIE
SCOTT MILBURN
COUNTY FAI
BOOTH # 27

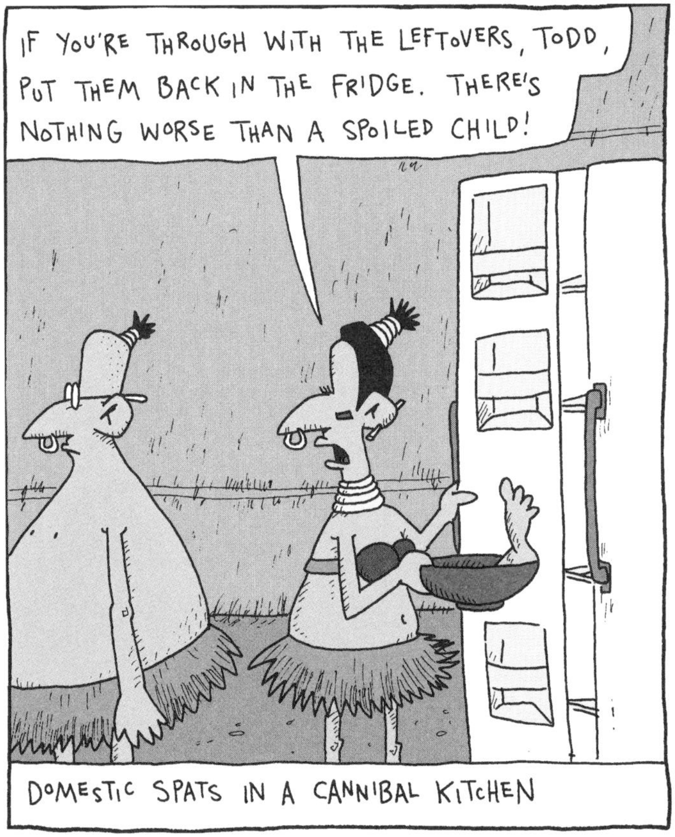
IF YOU'RE THROUGH WITH THE LEFTOVERS, TODD, PUT THEM BACK IN THE FRIDGE. THERE'S NOTHING WORSE THAN A SPOILED CHILD!
DOMESTIC SPATS IN A CANNIBAL KITCHEN

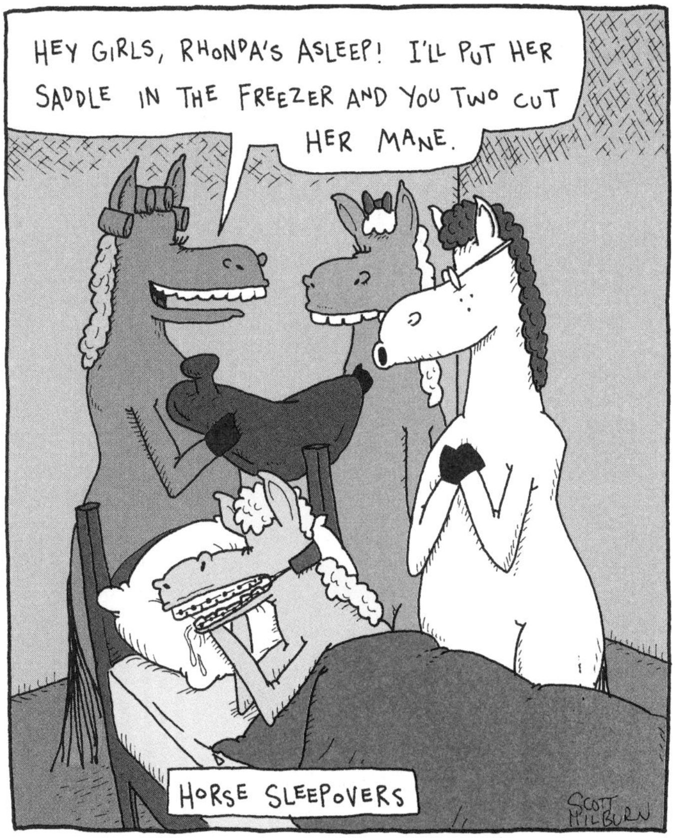
HEY GIRLS, RHONDA'S ASLEEP! I'LL PUT HER SADDLE IN THE FREEZER AND YOU TWO CUT HER MANE.
SCOTT HILBURN
HORSE SLEEPOVERS

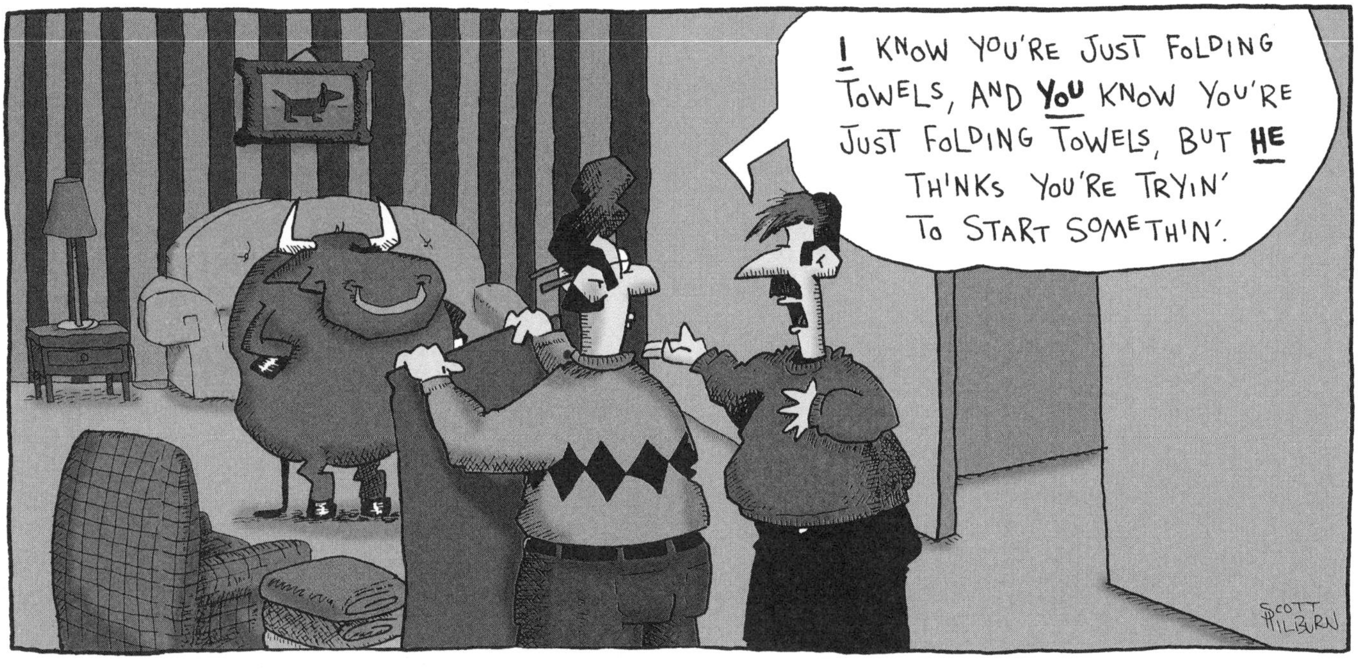
I KNOW YOU'RE JUST FOLDING TOWELS, AND YOU KNOW YOU'RE JUST FOLDING TOWELS, BUT HE THINKS YOU'RE TRYIN' TO START SOMETHIN'.
SCOTT HILBURN

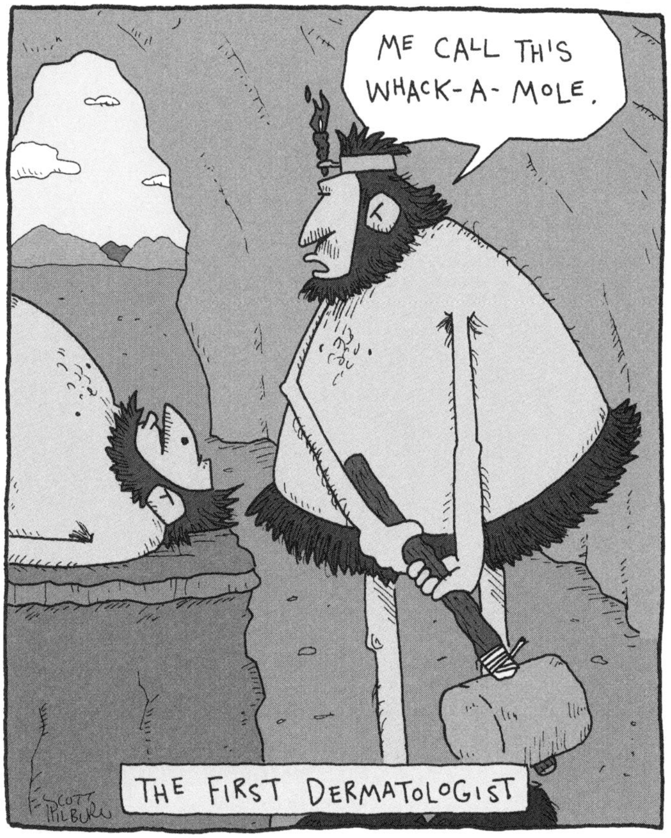
ME CALL THIS WHACK-A-MOLE.
SCOTT HILBURN
THE FIRST DERMATOLOGIST

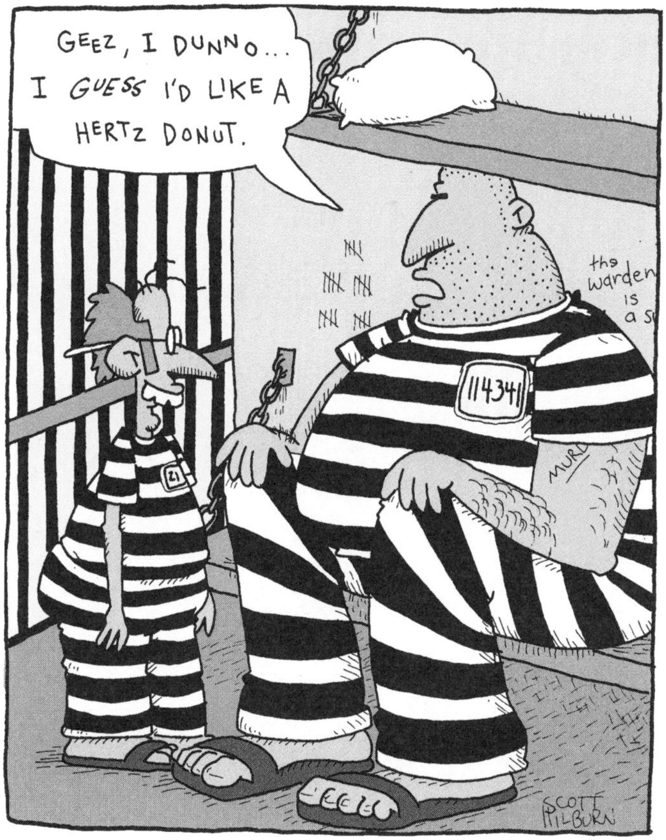
GEEZ, I DUNNO... I *GUESS* I'D LIKE A HERTZ DONUT.
the warden is a
114341
21
SCOTT HILBURN

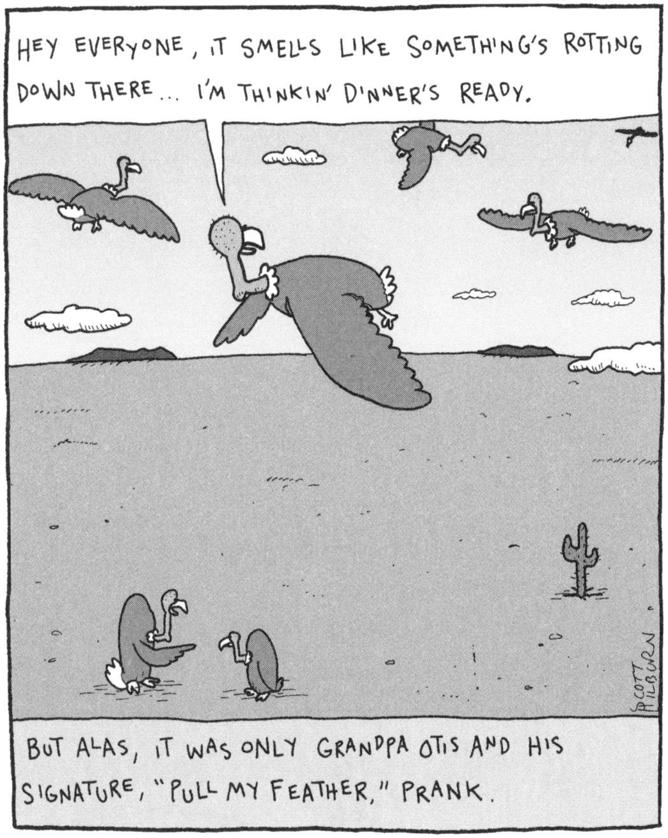
HEY EVERYONE, IT SMELLS LIKE SOMETHING'S ROTTING DOWN THERE... I'M THINKIN' DINNER'S READY.
BUT ALAS, IT WAS ONLY GRANDPA OTIS AND HIS SIGNATURE, "PULL MY FEATHER," PRANK.
SCOTT HILBURN

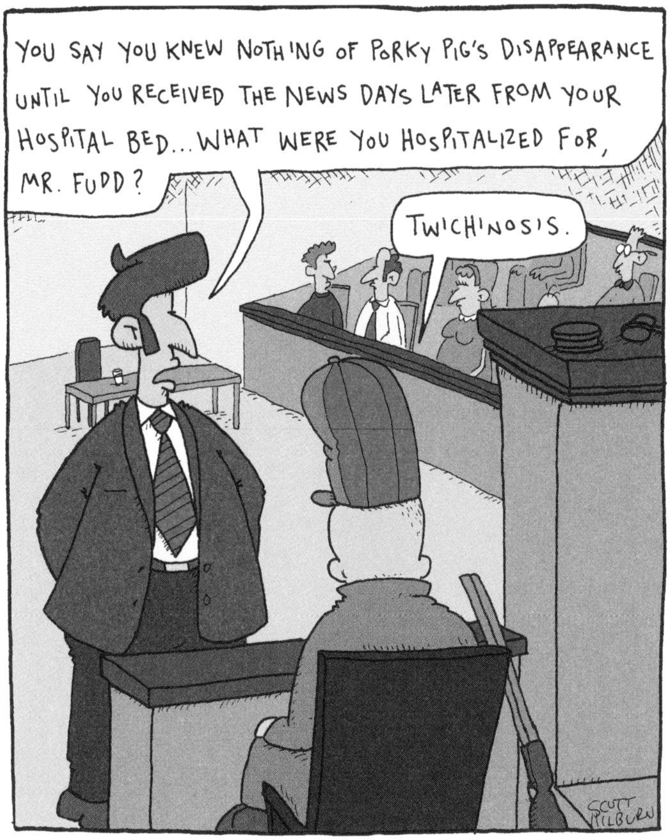
YOU SAY YOU KNEW NOTHING OF PORKY PIG'S DISAPPEARANCE UNTIL YOU RECEIVED THE NEWS DAYS LATER FROM YOUR HOSPITAL BED... WHAT WERE YOU HOSPITALIZED FOR, MR. FUDD?
TWICHINOSIS.
SCOTT HILBURN

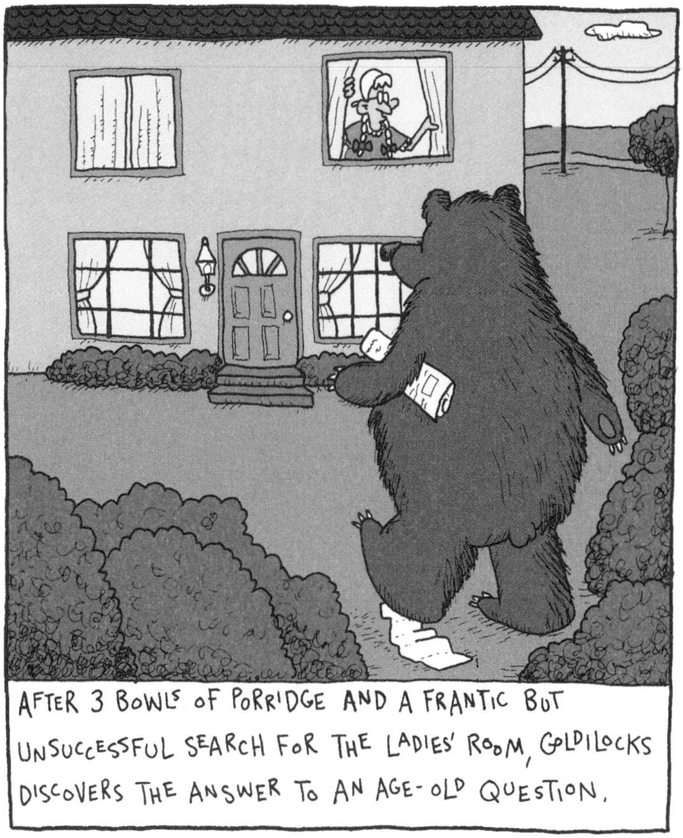
AFTER 3 BOWLS OF PORRIDGE AND A FRANTIC BUT UNSUCCESSFUL SEARCH FOR THE LADIES' ROOM, GOLDILOCKS DISCOVERS THE ANSWER TO AN AGE-OLD QUESTION.

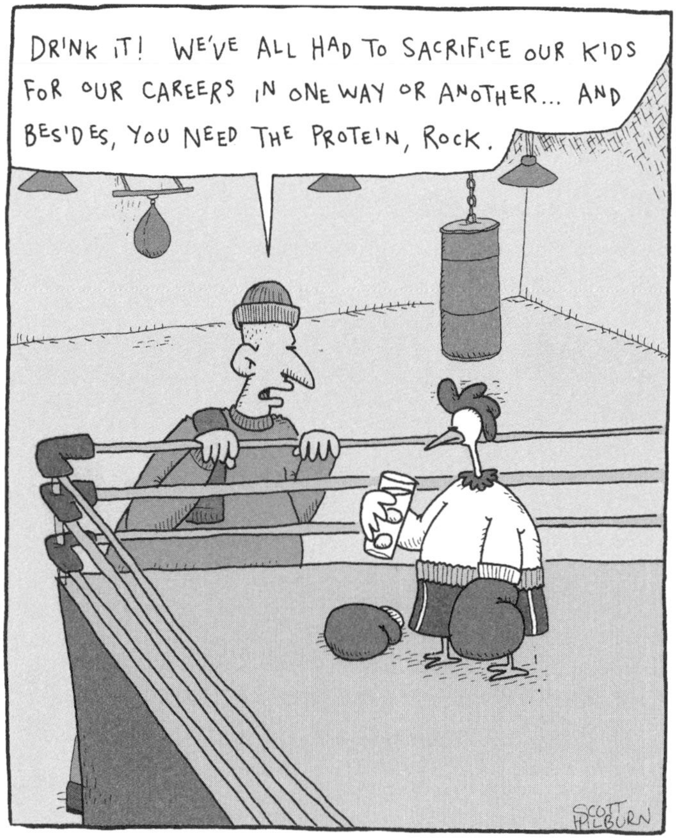
DRINK IT! WE'VE ALL HAD TO SACRIFICE OUR KIDS FOR OUR CAREERS IN ONE WAY OR ANOTHER... AND BESIDES, YOU NEED THE PROTEIN, ROCK.
SCOTT HILBURN

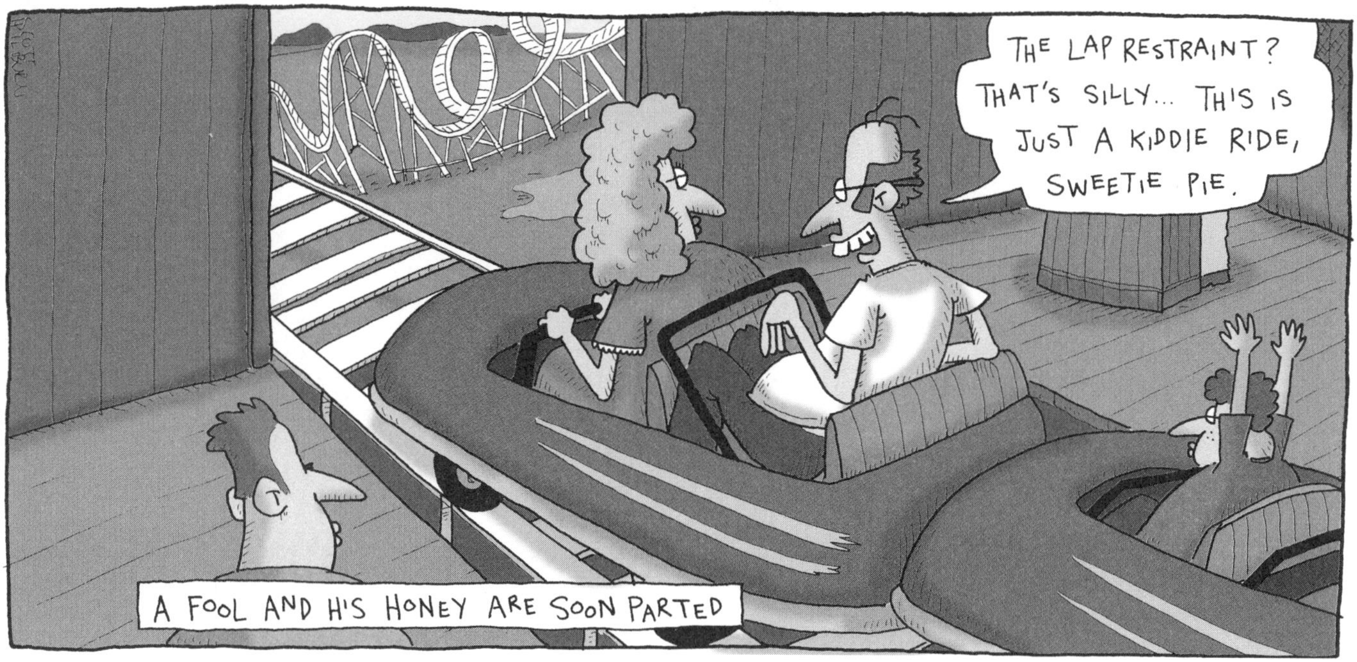
THE LAP RESTRAINT? THAT'S SILLY... THIS IS JUST A KIDDIE RIDE, SWEETIE PIE.
A FOOL AND HIS HONEY ARE SOON PARTED

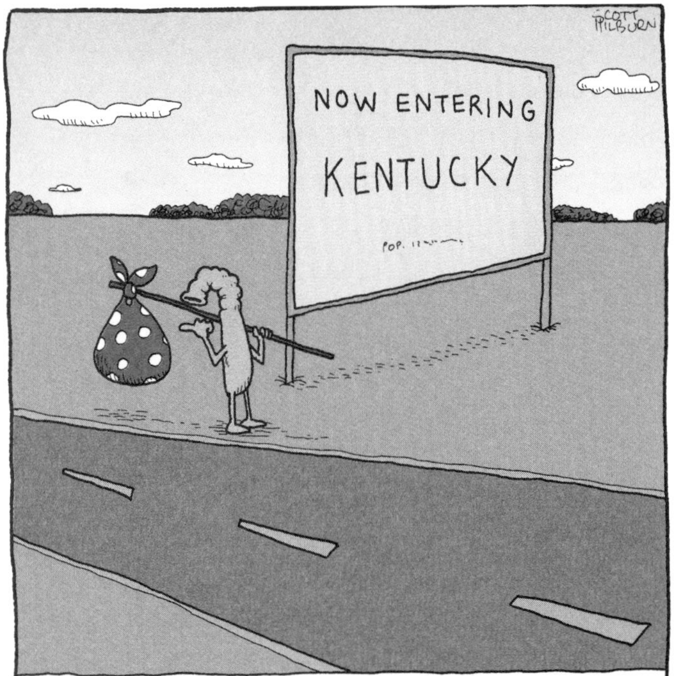
NOW ENTERING
KENTUCKY

FORCIBLY REMOVED FROM HIS HOME AND HIS PERSONAL LIFE RUPTURED, THE APPENDIX HITCHHIKES ACROSS AMERICA, SEARCHING FOR HIS PURPOSE.

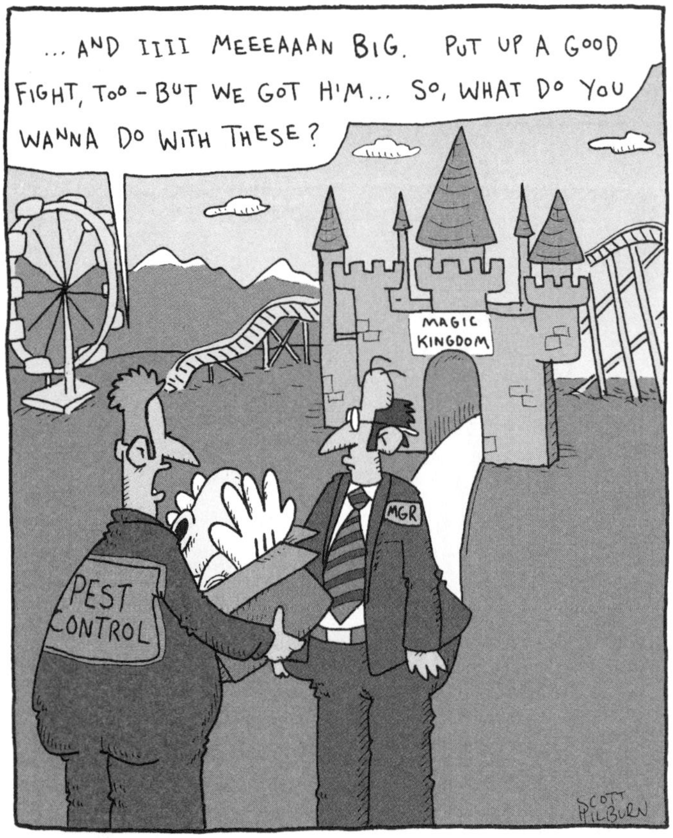
... AND IIII MEEEAAAN BIG. PUT UP A GOOD FIGHT, TOO - BUT WE GOT HIM... SO, WHAT DO YOU WANNA DO WITH THESE?
MAGIC KINGDOM
PEST CONTROL
MGR

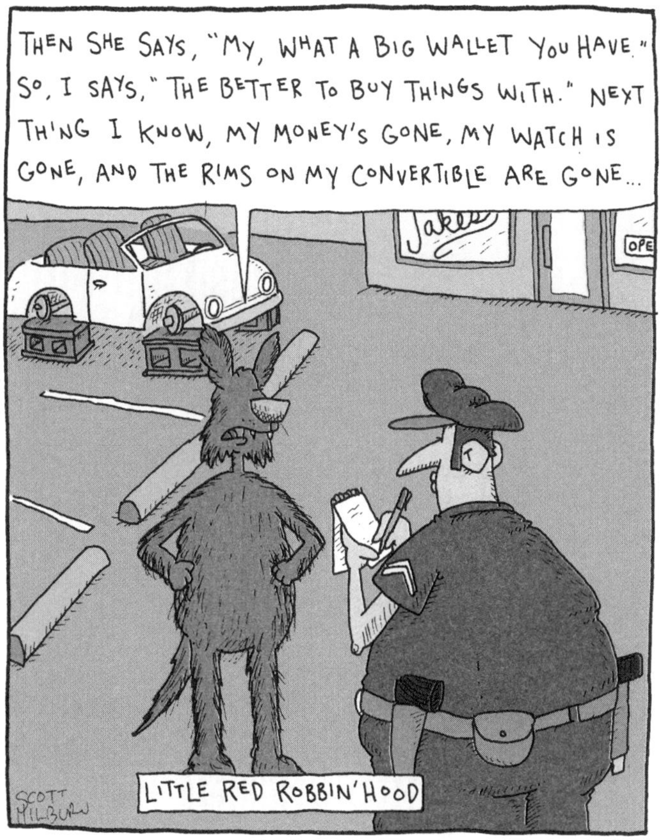
THEN SHE SAYS, "MY, WHAT A BIG WALLET YOU HAVE." SO, I SAYS," THE BETTER TO BUY THINGS WITH." NEXT THING I KNOW, MY MONEY'S GONE, MY WATCH IS GONE, AND THE RIMS ON MY CONVERTIBLE ARE GONE...
Jake's
OPE
SCOTT HILBURN
LITTLE RED ROBBIN' HOOD

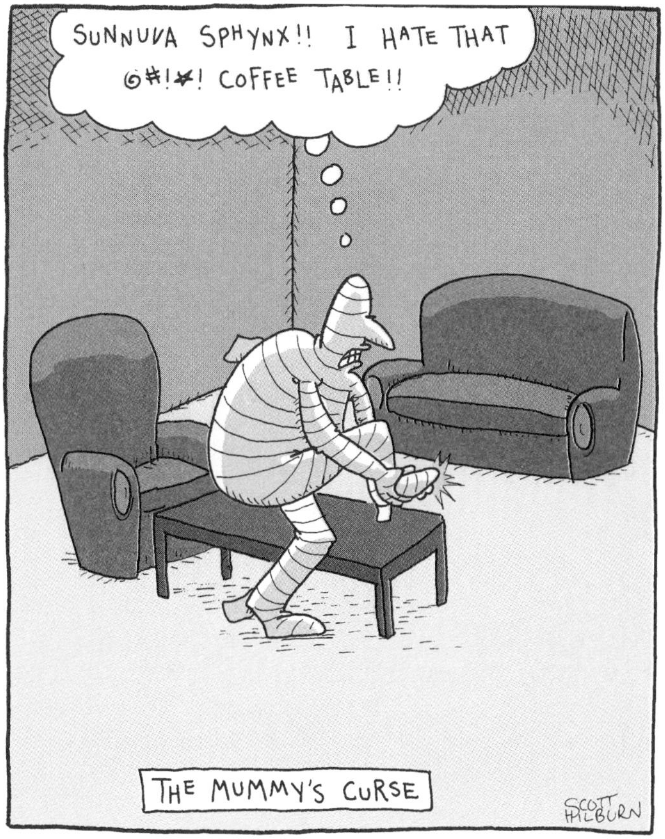
SUNNUVA SPHYNX!! I HATE THAT @#!*! COFFEE TABLE!!
SCOTT HILBURN
THE MUMMY'S CURSE

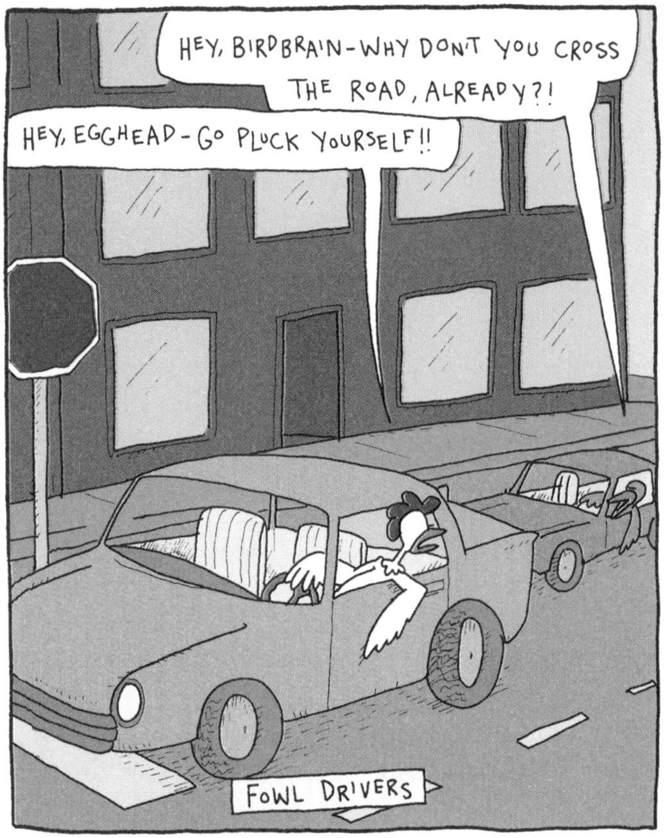
HEY, BIRDBRAIN - WHY DON'T YOU CROSS THE ROAD, ALREADY?!
HEY, EGGHEAD - GO PLUCK YOURSELF!!
FOWL DRIVERS

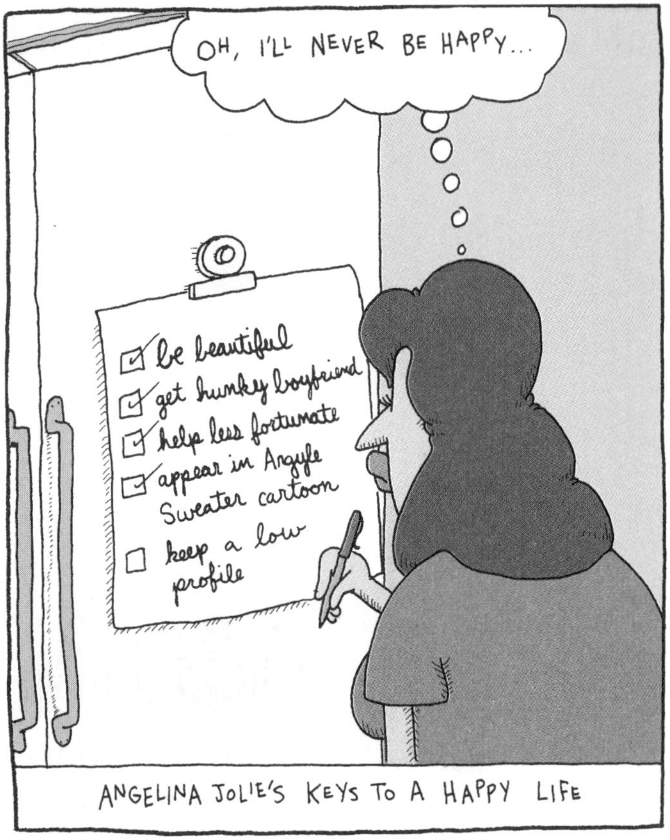
OH, I'LL NEVER BE HAPPY...
be beautiful
get hunkey boyfriend
help less fortunate
appear in Argyle Sweater cartoon
keep a low profile
ANGELINA JOLIE'S KEYS TO A HAPPY LIFE

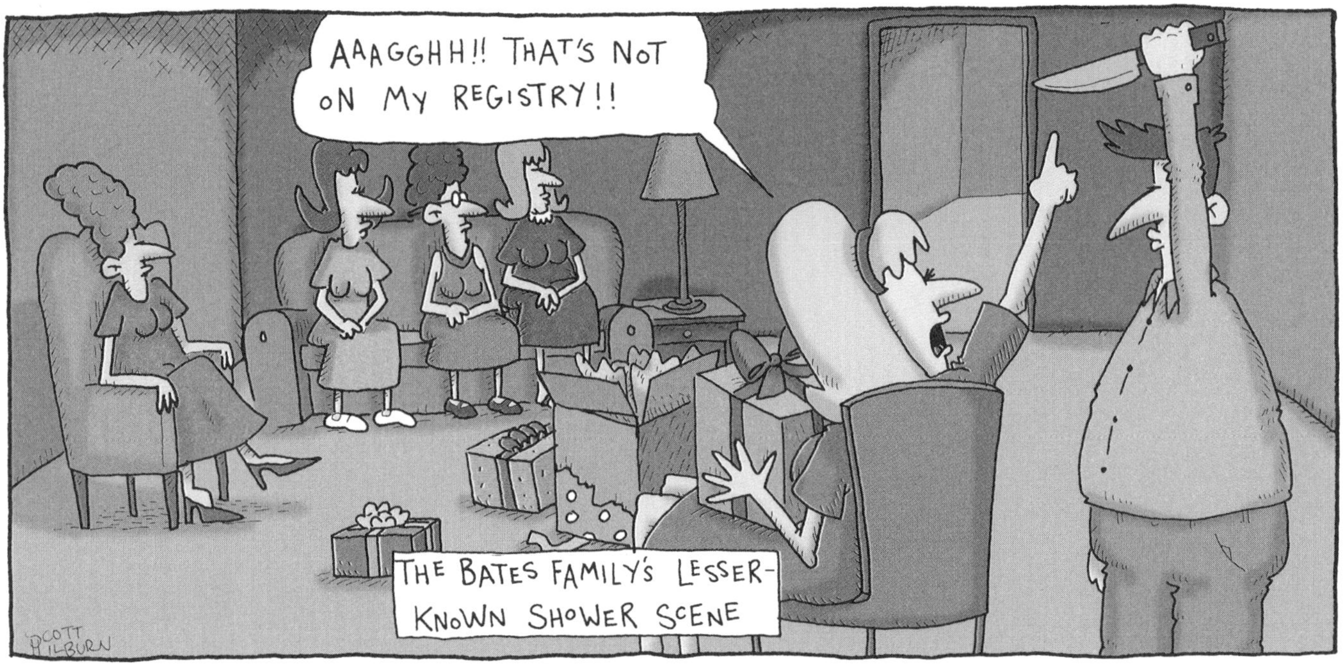
AAAGGHH!! THAT'S NOT ON MY REGISTRY!!
SCOTT HILBURN
THE BATES FAMILY'S LESSER-KNOWN SHOWER SCENE

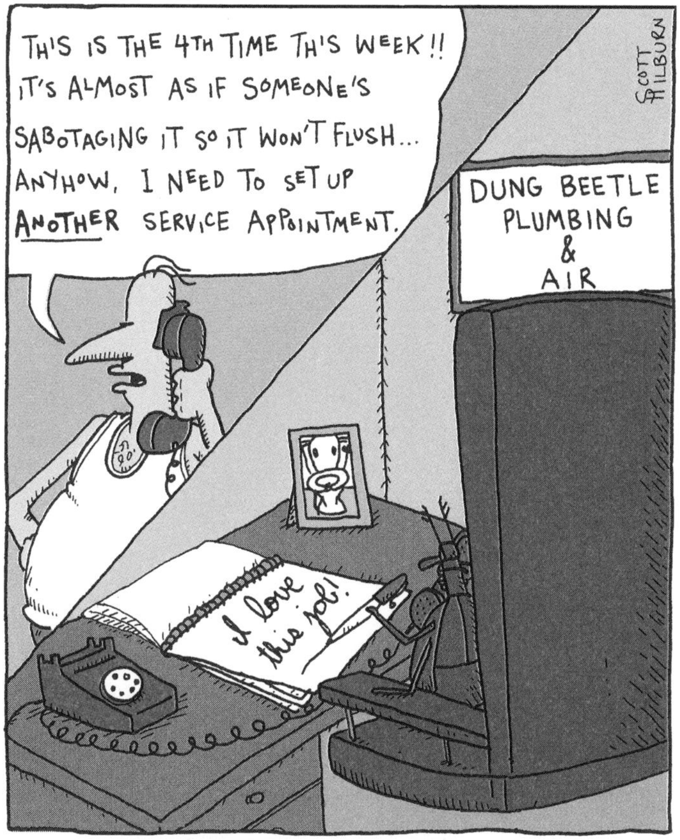
THIS IS THE 4TH TIME THIS WEEK!! IT'S ALMOST AS IF SOMEONE'S SABOTAGING IT SO IT WON'T FLUSH... ANYHOW, I NEED TO SET UP ANOTHER SERVICE APPOINTMENT.
DUNG BEETLE PLUMBING & AIR
I love this job!
SCOTT HILBURN

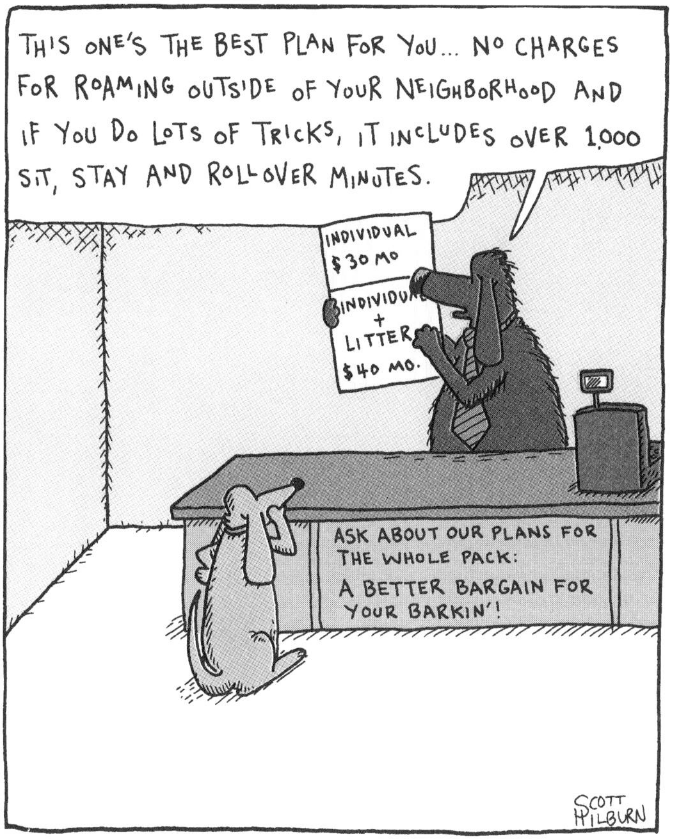
THIS ONE'S THE BEST PLAN FOR YOU... NO CHARGES FOR ROAMING OUTSIDE OF YOUR NEIGHBORHOOD AND IF YOU DO LOTS OF TRICKS, IT INCLUDES OVER 1,000 SIT, STAY AND ROLL OVER MINUTES.
INDIVIDUAL $30 MO
INDIVIDUAL + LITTER $40 MO.
ASK ABOUT OUR PLANS FOR THE WHOLE PACK:
A BETTER BARGAIN FOR YOUR BARKIN'!
SCOTT HILBURN

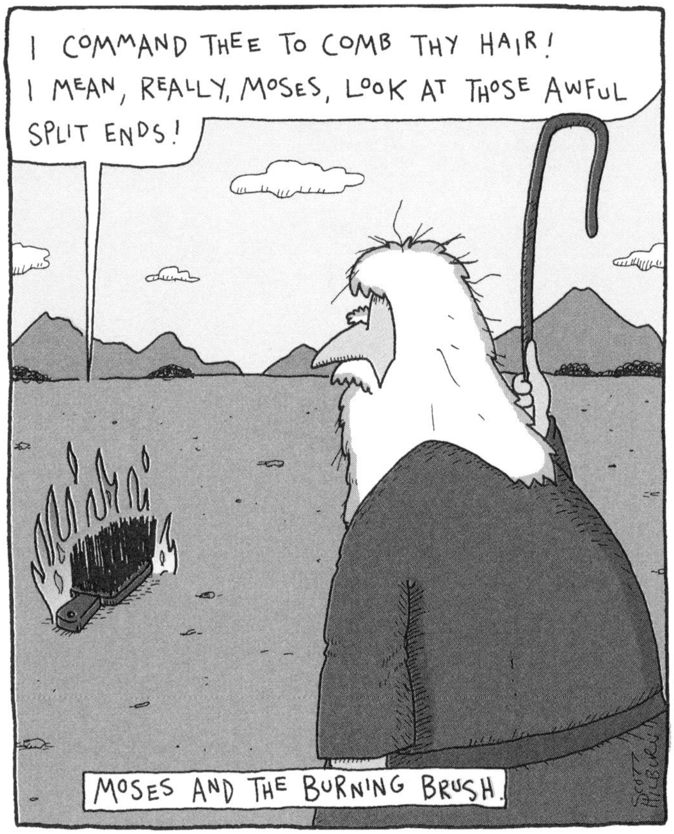
I COMMAND THEE TO COMB THY HAIR! I MEAN, REALLY, MOSES, LOOK AT THOSE AWFUL SPLIT ENDS!
MOSES AND THE BURNING BRUSH.

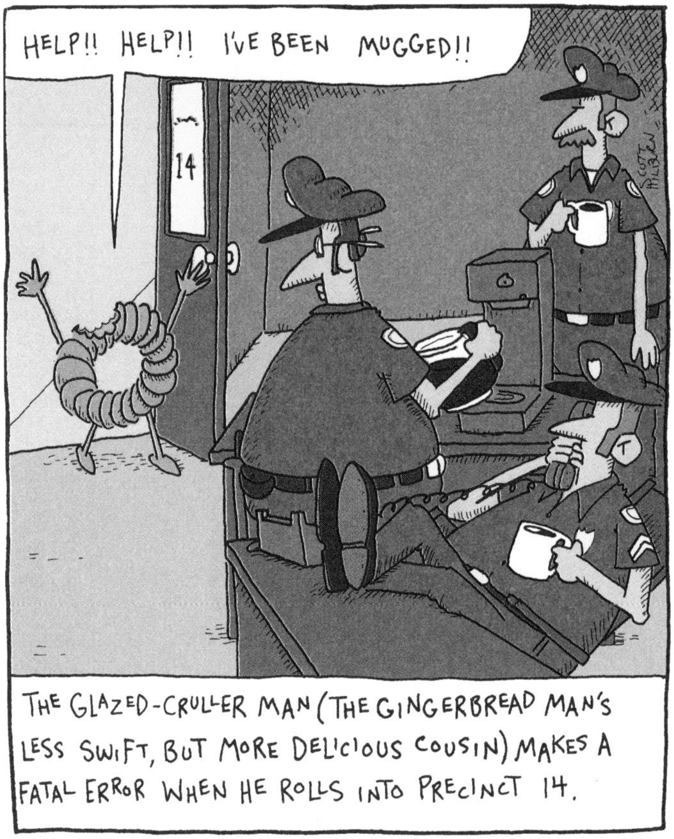
HELP!! HELP!! I'VE BEEN MUGGED!!
14
THE GLAZED-CRULLER MAN (THE GINGERBREAD MAN'S LESS SWIFT, BUT MORE DELICIOUS COUSIN) MAKES A FATAL ERROR WHEN HE ROLLS INTO PRECINCT 14.

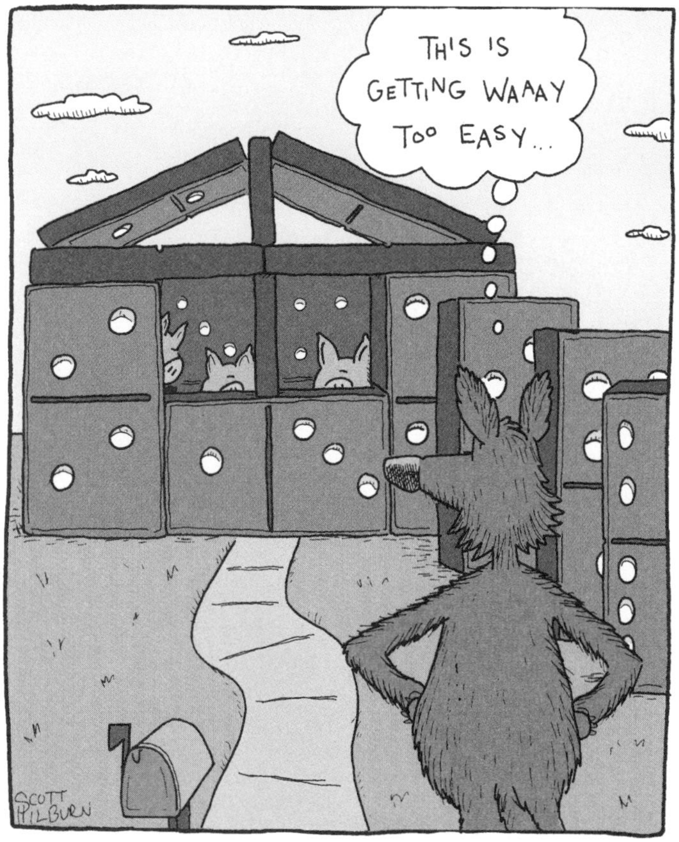
THIS IS GETTING WAAAY TOO EASY...
SCOTT HILBURN

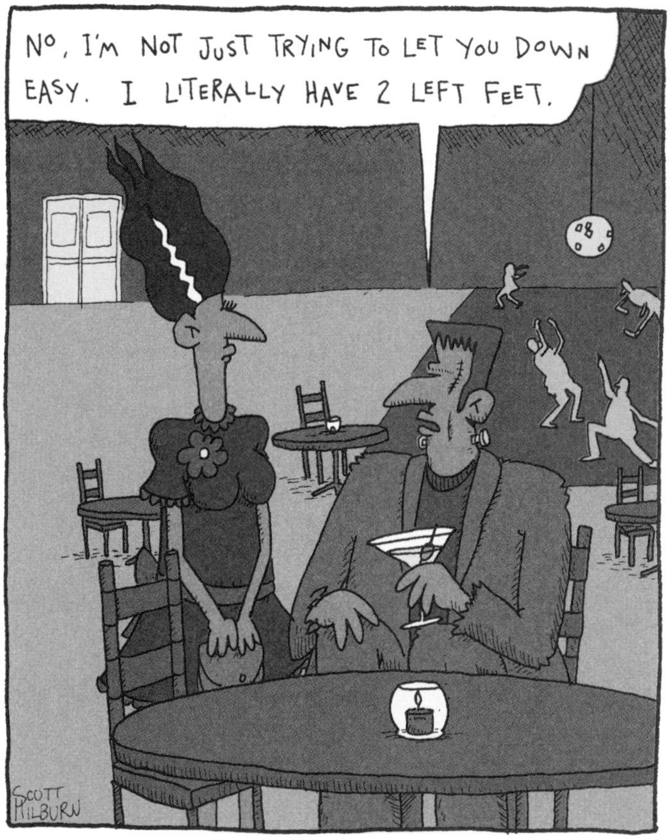
NO, I'M NOT JUST TRYING TO LET YOU DOWN EASY. I LITERALLY HAVE 2 LEFT FEET.
SCOTT HILBURN

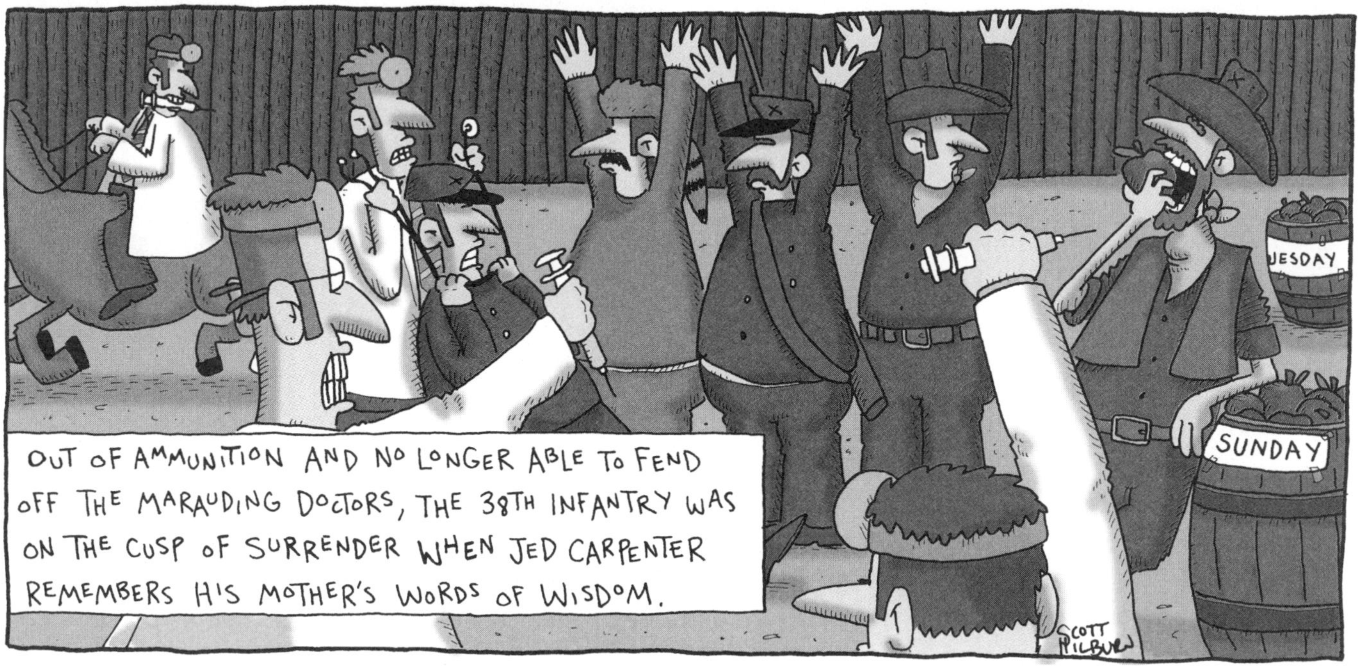
OUT OF AMMUNITION AND NO LONGER ABLE TO FEND OFF THE MARAUDING DOCTORS, THE 38TH INFANTRY WAS ON THE CUSP OF SURRENDER WHEN JED CARPENTER REMEMBERS HIS MOTHER'S WORDS OF WISDOM.
SUNDAY
SCOTT HILBURN

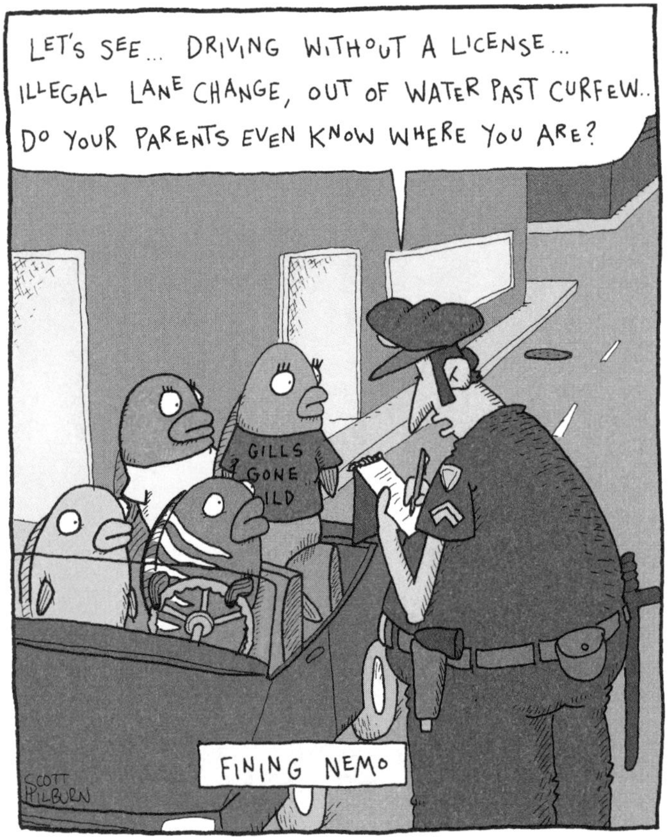
LET'S SEE... DRIVING WITHOUT A LICENSE... ILLEGAL LANE CHANGE, OUT OF WATER PAST CURFEW... DO YOUR PARENTS EVEN KNOW WHERE YOU ARE?
GILLS GONE WILD
SCOTT HILBURN
FINING NEMO

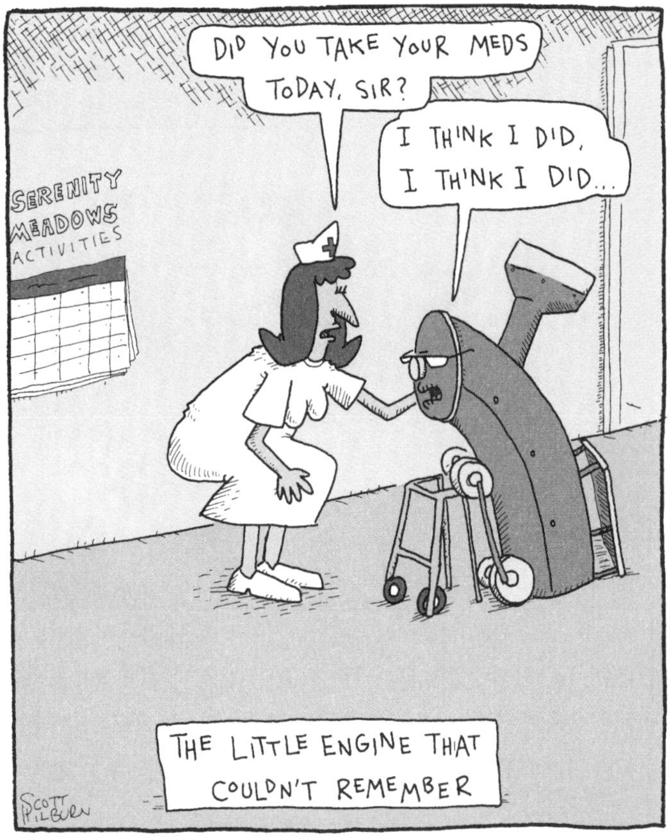
DID YOU TAKE YOUR MEDS TODAY, SIR?
I THINK I DID, I THINK I DID...
SERENITY MEADOWS ACTIVITIES
SCOTT HILBURN
THE LITTLE ENGINE THAT COULDN'T REMEMBER

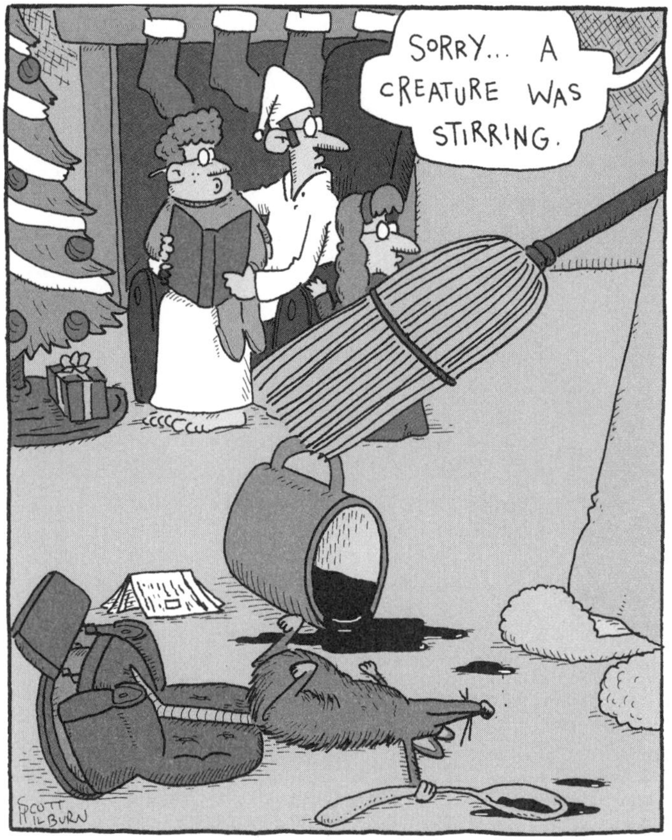
SORRY... A CREATURE WAS STIRRING.
SCOTT HILBURN

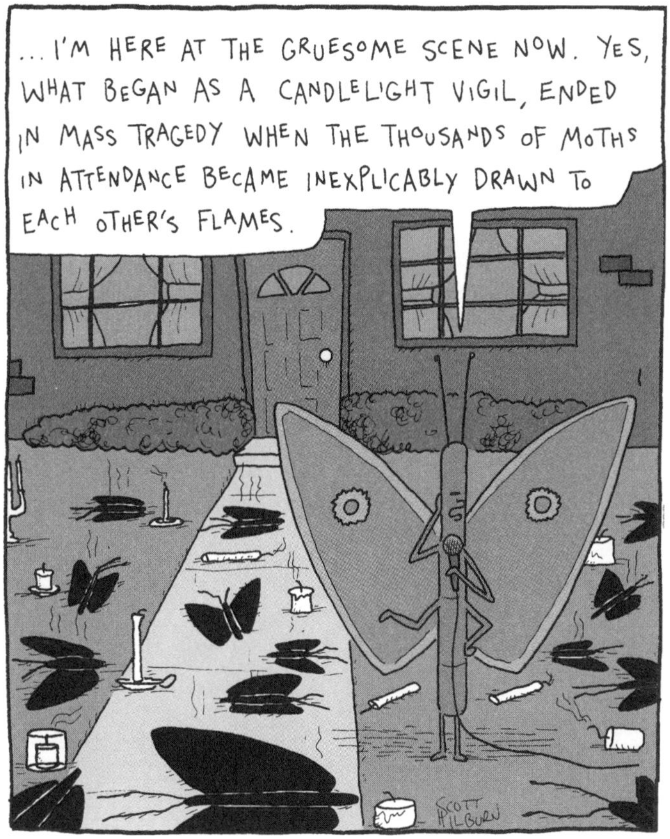
...I'M HERE AT THE GRUESOME SCENE NOW. YES, WHAT BEGAN AS A CANDLELIGHT VIGIL, ENDED IN MASS TRAGEDY WHEN THE THOUSANDS OF MOTHS IN ATTENDANCE BECAME INEXPLICABLY DRAWN TO EACH OTHER'S FLAMES.
SCOTT HILBURN

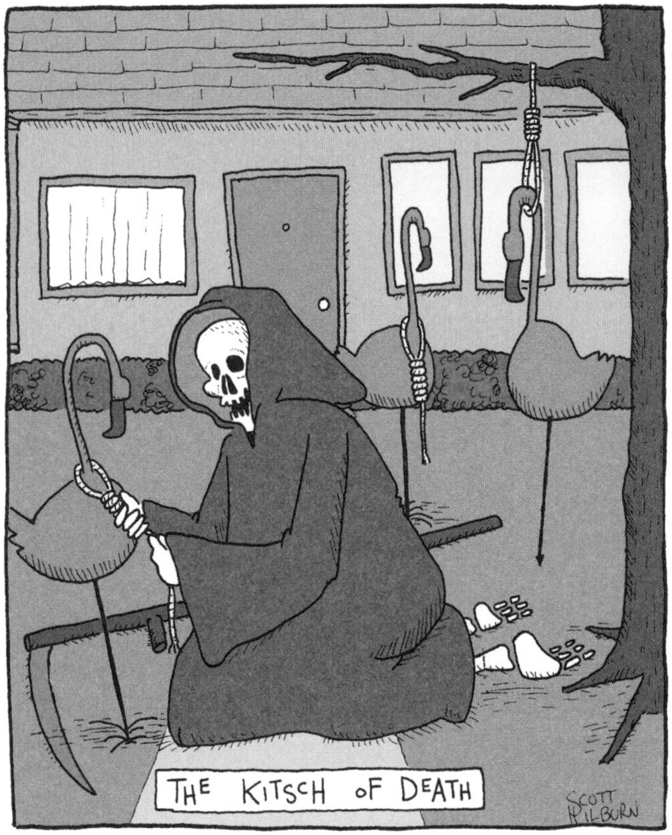
SCOTT HILBURN
THE KITSCH OF DEATH

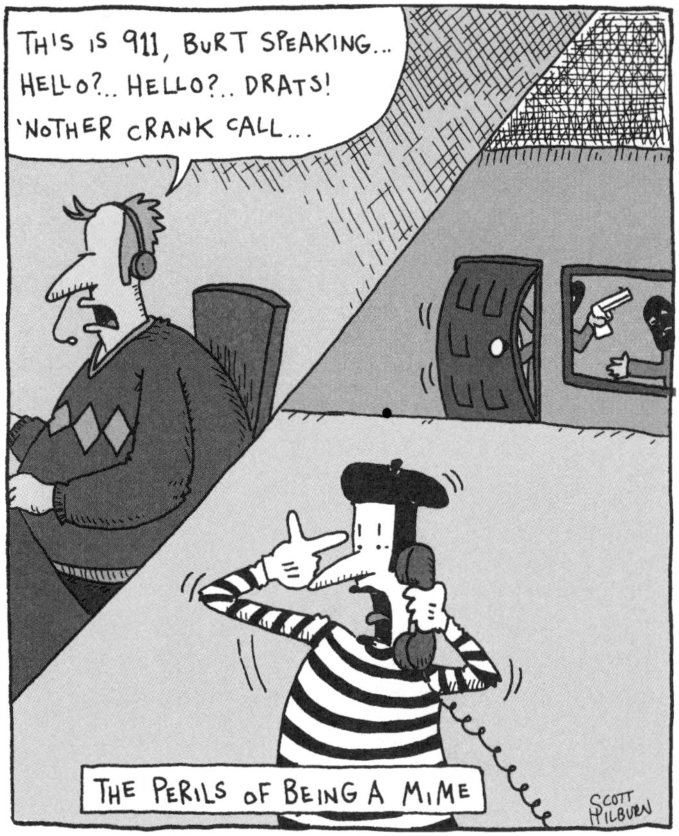
THIS IS 911, BURT SPEAKING... HELLO?.. HELLO?.. DRATS! 'NOTHER CRANK CALL...
SCOTT HILBURN
THE PERILS OF BEING A MIME

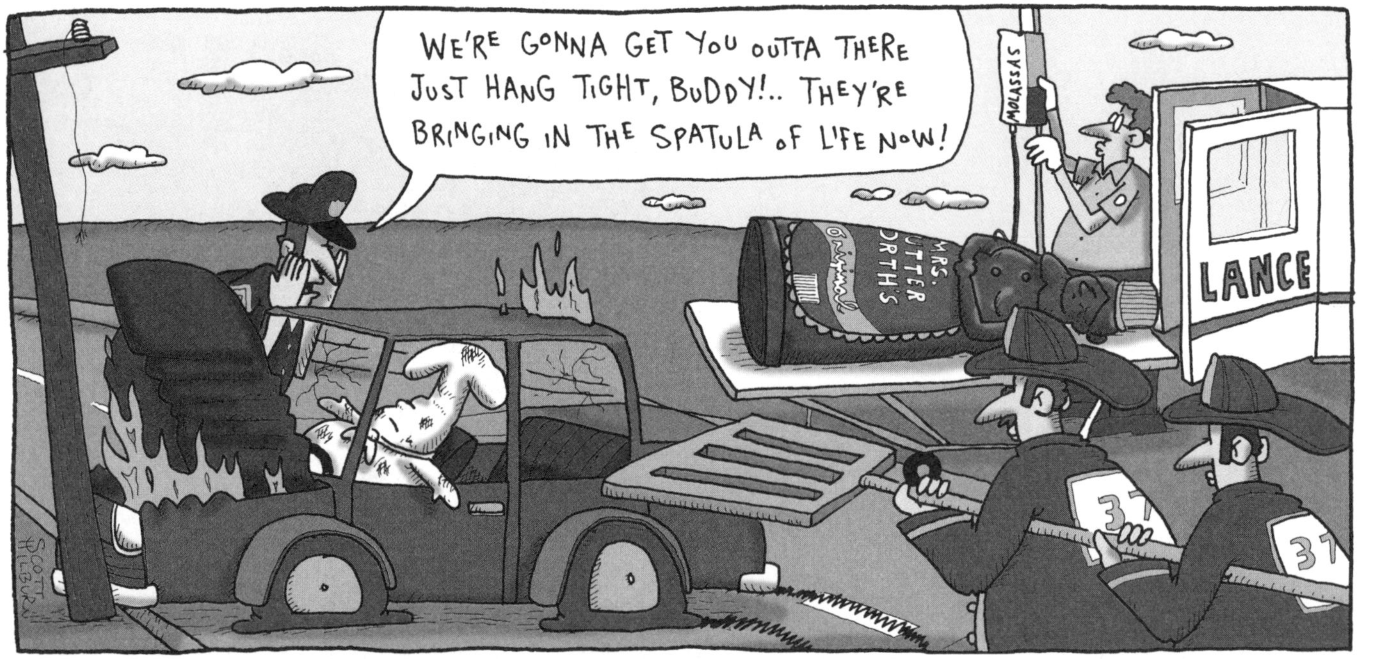
WE'RE GONNA GET YOU OUTTA THERE JUST HANG TIGHT, BUDDY!.. THEY'RE BRINGING IN THE SPATULA OF LIFE NOW!
MOLASSES
LANCE
37
37
SCOTT HILBURN

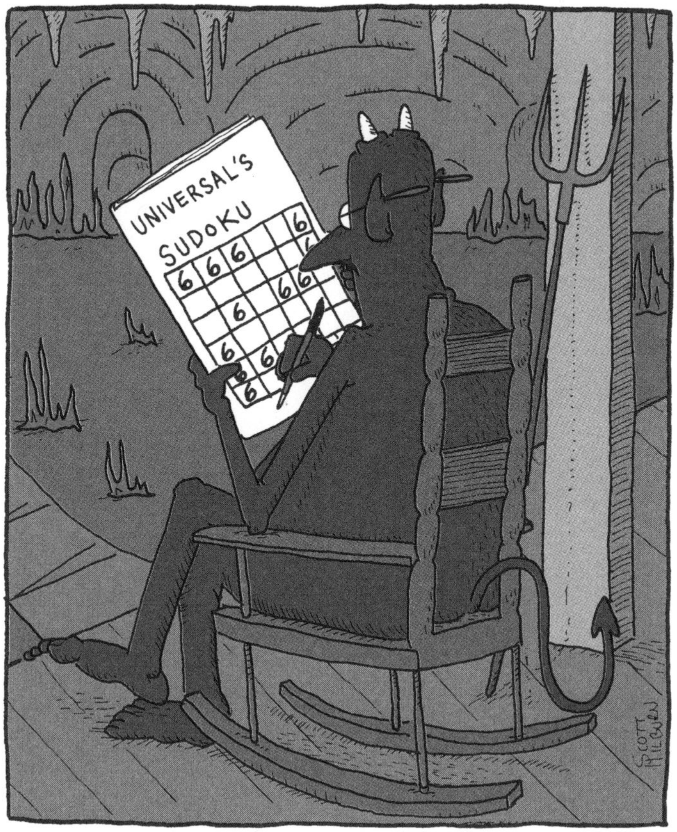
UNIVERSAL'S SUDOKU
SCOTT HILBURN

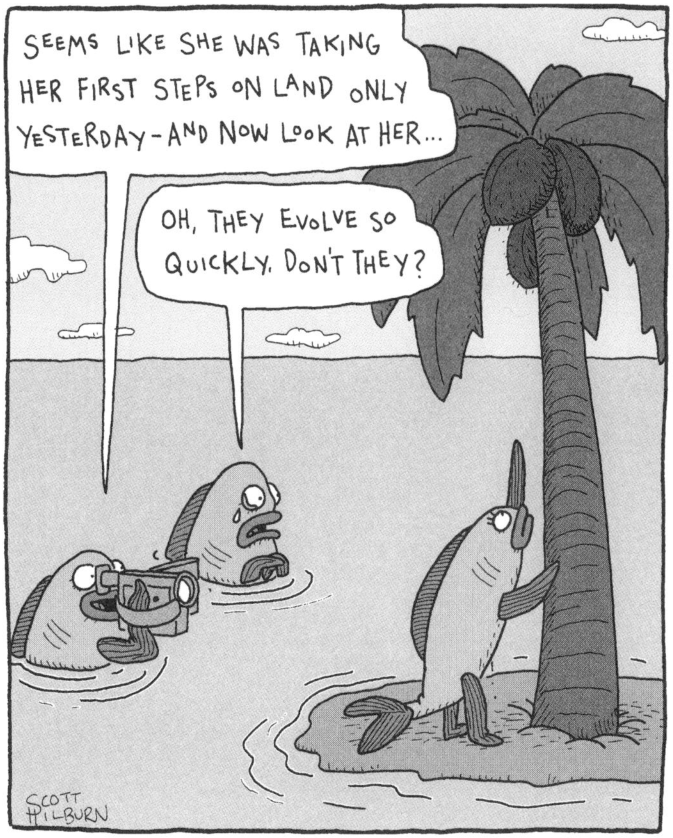
SEEMS LIKE SHE WAS TAKING HER FIRST STEPS ON LAND ONLY YESTERDAY - AND NOW LOOK AT HER...
OH, THEY EVOLVE SO QUICKLY. DON'T THEY?
SCOTT HILBURN

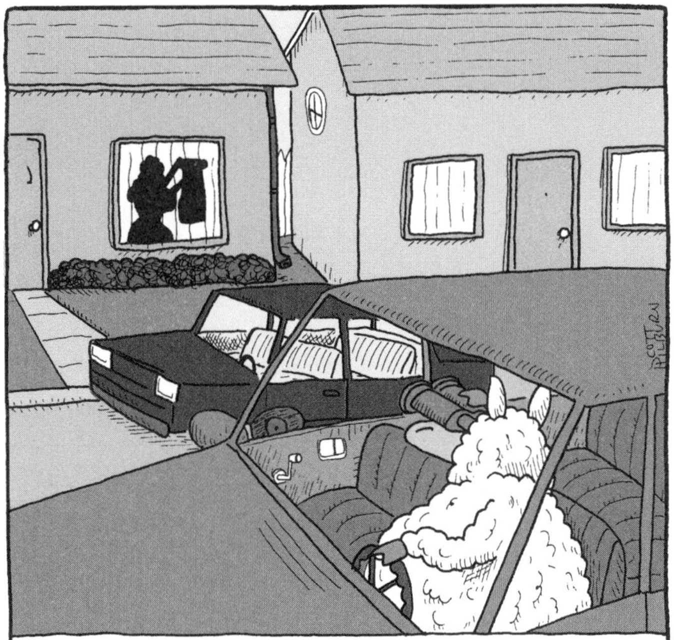
SCOTT HILBURN

H'S INFATUATION TURNED TO OBSESSION. HE WOULD WATCH HER AT WORK... HE WOULD FOLLOW HER HOME... YES, EVERYWHERE THAT MARY WENT, THE LAMB WAS SURE TO GO.

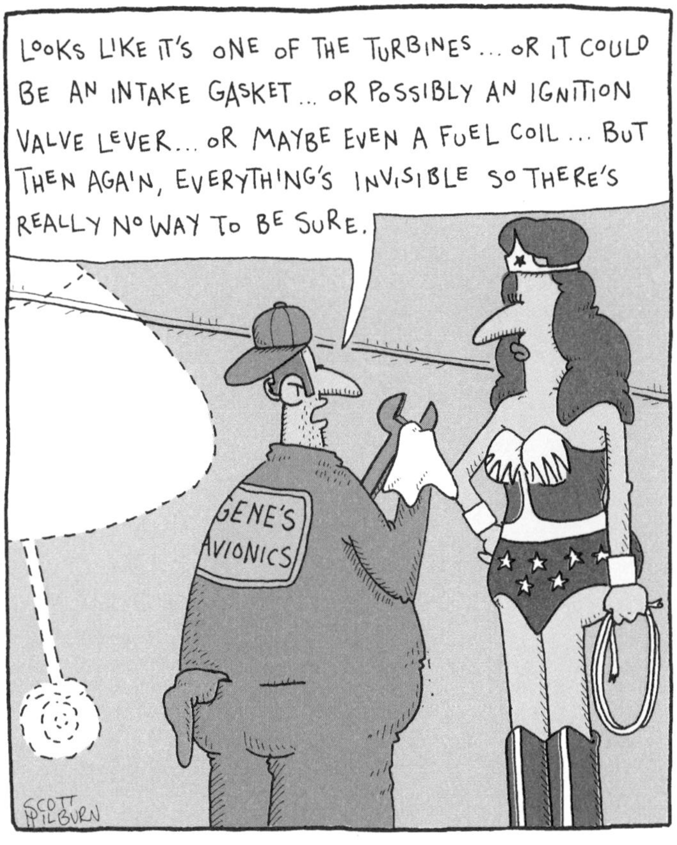
LOOKS LIKE IT'S ONE OF THE TURBINES... OR IT COULD BE AN INTAKE GASKET... OR POSSIBLY AN IGNITION VALVE LEVER... OR MAYBE EVEN A FUEL COIL... BUT THEN AGAIN, EVERYTHING'S INVISIBLE SO THERE'S REALLY NO WAY TO BE SURE.
GENE'S AVIONICS
SCOTT HILBURN

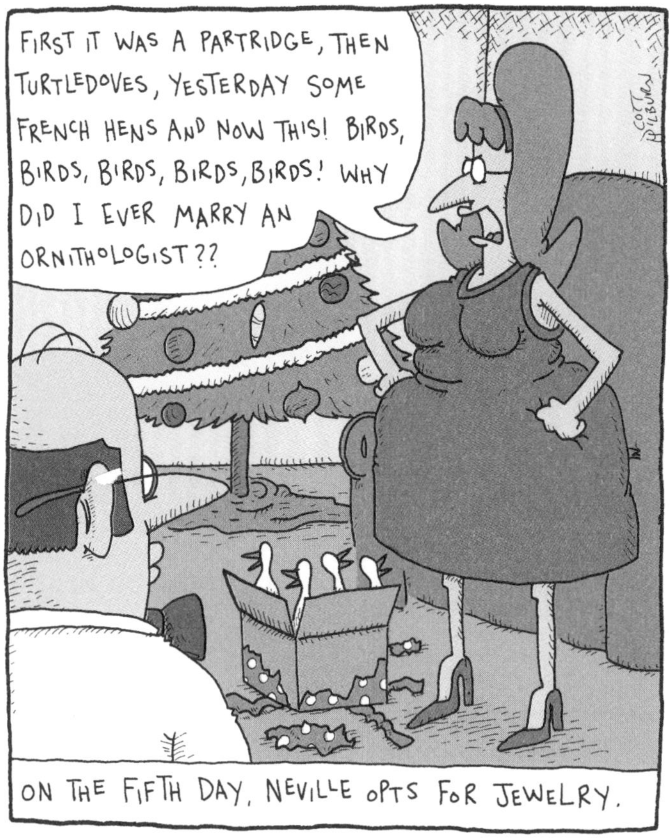
FIRST IT WAS A PARTRIDGE, THEN TURTLEDOVES, YESTERDAY SOME FRENCH HENS AND NOW THIS! BIRDS, BIRDS, BIRDS, BIRDS, BIRDS! WHY DID I EVER MARRY AN ORNITHOLOGIST??
SCOTT HILBURN

ON THE FIFTH DAY, NEVILLE OPTS FOR JEWELRY.

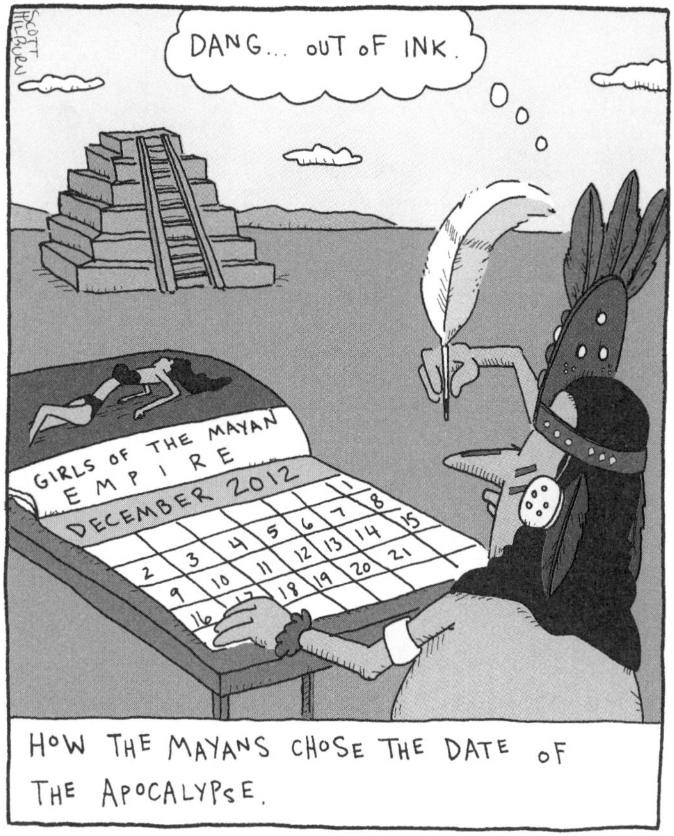
SCOTT HILBURN
DANG... OUT OF INK.
GIRLS OF THE MAYAN EMPIRE
DECEMBER 2012

HOW THE MAYANS CHOSE THE DATE OF THE APOCALYPSE.

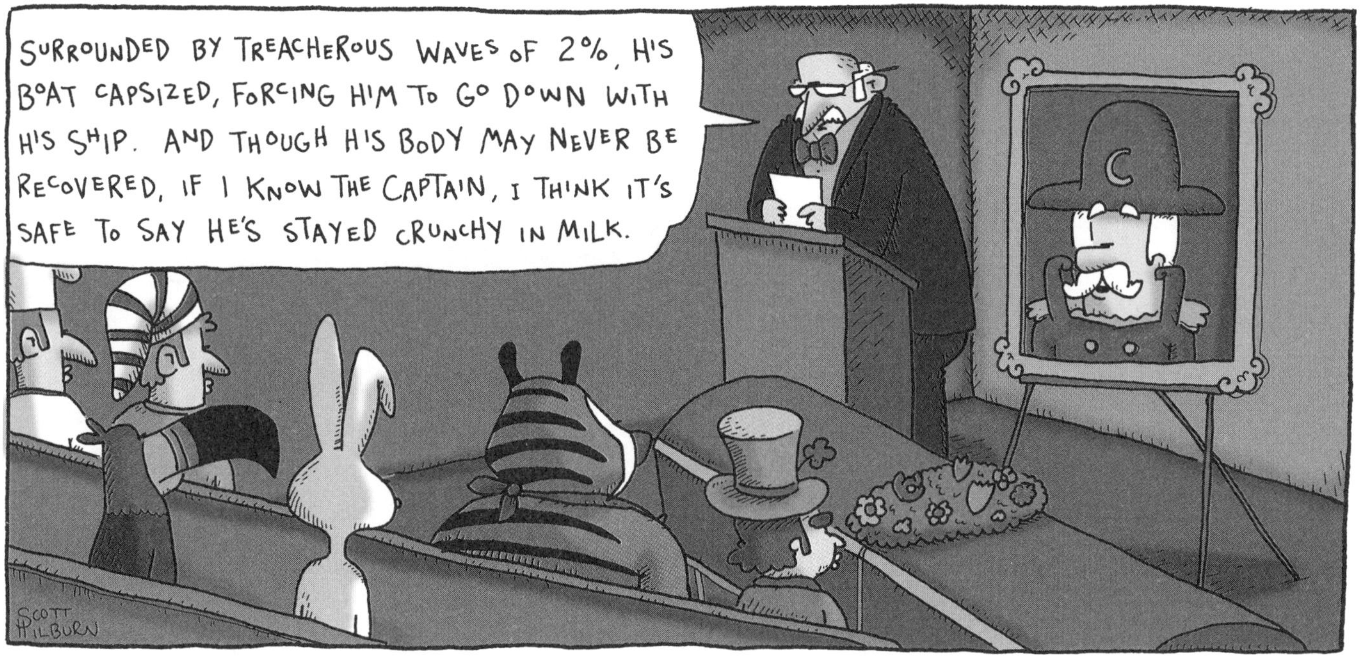
SURROUNDED BY TREACHEROUS WAVES OF 2%, HIS BOAT CAPSIZED, FORCING HIM TO GO DOWN WITH HIS SHIP. AND THOUGH HIS BODY MAY NEVER BE RECOVERED, IF I KNOW THE CAPTAIN, I THINK IT'S SAFE TO SAY HE'S STAYED CRUNCHY IN MILK.
C
SCOTT HILBURN

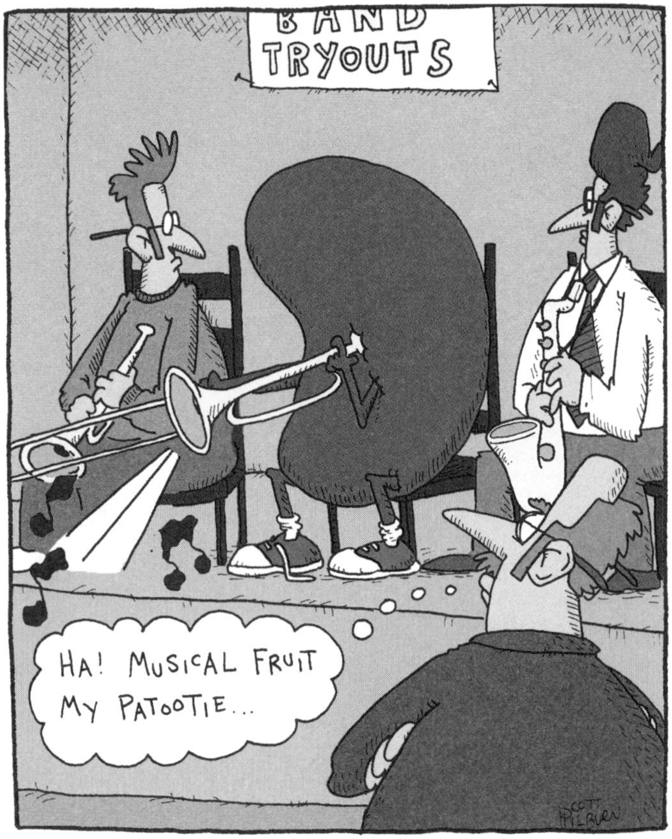
BAND TRYOUTS
HA! MUSICAL FRUIT MY PATOOTIE...
SCOTT HILBURN

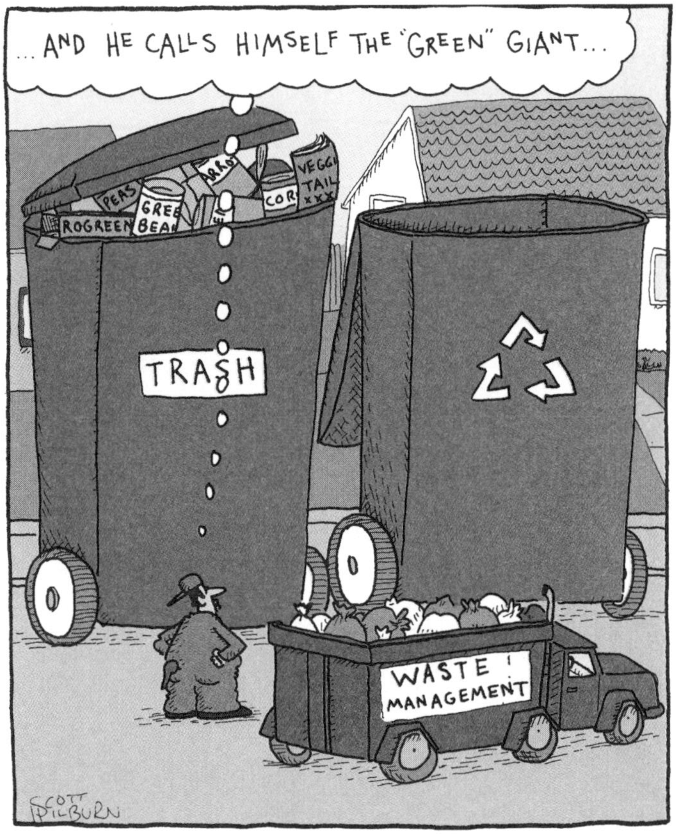
...AND HE CALLS HIMSELF THE "GREEN" GIANT...
PEAS
GREE BEA
ROGREEN
COR
VEGG TAIL
TRASH
WASTE MANAGEMENT
SCOTT HILBURN

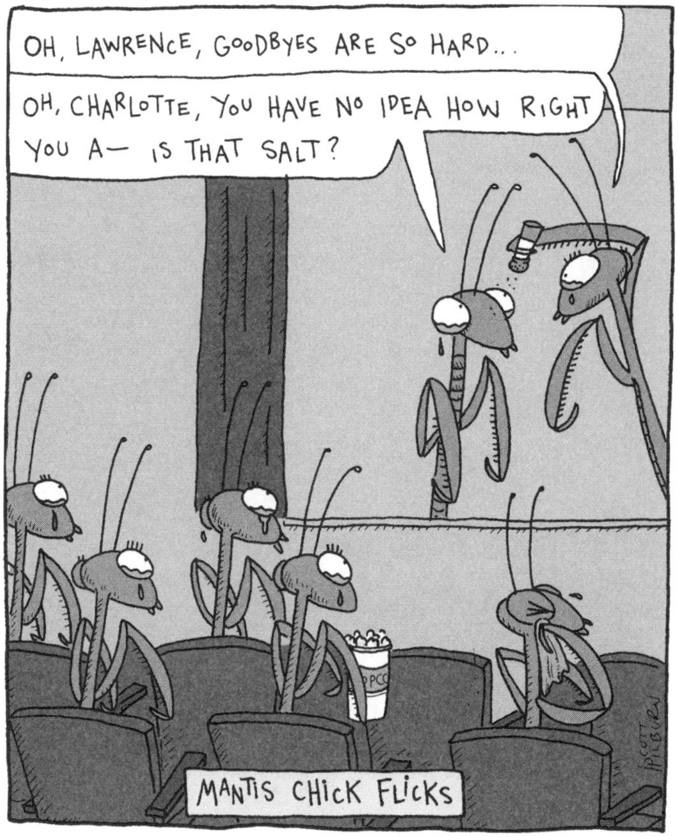
OH, LAWRENCE, GOODBYES ARE SO HARD...
OH, CHARLOTTE, YOU HAVE NO IDEA HOW RIGHT YOU A— IS THAT SALT?
MANTIS CHICK FLICKS

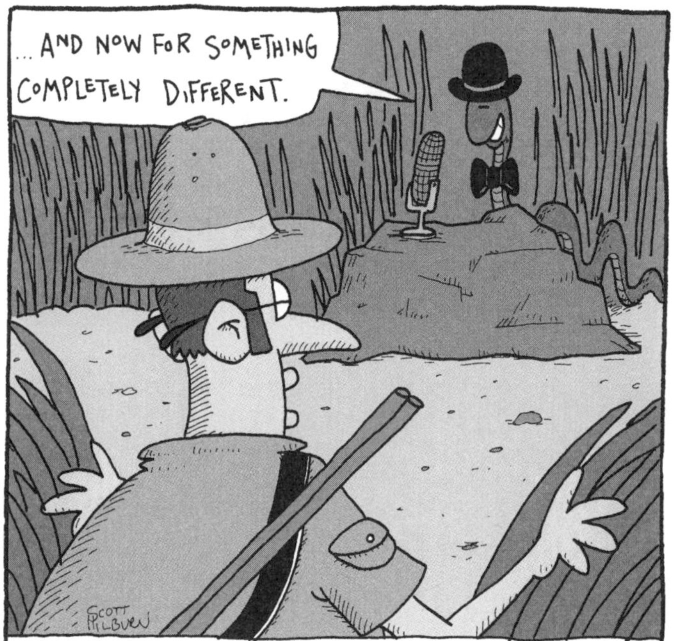
...AND NOW FOR SOMETHING COMPLETELY DIFFERENT.

HE INSTANTLY REALIZED THAT THE SNAKE HE HAD STUMBLED UPON WASN'T THE ORDINARY, NONVENOMOUS PYTHON BUT THE FEARED MONTY PYTHON. HOWEVER, IMPERVIOUS TO BRITISH HUMOR, WALTER WALKED AWAY UNSCATHED.

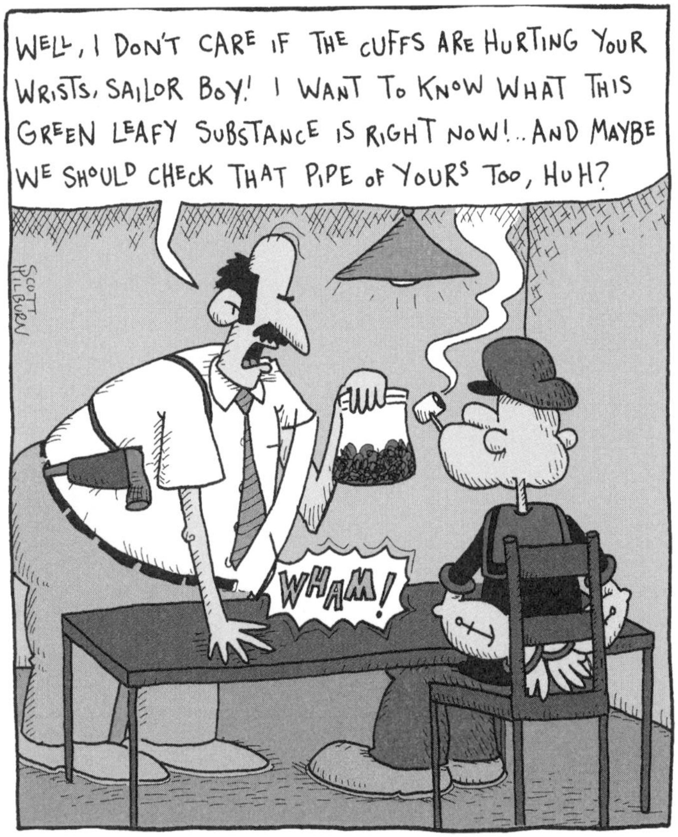
WELL, I DON'T CARE IF THE CUFFS ARE HURTING YOUR WRISTS, SAILOR BOY! I WANT TO KNOW WHAT THIS GREEN LEAFY SUBSTANCE IS RIGHT NOW!.. AND MAYBE WE SHOULD CHECK THAT PIPE OF YOURS TOO, HUH?
WHAM!
SCOTT HILBURN

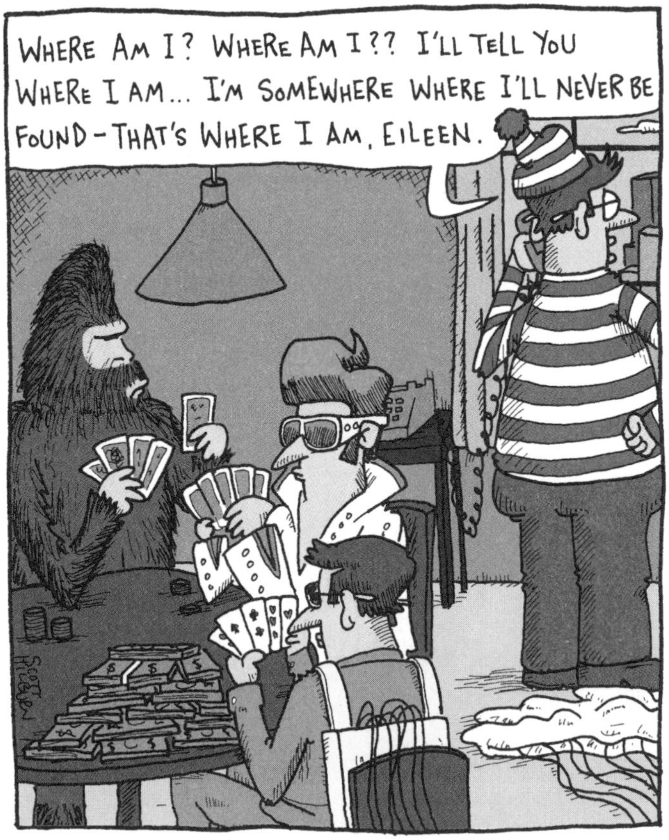
WHERE AM I? WHERE AM I?? I'LL TELL YOU WHERE I AM... I'M SOMEWHERE WHERE I'LL NEVER BE FOUND - THAT'S WHERE I AM, EILEEN.
SCOTT HILBURN

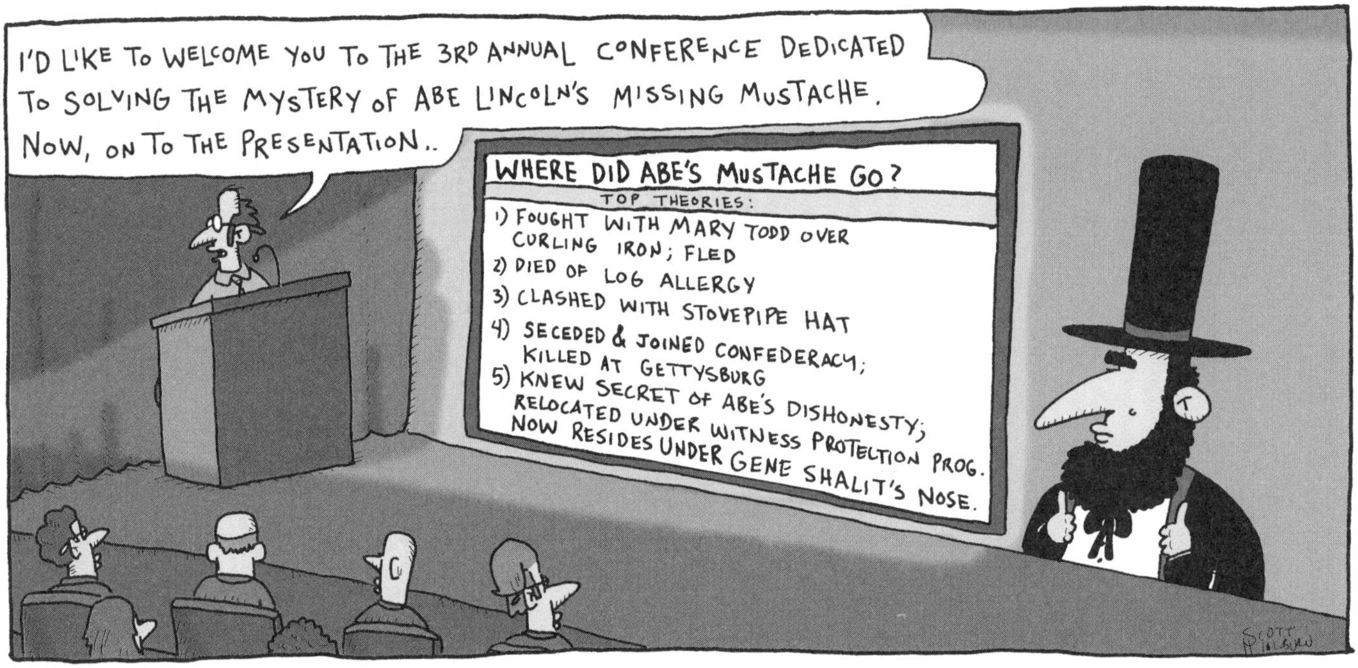
I'D LIKE TO WELCOME YOU TO THE 3RD ANNUAL CONFERENCE DEDICATED TO SOLVING THE MYSTERY OF ABE LINCOLN'S MISSING MUSTACHE. NOW, ON TO THE PRESENTATION..
WHERE DID ABE'S MUSTACHE GO?
TOP THEORIES:
1) FOUGHT WITH MARY TODD OVER CURLING IRON; FLED
2) DIED OF LOG ALLERGY
3) CLASHED WITH STOVEPIPE HAT
4) SECEDED & JOINED CONFEDERACY; KILLED AT GETTYSBURG
5) KNEW SECRET OF ABE'S DISHONESTY; RELOCATED UNDER WITNESS PROTECTION PROG. NOW RESIDES UNDER GENE SHALIT'S NOSE.
SCOTT HILBURN

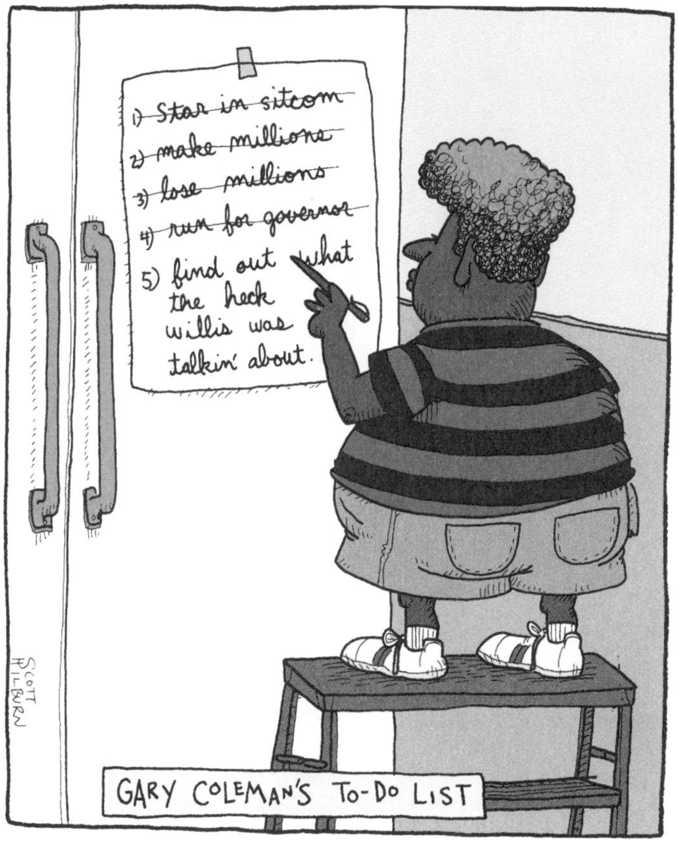
1) Star in sitcom
2) make millions
3) lose millions
4) run for governor
5) find out what the heck willis was talkin' about.
SCOTT HILBURN
GARY COLEMAN'S TO-DO LIST

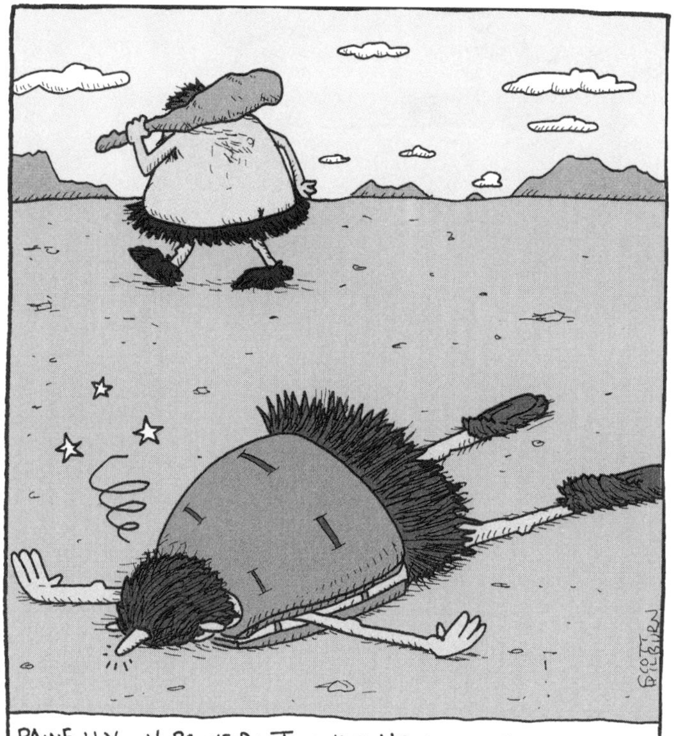
SCOTT HILBURN
PAINFULLY OVERCONFIDENT IN HIS NEW INVENTION, TOG MISCALCULATES THE EFFECTIVENESS OF HIS CLUB-PROOF VEST.

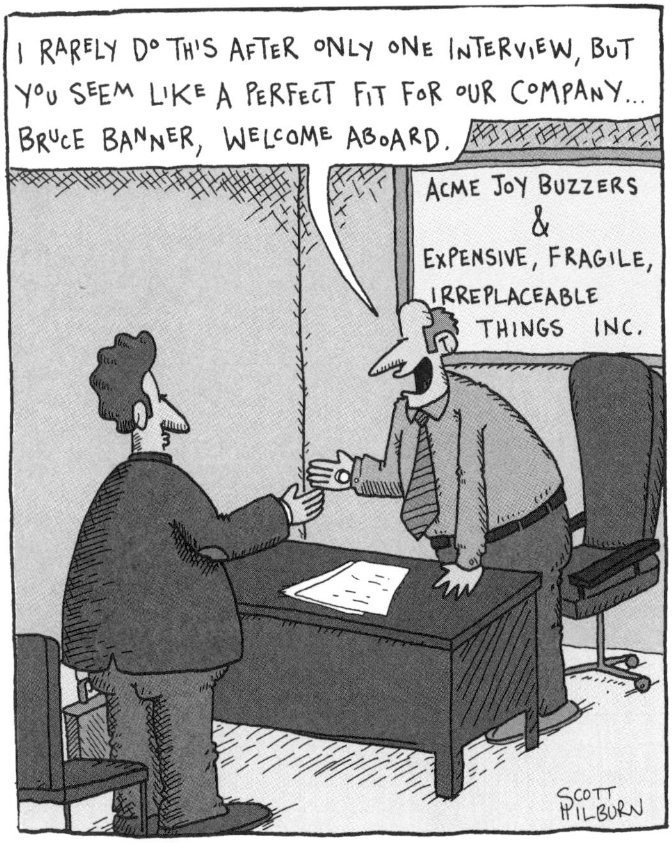
I RARELY DO THIS AFTER ONLY ONE INTERVIEW, BUT YOU SEEM LIKE A PERFECT FIT FOR OUR COMPANY... BRUCE BANNER, WELCOME ABOARD.
ACME JOY BUZZERS & EXPENSIVE, FRAGILE, IRREPLACEABLE THINGS INC.
SCOTT HILBURN

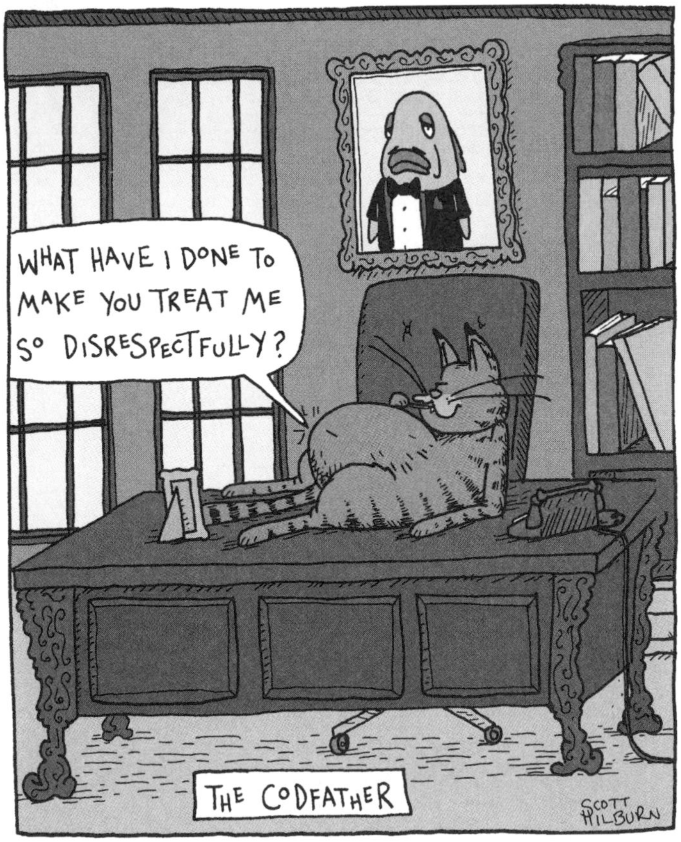
WHAT HAVE I DONE TO MAKE YOU TREAT ME SO DISRESPECTFULLY?
THE CODFATHER
SCOTT HILBURN

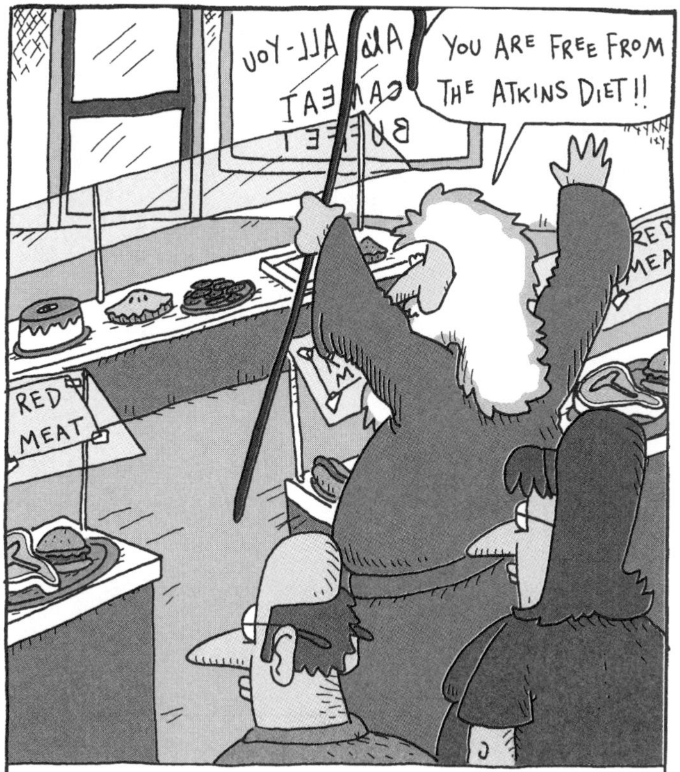
YOU ARE FREE FROM THE ATKINS DIET!!
RED MEAT
RED MEA
MOSES LEADS HIS PEOPLE TO THE DESSERT

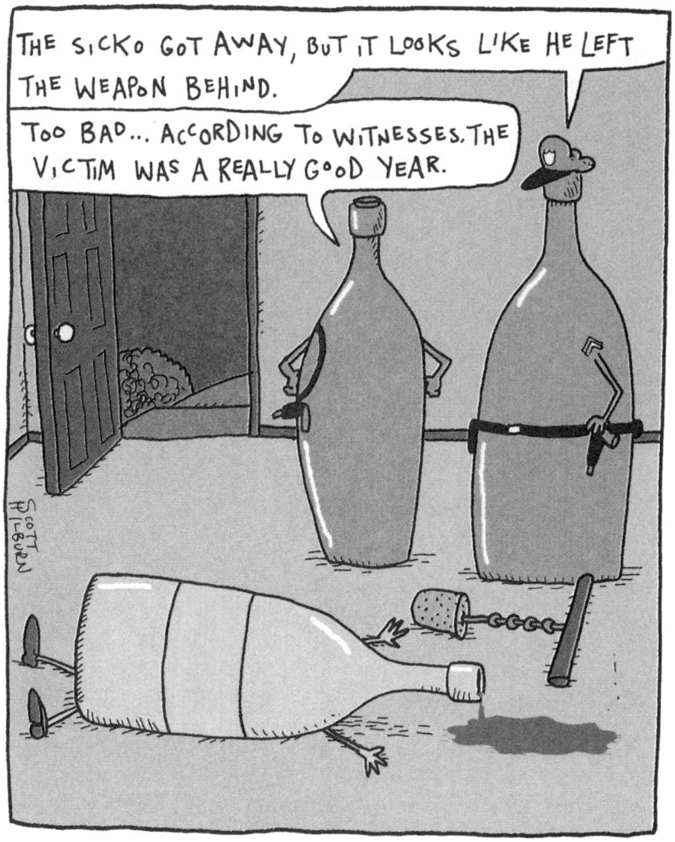
THE SICKO GOT AWAY, BUT IT LOOKS LIKE HE LEFT THE WEAPON BEHIND.
TOO BAD... ACCORDING TO WITNESSES, THE VICTIM WAS A REALLY GOOD YEAR.
SCOTT HILBURN

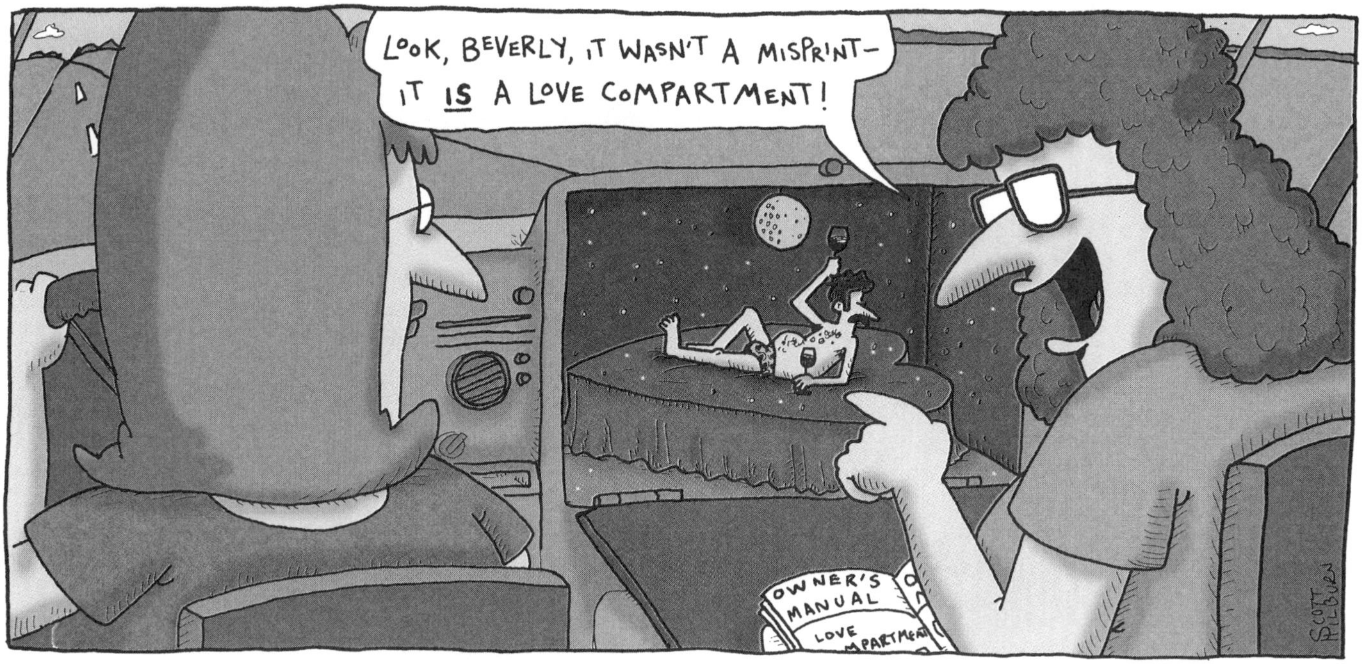
LOOK, BEVERLY, IT WASN'T A MISPRINT— IT IS A LOVE COMPARTMENT!
OWNER'S MANUAL
LOVE COMPARTMENT
SCOTT HILBURN

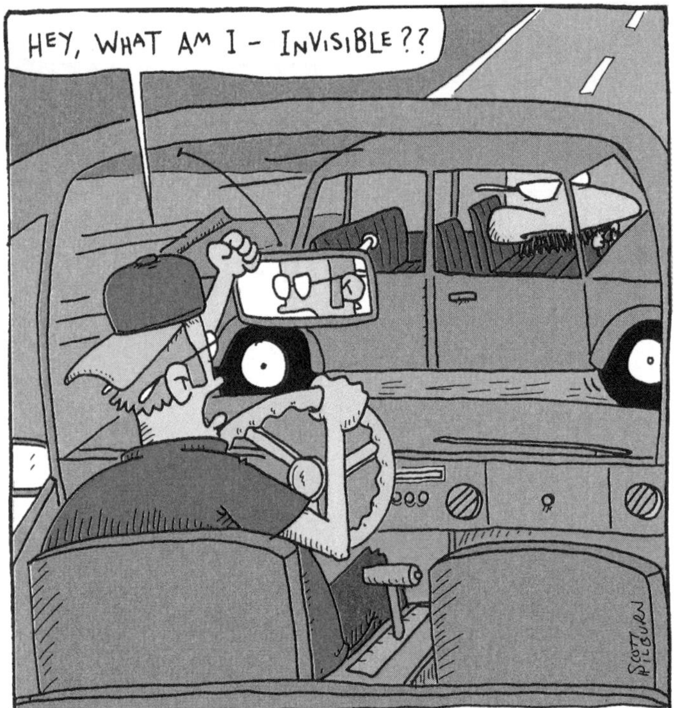
HEY, WHAT AM I - INVISIBLE??
SCOTT HILBURN

ANDREW'S OWN NOSE CUTS HIM OFF JUST TO SPITE HIS FACE.

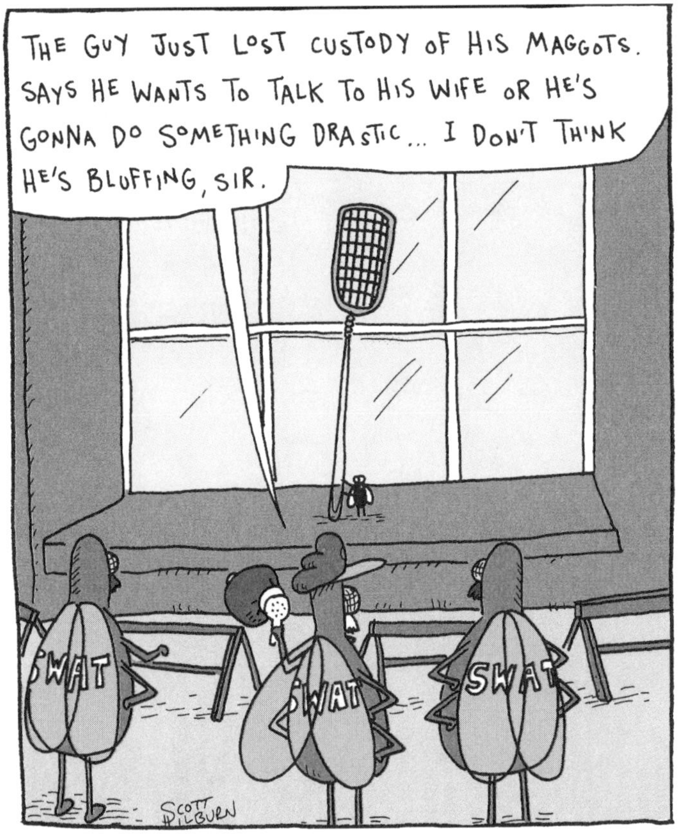
THE GUY JUST LOST CUSTODY OF HIS MAGGOTS. SAYS HE WANTS TO TALK TO HIS WIFE OR HE'S GONNA DO SOMETHING DRASTIC... I DON'T THINK HE'S BLUFFING, SIR.
SWAT
SWAT
SWAT
SCOTT HILBURN

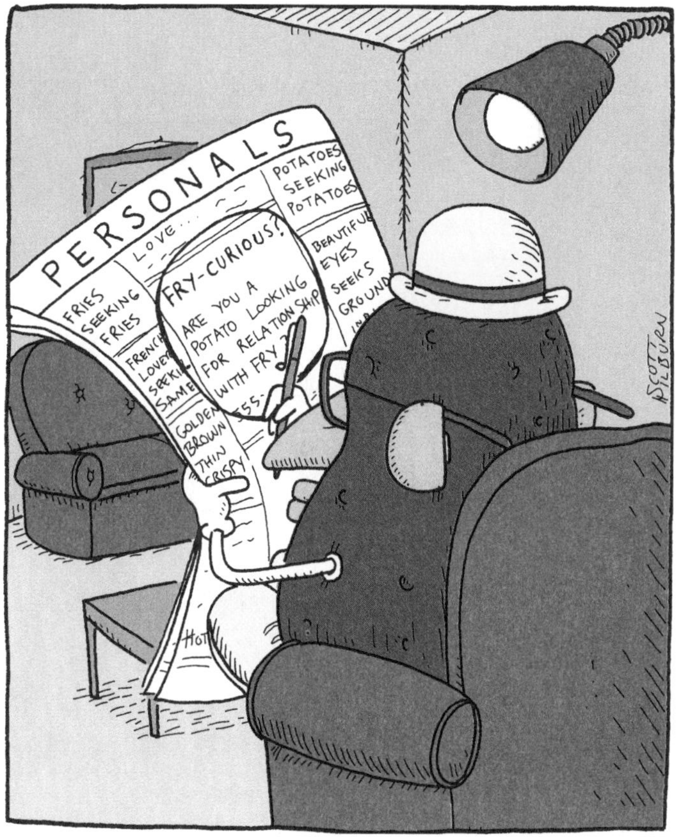
PERSONALS
FRIES SEEKING FRIES
LOVE...
FRY-CURIOUS? ARE YOU A POTATO LOOKING FOR RELATIONSHIP WITH FRY
POTATOES SEEKING POTATOES
BEAUTIFUL EYES SEEKS GROUND
GOLDEN BROWN THIN CRISPY
SCOTT HILBURN

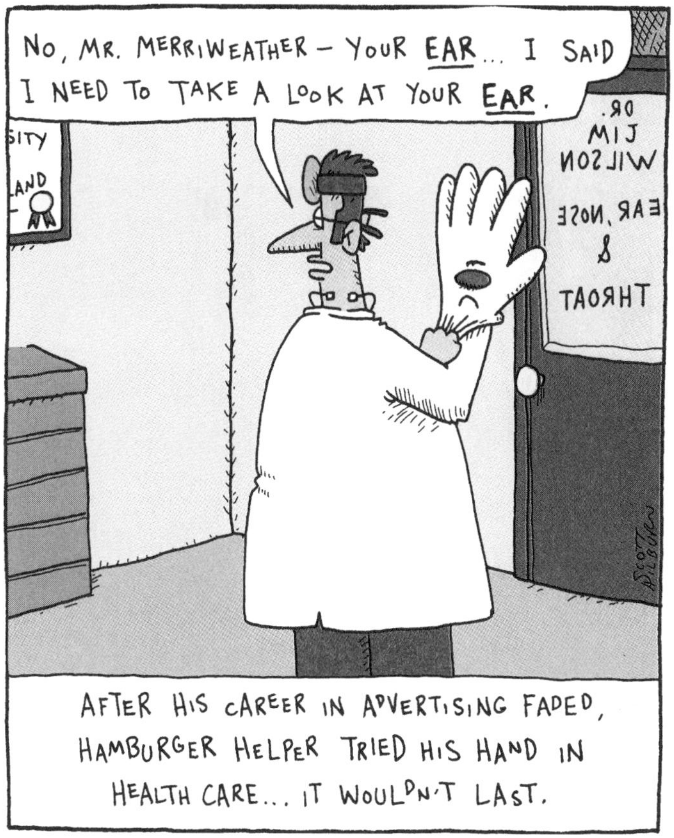
NO, MR. MERRIWEATHER – YOUR EAR... I SAID I NEED TO TAKE A LOOK AT YOUR EAR.
DR. JIM WILSON EAR, NOSE & THROAT
SCOTT HILBURN
AFTER HIS CAREER IN ADVERTISING FADED, HAMBURGER HELPER TRIED HIS HAND IN HEALTH CARE... IT WOULDN'T LAST.

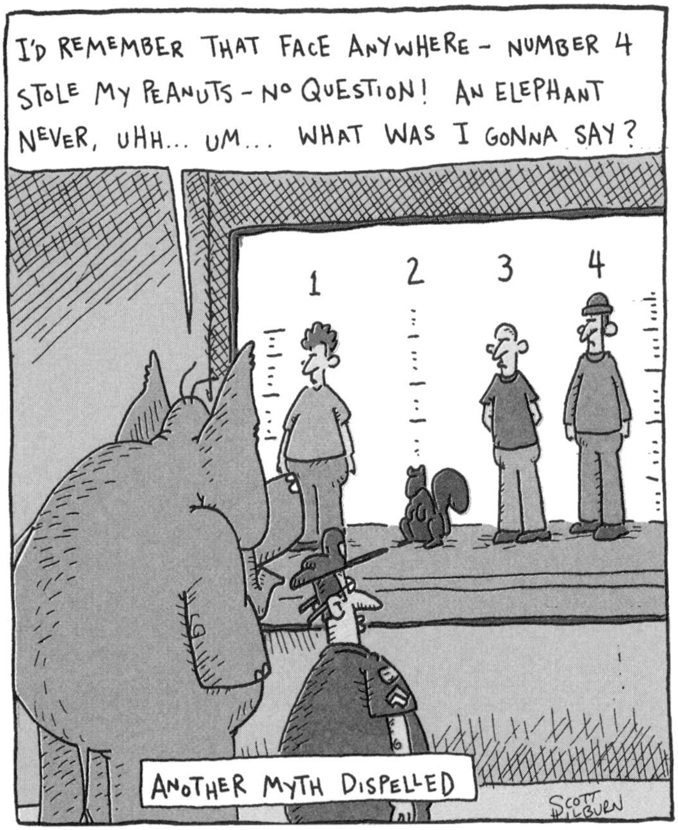
I'D REMEMBER THAT FACE ANYWHERE - NUMBER 4 STOLE MY PEANUTS - NO QUESTION! AN ELEPHANT NEVER, UHH... UM... WHAT WAS I GONNA SAY?
1
2
3
4
ANOTHER MYTH DISPELLED
SCOTT HILBURN

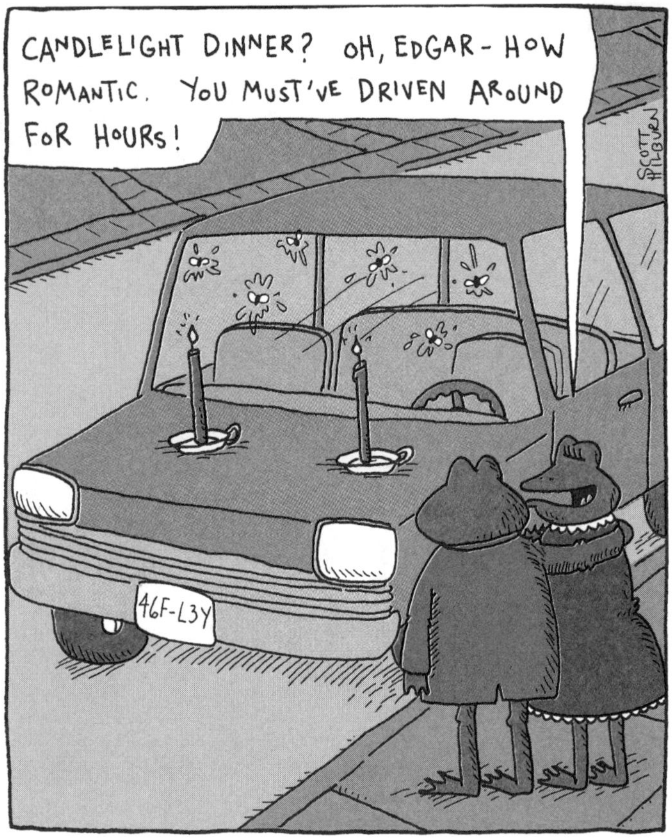
CANDLELIGHT DINNER? OH, EDGAR - HOW ROMANTIC. YOU MUST'VE DRIVEN AROUND FOR HOURS!
46F-L3Y
SCOTT HILBURN

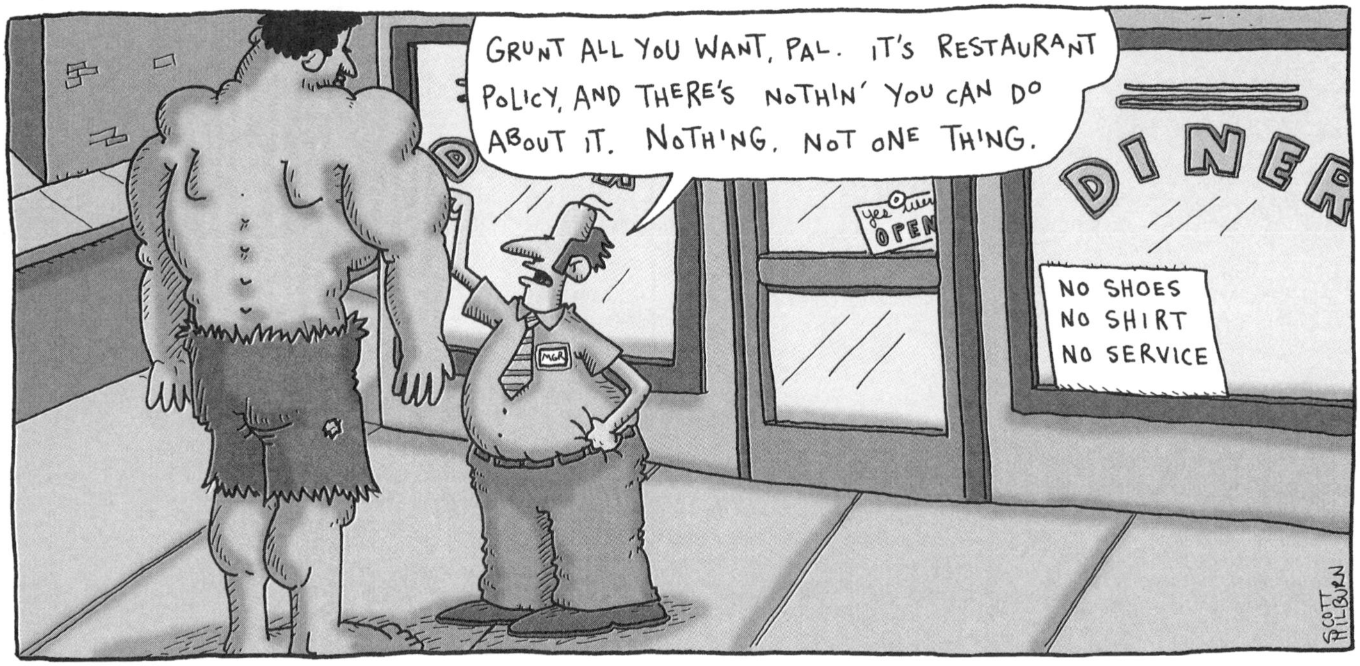
GRUNT ALL YOU WANT, PAL. IT'S RESTAURANT POLICY, AND THERE'S NOTHIN' YOU CAN DO ABOUT IT. NOTHING. NOT ONE THING.
DINER
OPEN
MGR
NO SHOES
NO SHIRT
NO SERVICE
SCOTT HILBURN

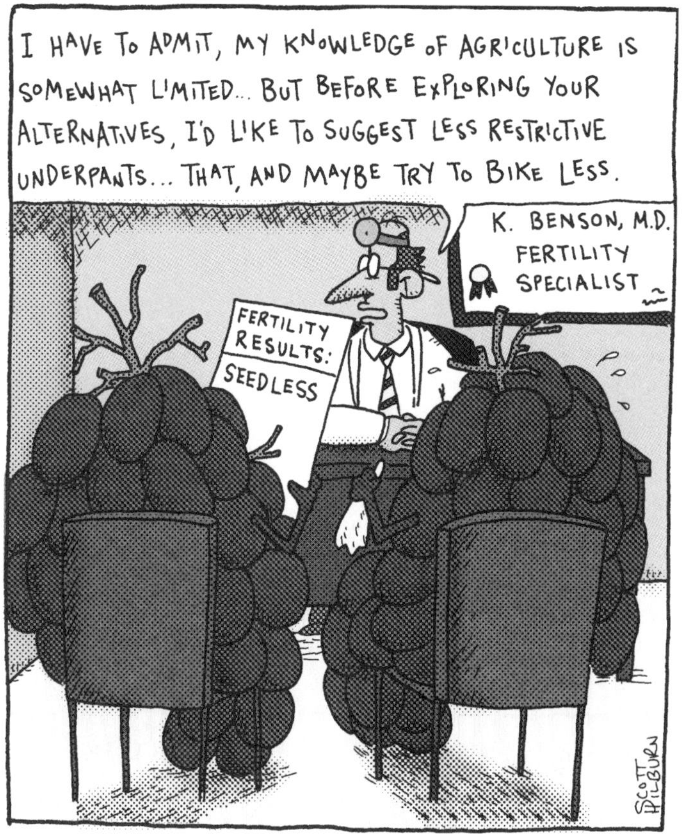
I HAVE TO ADMIT, MY KNOWLEDGE OF AGRICULTURE IS SOMEWHAT LIMITED... BUT BEFORE EXPLORING YOUR ALTERNATIVES, I'D LIKE TO SUGGEST LESS RESTRICTIVE UNDERPANTS... THAT, AND MAYBE TRY TO BIKE LESS.
K. BENSON, M.D.
FERTILITY
SPECIALIST
FERTILITY
RESULTS:
SEEDLESS
SCOTT
HILBURN

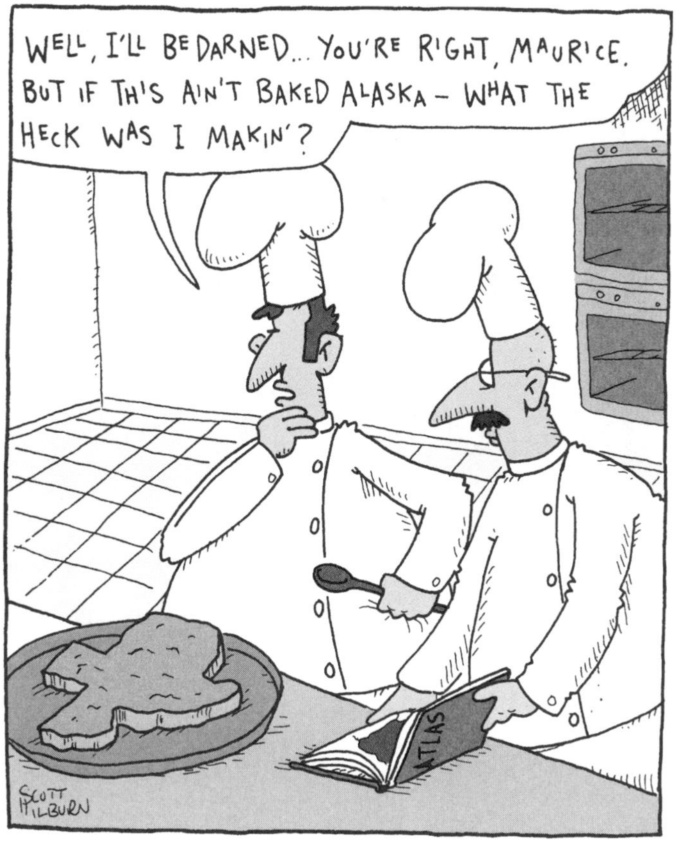
WELL, I'LL BE DARNED... YOU'RE RIGHT, MAURICE. BUT IF THIS AIN'T BAKED ALASKA – WHAT THE HECK WAS I MAKIN'?
ATLAS
SCOTT
HILBURN

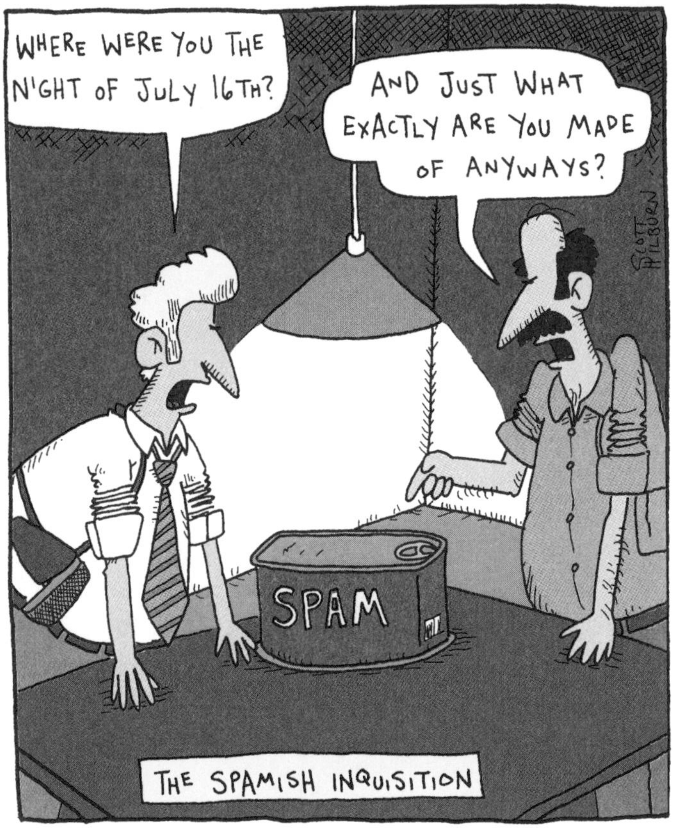
WHERE WERE YOU THE NIGHT OF JULY 16TH?
AND JUST WHAT EXACTLY ARE YOU MADE OF ANYWAYS?
SPAM
THE SPAMISH INQUISITION
SCOTT HILBURN

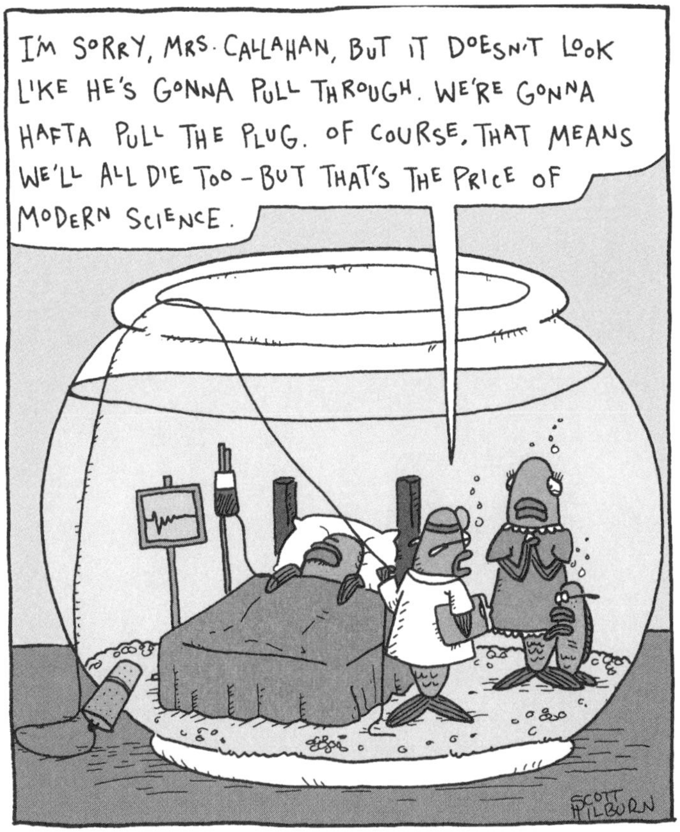
I'M SORRY, MRS. CALLAHAN, BUT IT DOESN'T LOOK LIKE HE'S GONNA PULL THROUGH. WE'RE GONNA HAFTA PULL THE PLUG. OF COURSE, THAT MEANS WE'LL ALL DIE TOO – BUT THAT'S THE PRICE OF MODERN SCIENCE.
SCOTT HILBURN

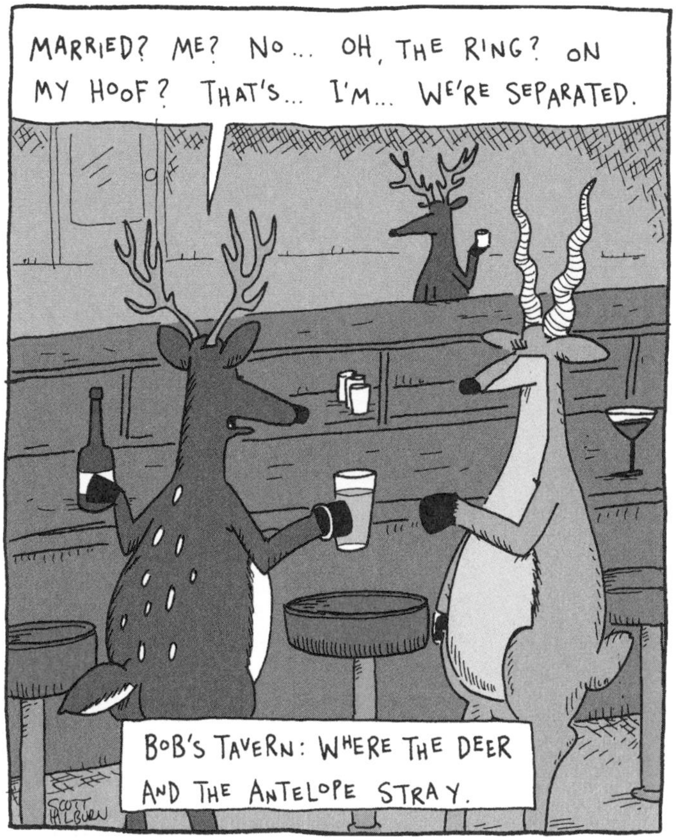
MARRIED? ME? NO... OH, THE RING? ON MY HOOF? THAT'S... I'M... WE'RE SEPARATED.
BOB'S TAVERN: WHERE THE DEER AND THE ANTELOPE STRAY.
SCOTT HILBURN

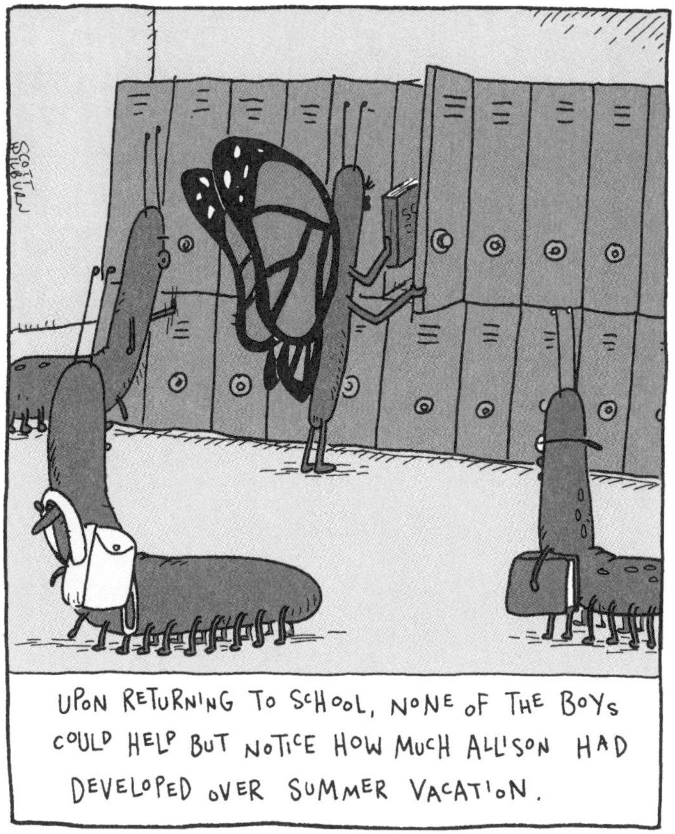
SCOTT HILBURN
UPON RETURNING TO SCHOOL, NONE OF THE BOYS COULD HELP BUT NOTICE HOW MUCH ALLISON HAD DEVELOPED OVER SUMMER VACATION.

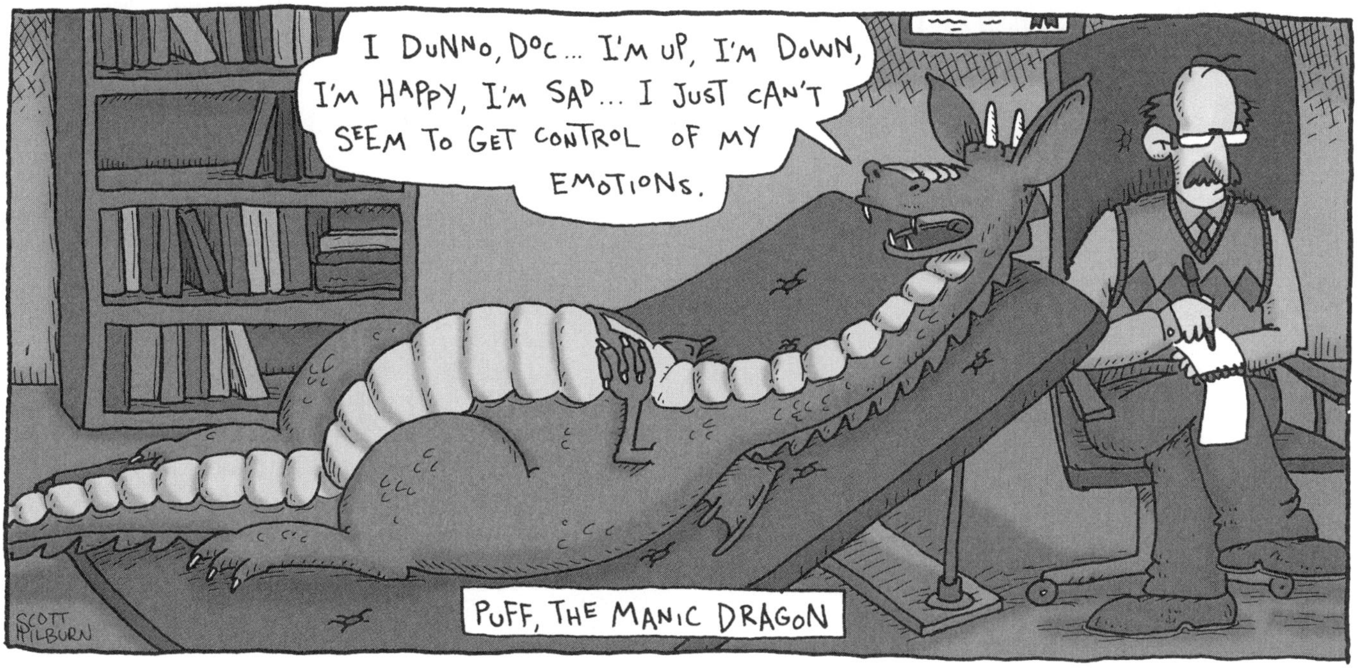
I DUNNO, DOC... I'M UP, I'M DOWN, I'M HAPPY, I'M SAD... I JUST CAN'T SEEM TO GET CONTROL OF MY EMOTIONS.
PUFF, THE MANIC DRAGON
SCOTT HILBURN

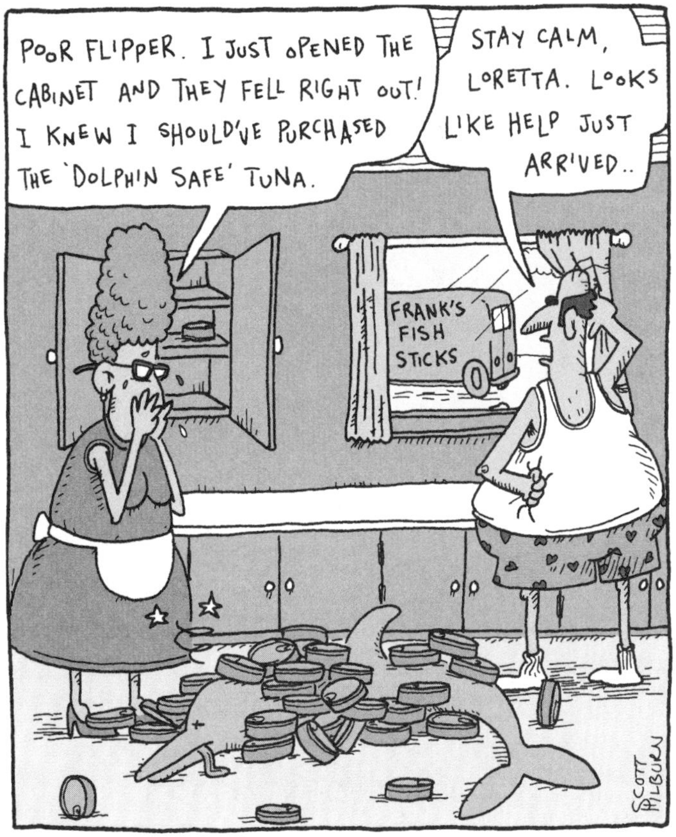
POOR FLIPPER. I JUST OPENED THE CABINET AND THEY FELL RIGHT OUT! I KNEW I SHOULD'VE PURCHASED THE 'DOLPHIN SAFE' TUNA.
STAY CALM, LORETTA. LOOKS LIKE HELP JUST ARRIVED..
FRANK'S FISH STICKS
SCOTT HILBURN

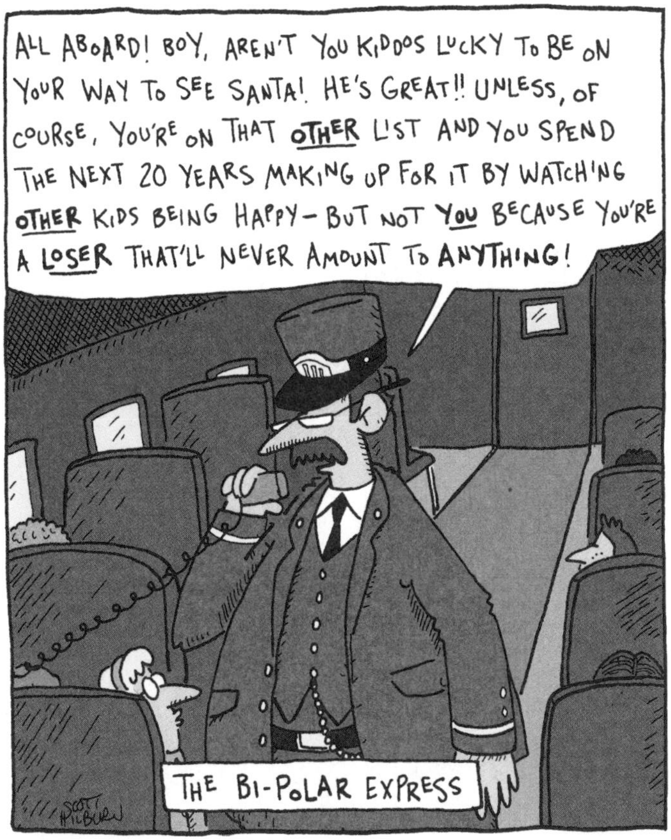
ALL ABOARD! BOY, AREN'T YOU KIDDOS LUCKY TO BE ON YOUR WAY TO SEE SANTA! HE'S GREAT!! UNLESS, OF COURSE, YOU'RE ON THAT OTHER LIST AND YOU SPEND THE NEXT 20 YEARS MAKING UP FOR IT BY WATCHING OTHER KIDS BEING HAPPY – BUT NOT YOU BECAUSE YOU'RE A LOSER THAT'LL NEVER AMOUNT TO ANYTHING!
THE BI-POLAR EXPRESS
SCOTT HILBURN

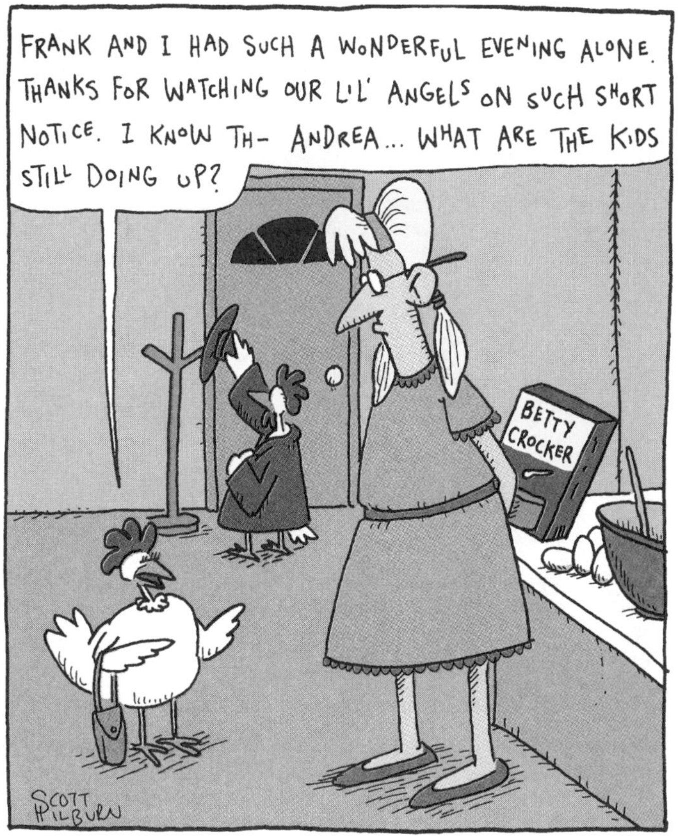
FRANK AND I HAD SUCH A WONDERFUL EVENING ALONE. THANKS FOR WATCHING OUR LIL' ANGELS ON SUCH SHORT NOTICE. I KNOW TH- ANDREA... WHAT ARE THE KIDS STILL DOING UP?
BETTY CROCKER
SCOTT HILBURN

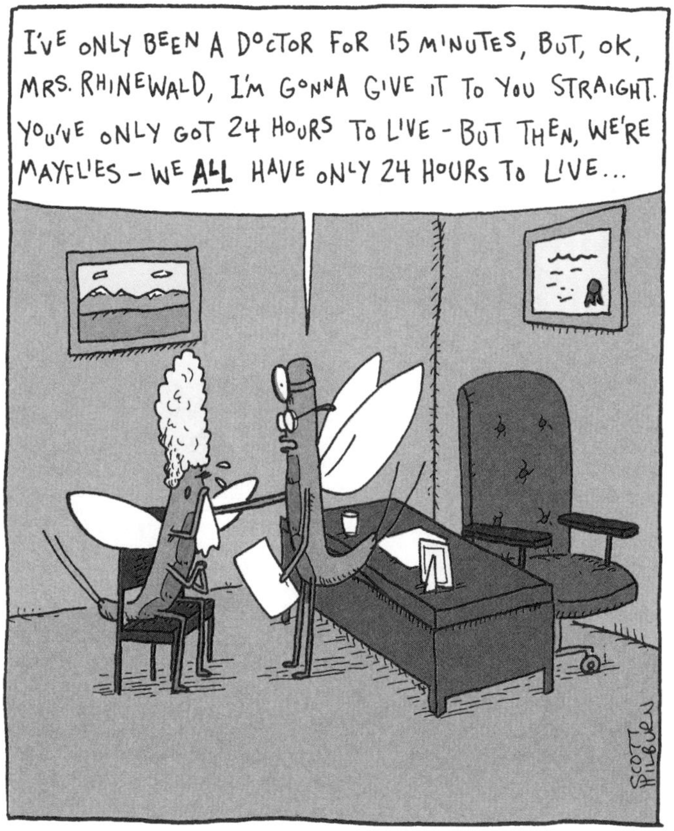
I'VE ONLY BEEN A DOCTOR FOR 15 MINUTES, BUT, OK, MRS. RHINEWALD, I'M GONNA GIVE IT TO YOU STRAIGHT. YOU'VE ONLY GOT 24 HOURS TO LIVE - BUT THEN, WE'RE MAYFLIES - WE ALL HAVE ONLY 24 HOURS TO LIVE...
SCOTT HILBURN

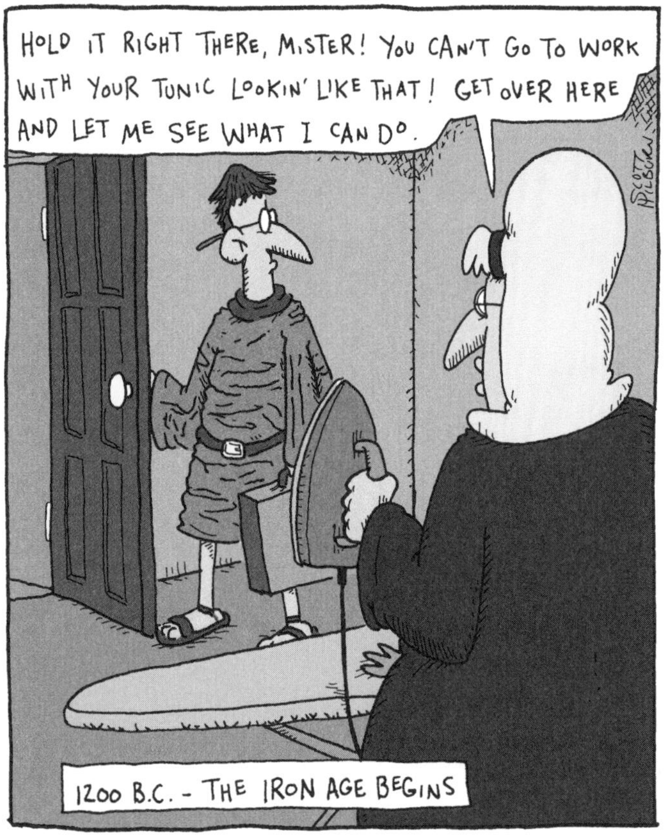
HOLD IT RIGHT THERE, MISTER! YOU CAN'T GO TO WORK WITH YOUR TUNIC LOOKIN' LIKE THAT! GET OVER HERE AND LET ME SEE WHAT I CAN DO.
SCOTT HILBURN
1200 B.C. - THE IRON AGE BEGINS

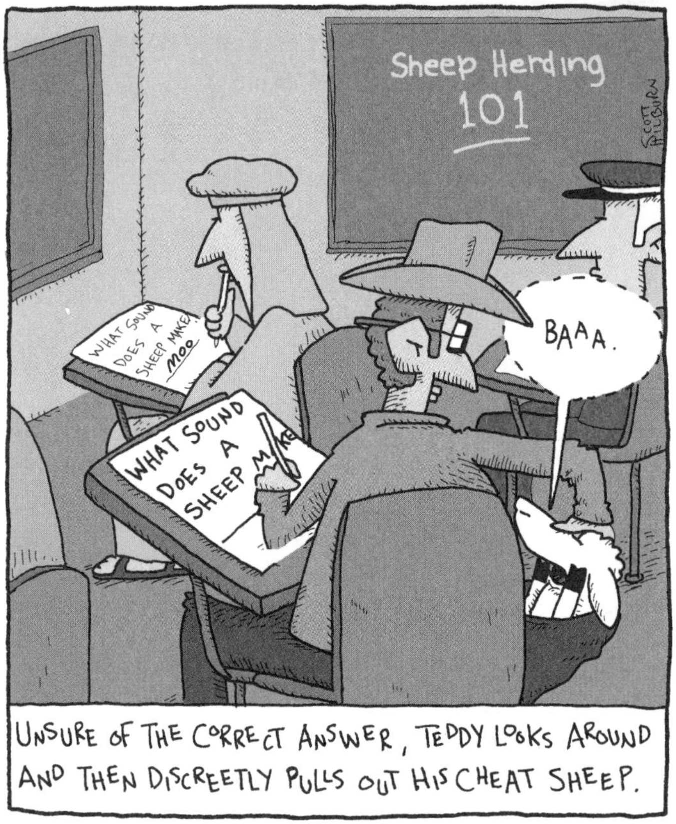
Sheep Herding 101
SCOTT HILBURN
WHAT SOUND DOES A SHEEP MAKE? MOO
WHAT SOUND DOES A SHEEP MAKE
BAAA.
UNSURE OF THE CORRECT ANSWER, TEDDY LOOKS AROUND AND THEN DISCREETLY PULLS OUT HIS CHEAT SHEEP.

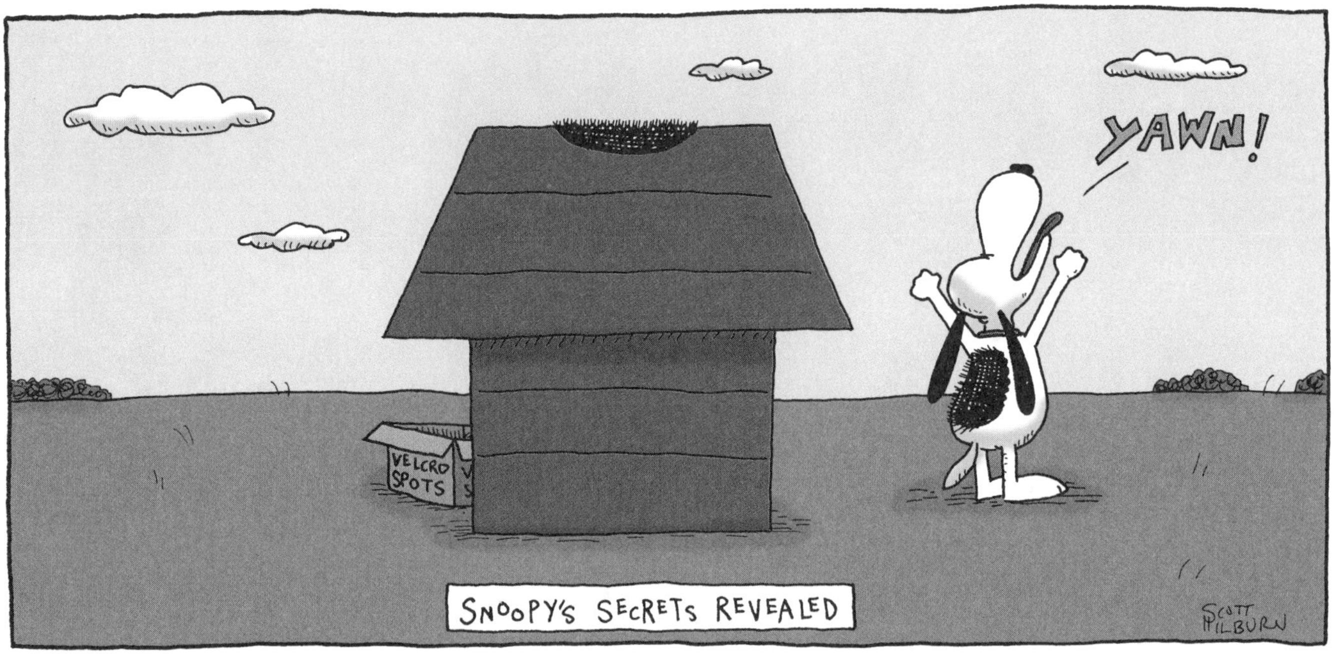
YAWN!
VELCRO SPOTS
SCOTT HILBURN
SNOOPY'S SECRETS REVEALED

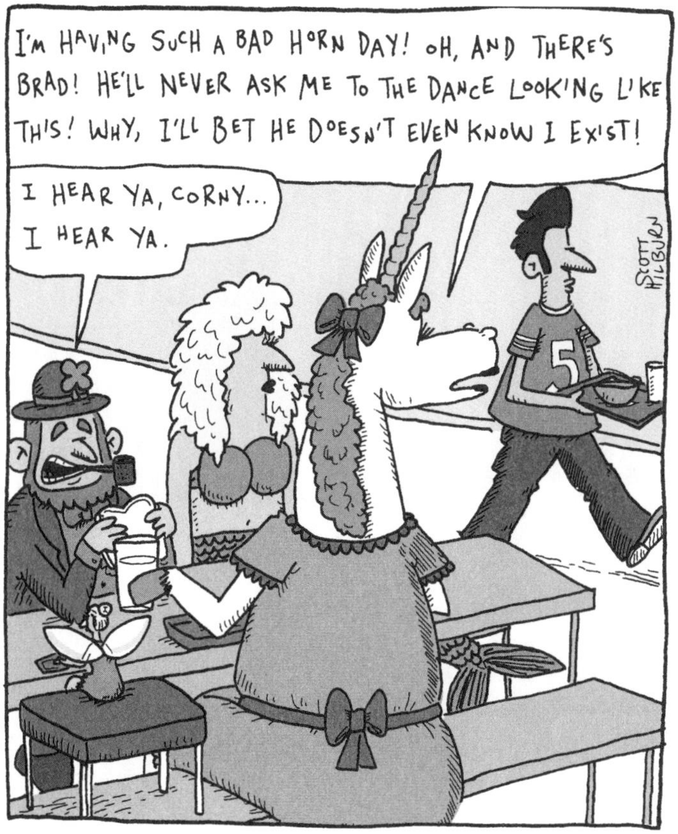
I'M HAVING SUCH A BAD HORN DAY! OH, AND THERE'S BRAD! HE'LL NEVER ASK ME TO THE DANCE LOOKING LIKE THIS! WHY, I'LL BET HE DOESN'T EVEN KNOW I EXIST!
I HEAR YA, CORNY... I HEAR YA.
5
SCOTT HILBURN

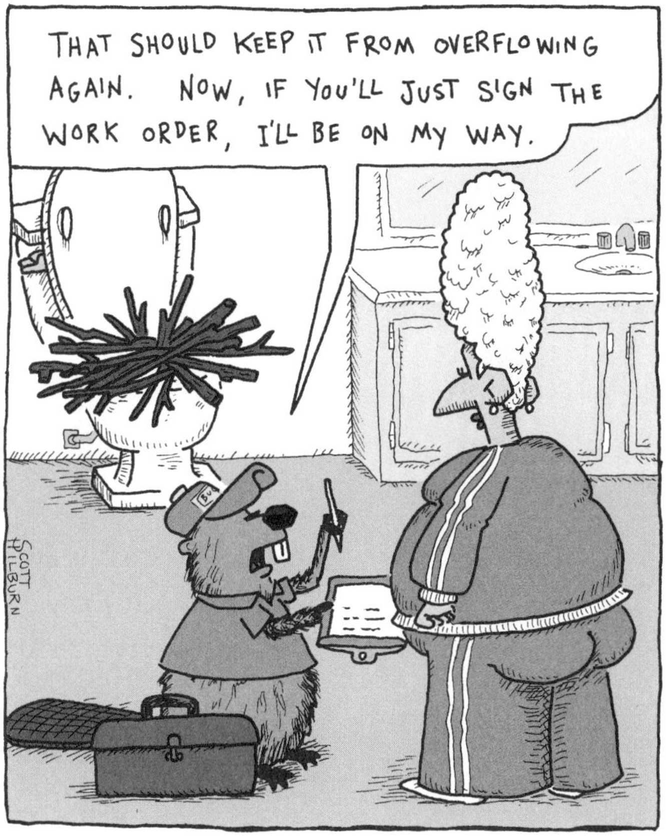
THAT SHOULD KEEP IT FROM OVERFLOWING AGAIN. NOW, IF YOU'LL JUST SIGN THE WORK ORDER, I'LL BE ON MY WAY.
SCOTT HILBURN

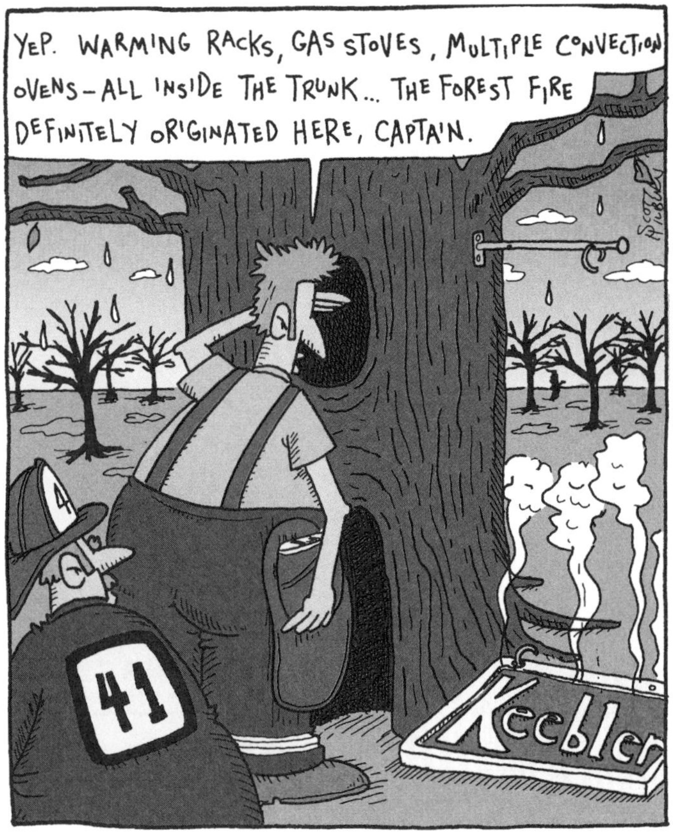
YEP. WARMING RACKS, GAS STOVES, MULTIPLE CONVECTION OVENS—ALL INSIDE THE TRUNK... THE FOREST FIRE DEFINITELY ORIGINATED HERE, CAPTAIN.
41
Keebler

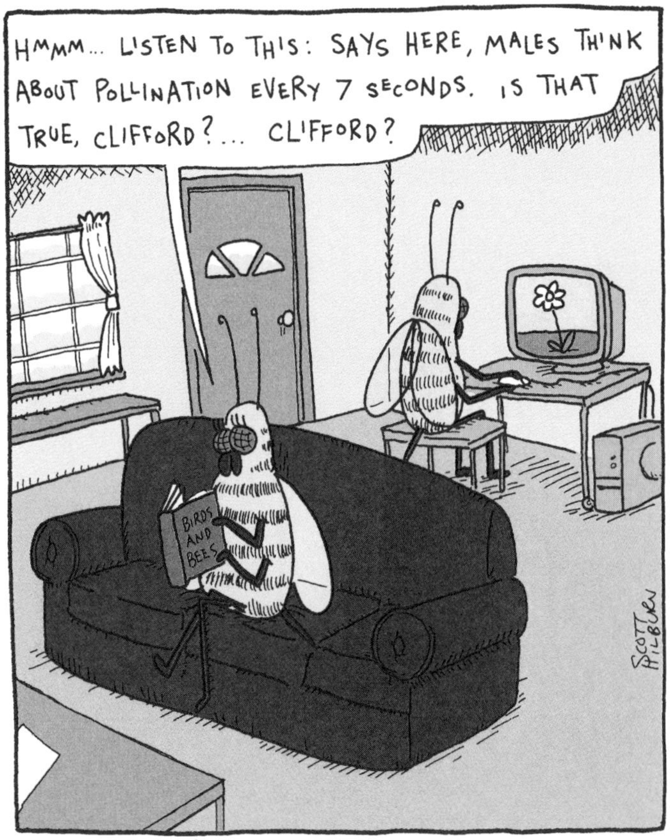
HMMM... LISTEN TO THIS: SAYS HERE, MALES THINK ABOUT POLLINATION EVERY 7 SECONDS. IS THAT TRUE, CLIFFORD?... CLIFFORD?
BIRDS AND BEES

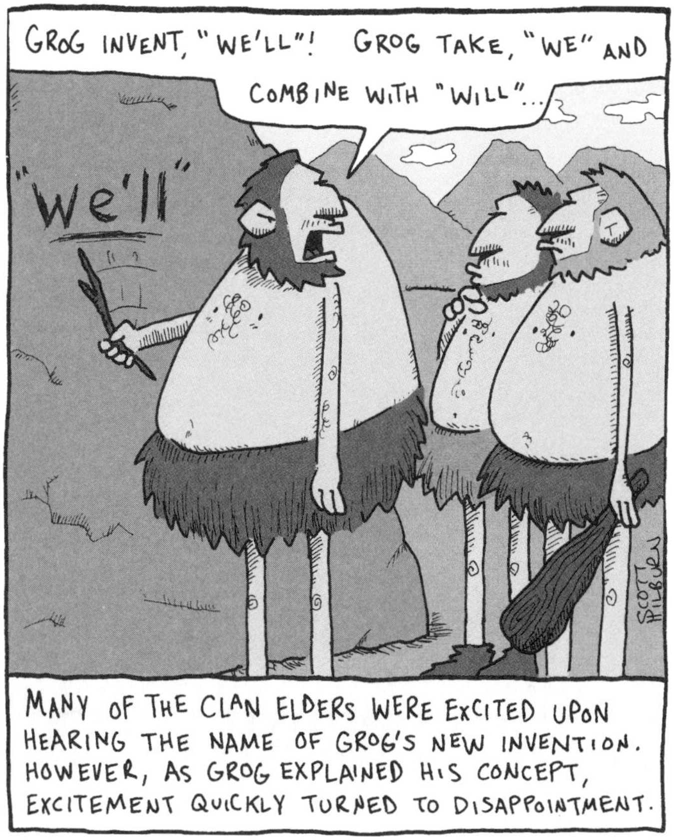
GROG INVENT, "WE'LL"! GROG TAKE, "WE" AND COMBINE WITH "WILL"...
"We'll"
SCOTT HILBURN
MANY OF THE CLAN ELDERS WERE EXCITED UPON HEARING THE NAME OF GROG'S NEW INVENTION. HOWEVER, AS GROG EXPLAINED HIS CONCEPT, EXCITEMENT QUICKLY TURNED TO DISAPPOINTMENT.

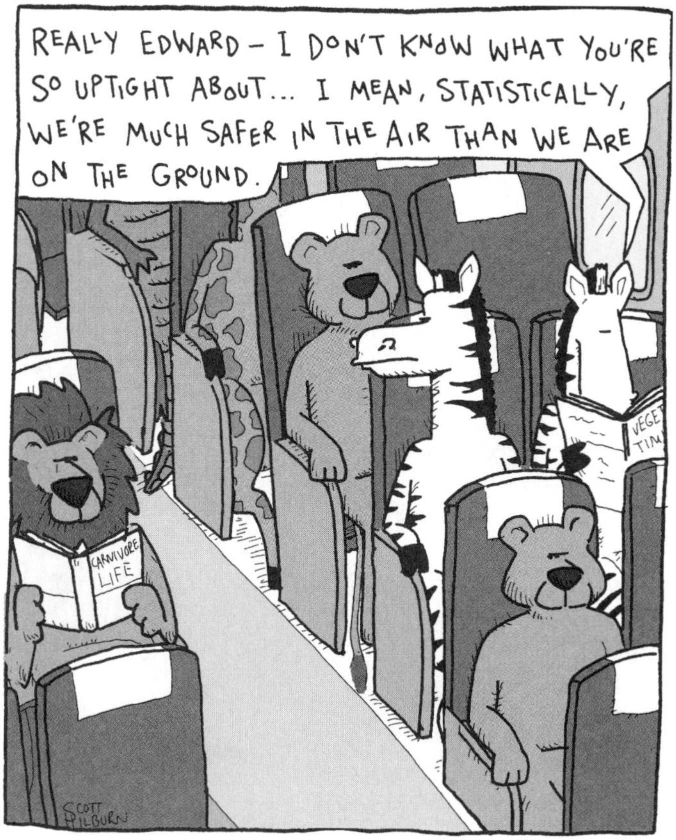
REALLY EDWARD – I DON'T KNOW WHAT YOU'RE SO UPTIGHT ABOUT... I MEAN, STATISTICALLY, WE'RE MUCH SAFER IN THE AIR THAN WE ARE ON THE GROUND.
CARNIVORE LIFE
SCOTT HILBURN

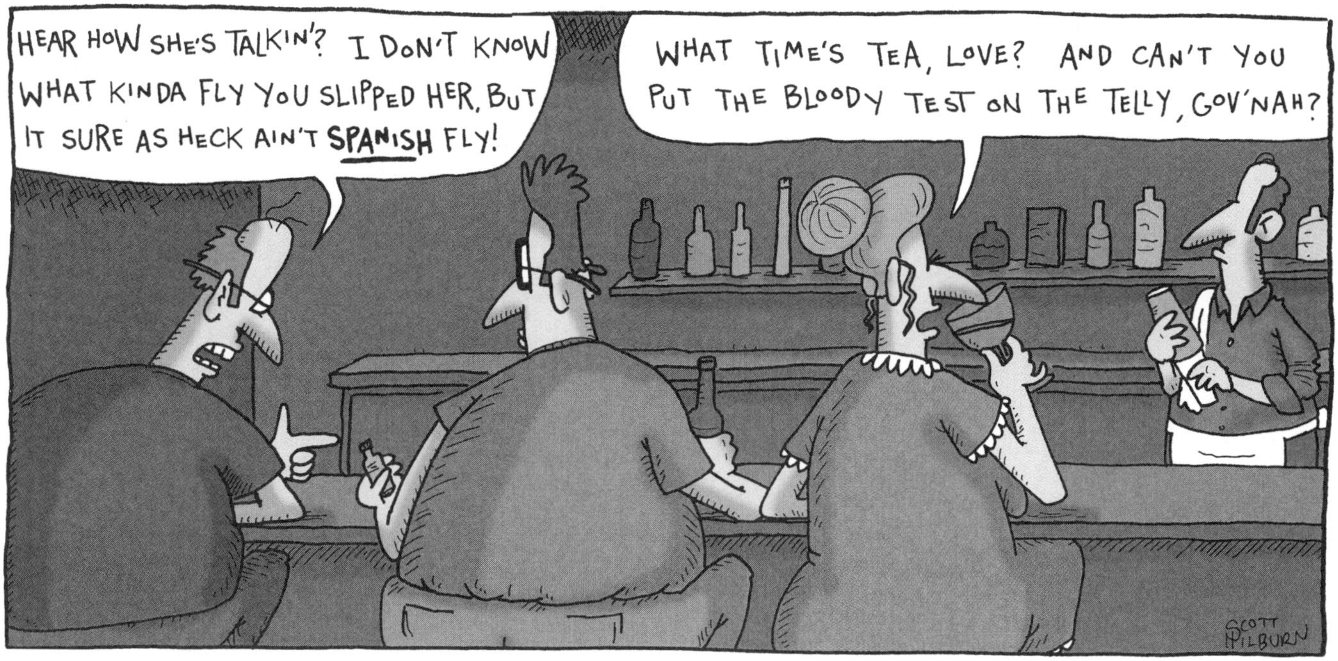
HEAR HOW SHE'S TALKIN'? I DON'T KNOW WHAT KINDA FLY YOU SLIPPED HER, BUT IT SURE AS HECK AIN'T SPANISH FLY!
WHAT TIME'S TEA, LOVE? AND CAN'T YOU PUT THE BLOODY TEST ON THE TELLY, GOV'NAH?
SCOTT HILBURN

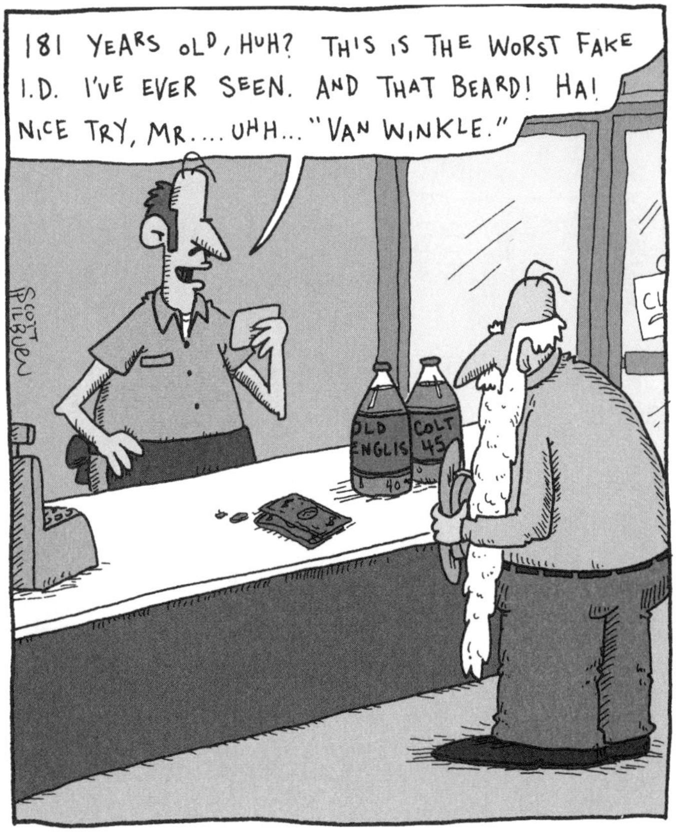
181 YEARS OLD, HUH? THIS IS THE WORST FAKE I.D. I'VE EVER SEEN. AND THAT BEARD! HA! NICE TRY, MR.... UHH... "VAN WINKLE."
OLD ENGLISH
COLT 45
SCOTT HILBURN

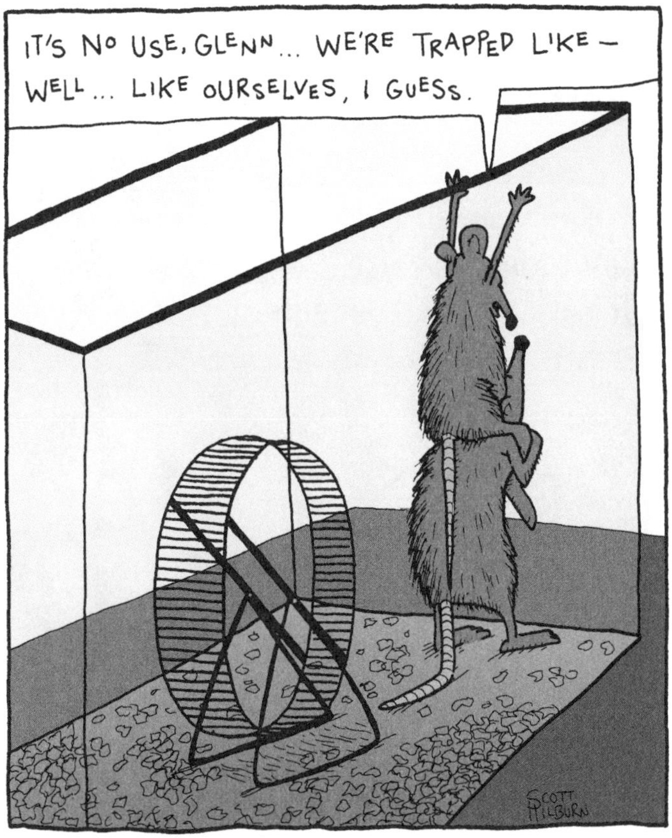
IT'S NO USE, GLENN... WE'RE TRAPPED LIKE— WELL... LIKE OURSELVES, I GUESS.
SCOTT HILBURN

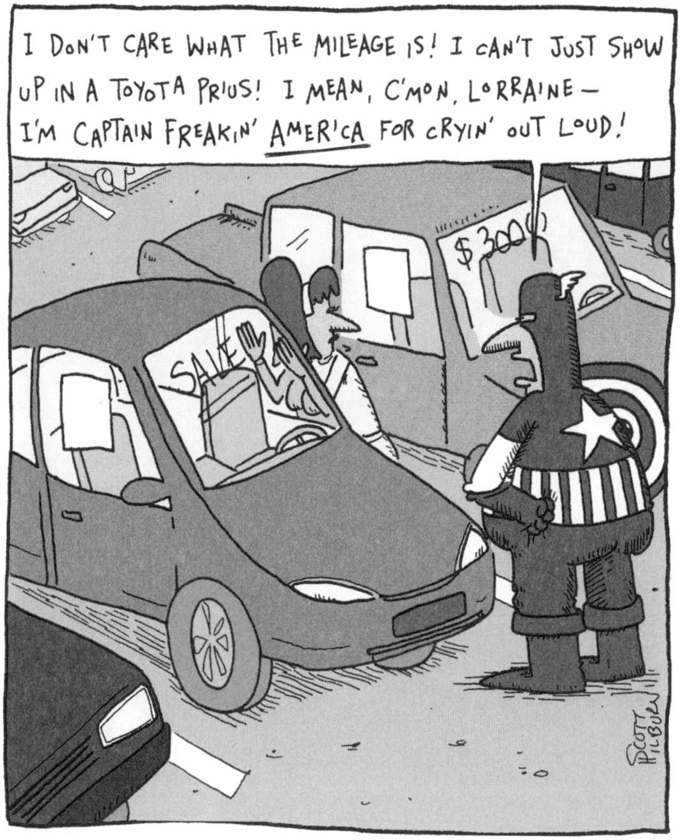
I DON'T CARE WHAT THE MILEAGE IS! I CAN'T JUST SHOW UP IN A TOYOTA PRIUS! I MEAN, C'MON, LORRAINE — I'M CAPTAIN FREAKIN' AMERICA FOR CRYIN' OUT LOUD!
SALE
SCOTT HILBURN

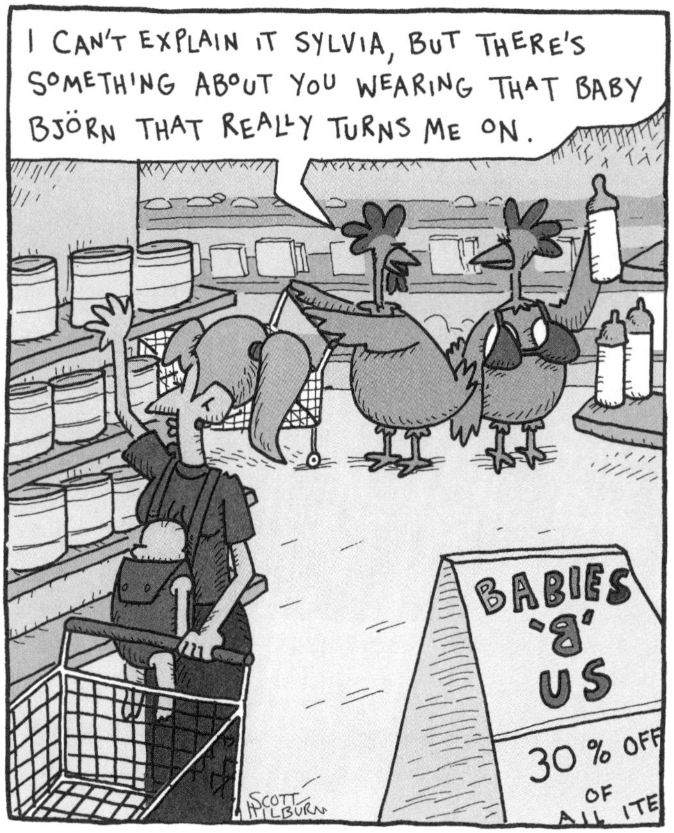
I CAN'T EXPLAIN IT SYLVIA, BUT THERE'S SOMETHING ABOUT YOU WEARING THAT BABY BJÖRN THAT REALLY TURNS ME ON.
BABIES 'Я' US
30 % OFF
SCOTT HILBURN

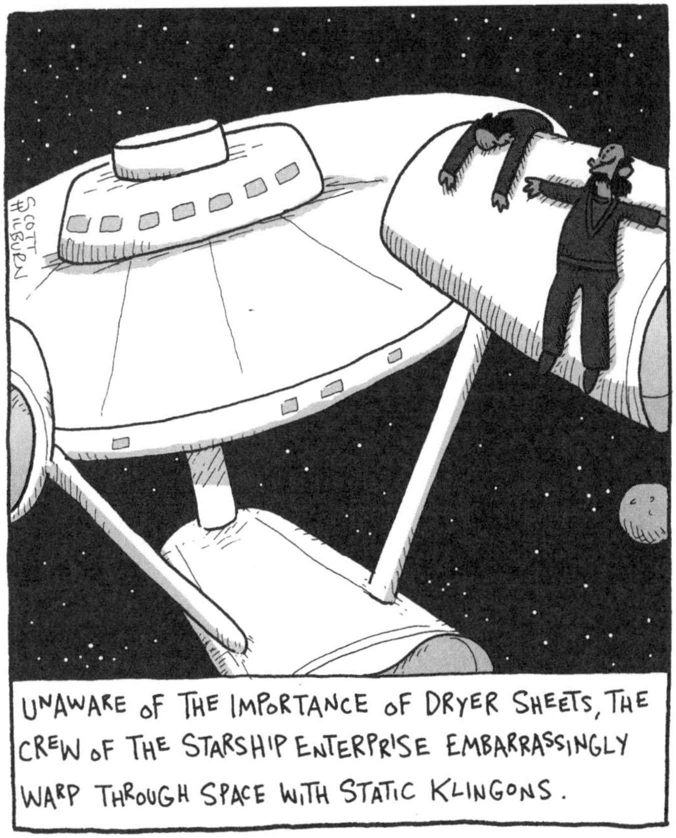
SCOTT HILBURN
UNAWARE OF THE IMPORTANCE OF DRYER SHEETS, THE CREW OF THE STARSHIP ENTERPRISE EMBARRASSINGLY WARP THROUGH SPACE WITH STATIC KLINGONS.

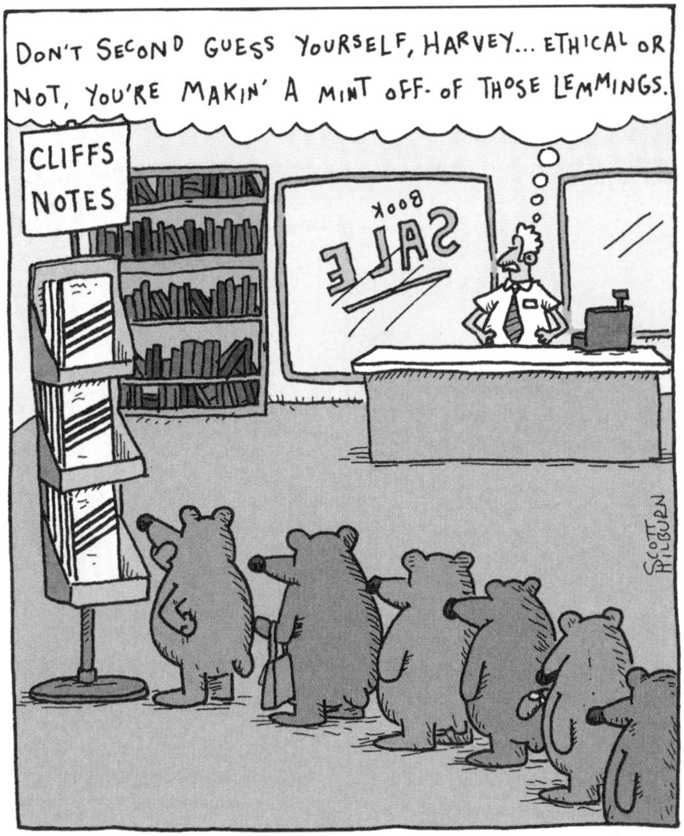
DON'T SECOND GUESS YOURSELF, HARVEY... ETHICAL OR NOT, YOU'RE MAKIN' A MINT OFF OF THOSE LEMMINGS.
CLIFFS NOTES
SCOTT HILBURN

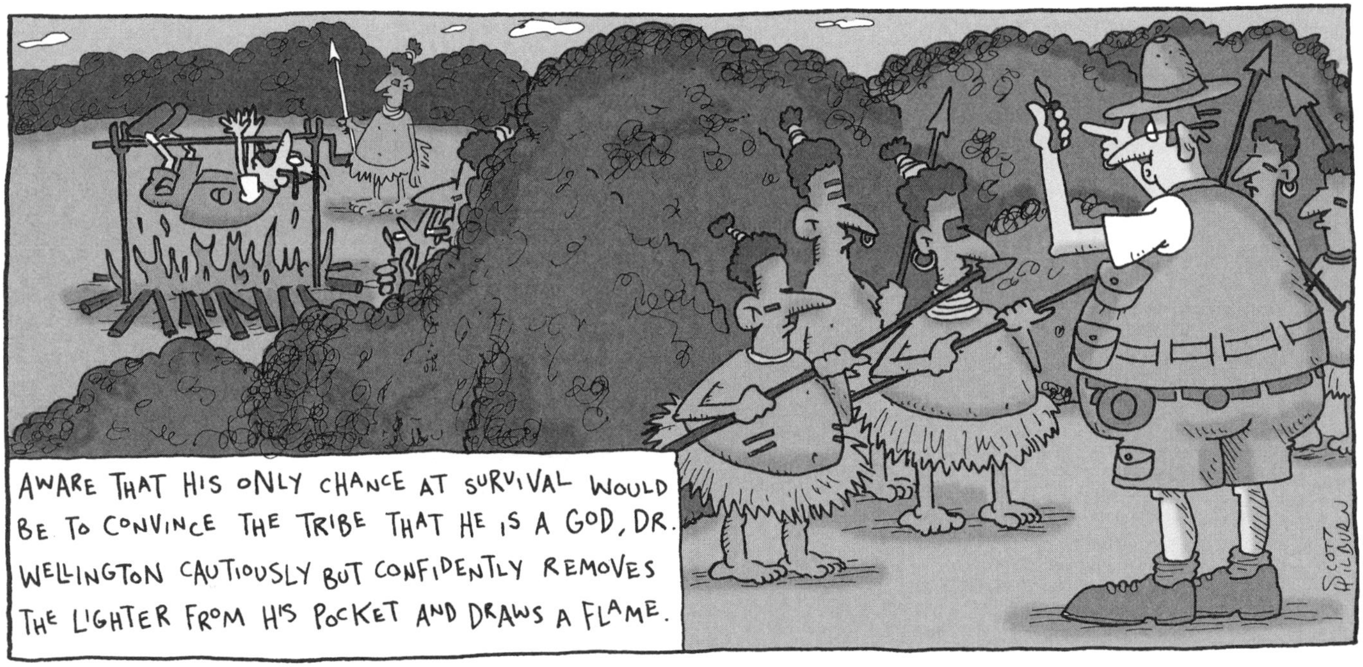
AWARE THAT HIS ONLY CHANCE AT SURVIVAL WOULD BE TO CONVINCE THE TRIBE THAT HE IS A GOD, DR. WELLINGTON CAUTIOUSLY BUT CONFIDENTLY REMOVES THE LIGHTER FROM HIS POCKET AND DRAWS A FLAME.
SCOTT HILBURN

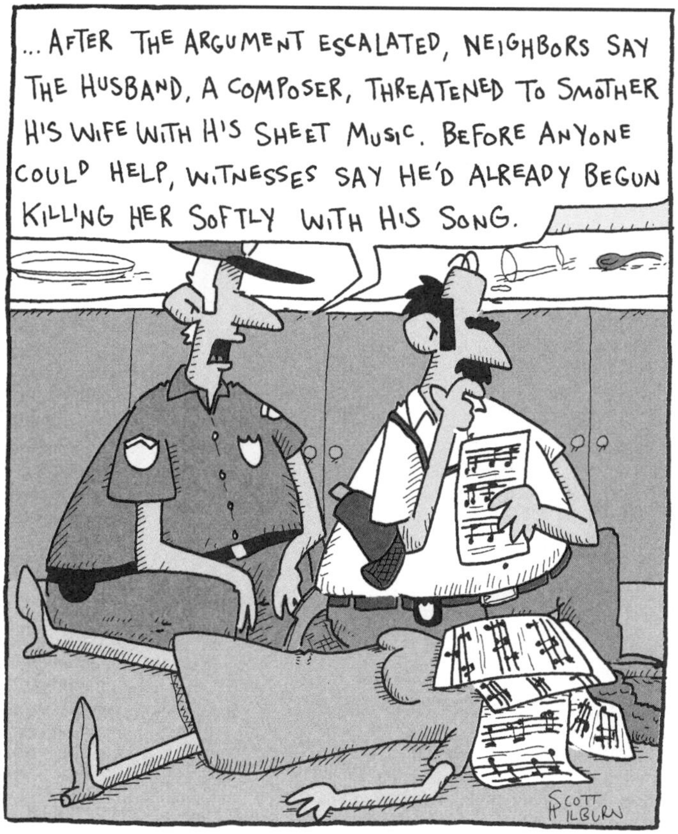
...AFTER THE ARGUMENT ESCALATED, NEIGHBORS SAY THE HUSBAND, A COMPOSER, THREATENED TO SMOTHER HIS WIFE WITH HIS SHEET MUSIC. BEFORE ANYONE COULD HELP, WITNESSES SAY HE'D ALREADY BEGUN KILLING HER SOFTLY WITH HIS SONG.
SCOTT HILBURN

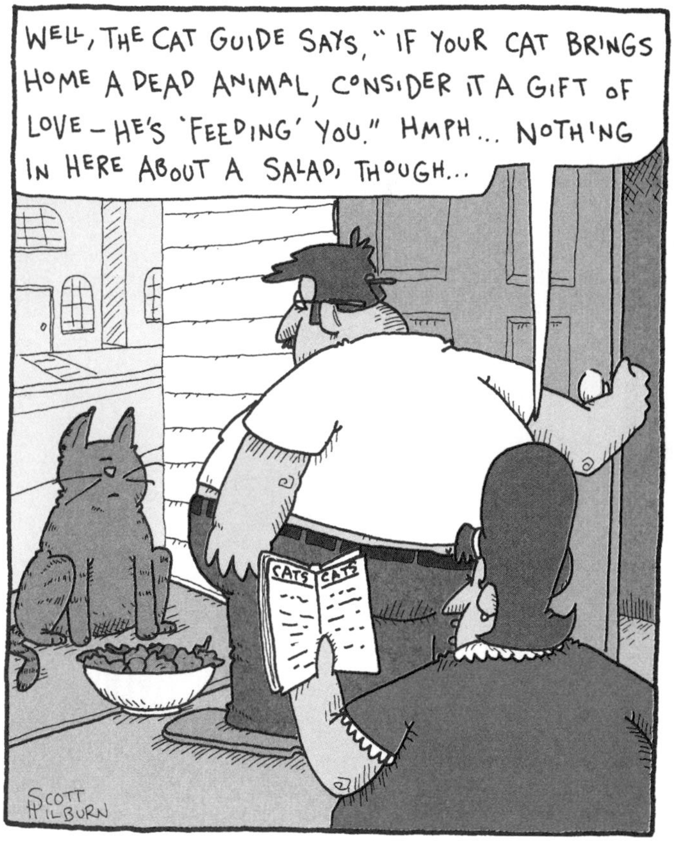
WELL, THE CAT GUIDE SAYS, "IF YOUR CAT BRINGS HOME A DEAD ANIMAL, CONSIDER IT A GIFT OF LOVE – HE'S 'FEEDING' YOU." HMPH... NOTHING IN HERE ABOUT A SALAD, THOUGH...
CATS
CATS
SCOTT HILBURN

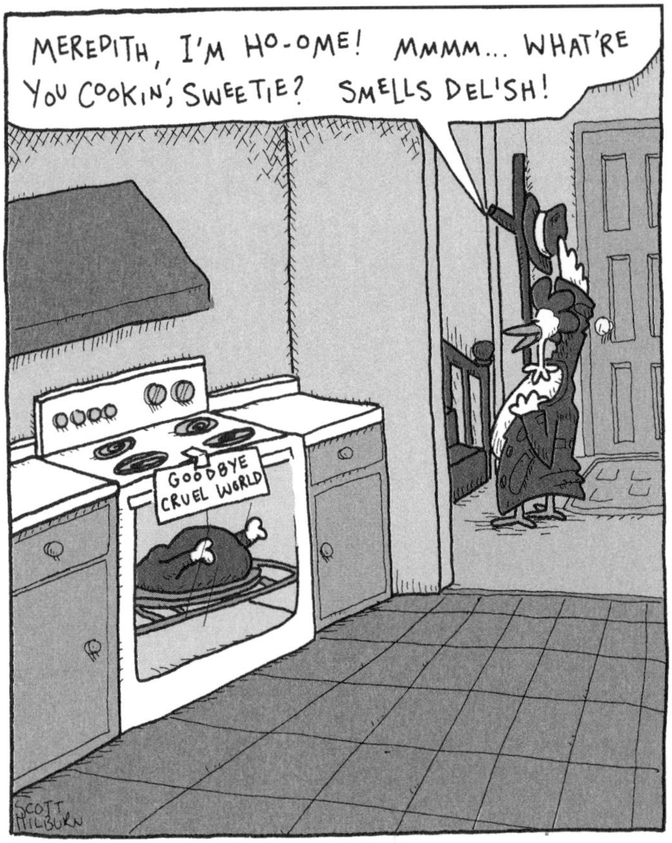
MEREDITH, I'M HO-OME! MMMM... WHAT'RE YOU COOKIN', SWEETIE? SMELLS DELISH!
GOODBYE CRUEL WORLD
SCOTT HILBURN

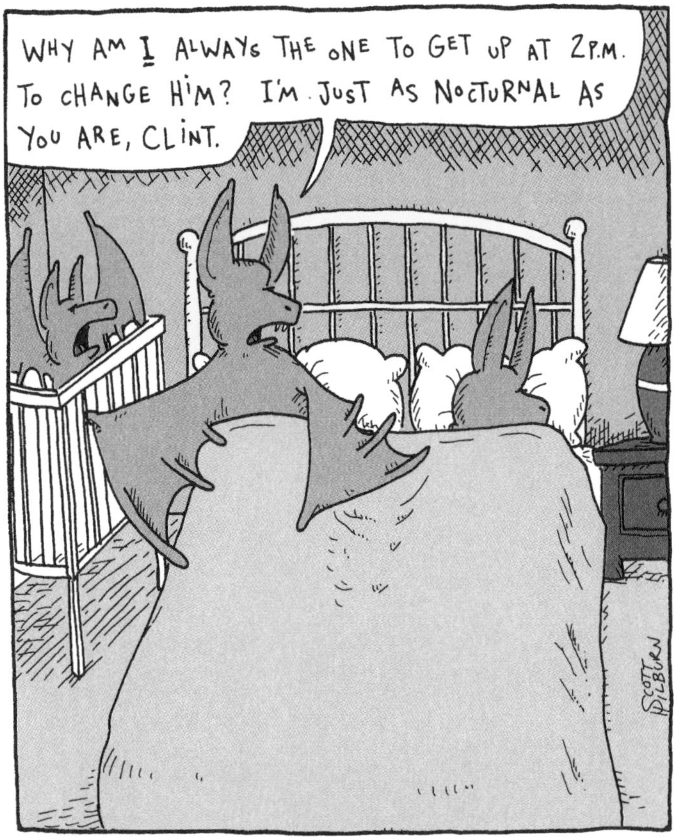
WHY AM I ALWAYS THE ONE TO GET UP AT 2P.M. TO CHANGE HIM? I'M JUST AS NOCTURNAL AS YOU ARE, CLINT.
SCOTT HILBURN

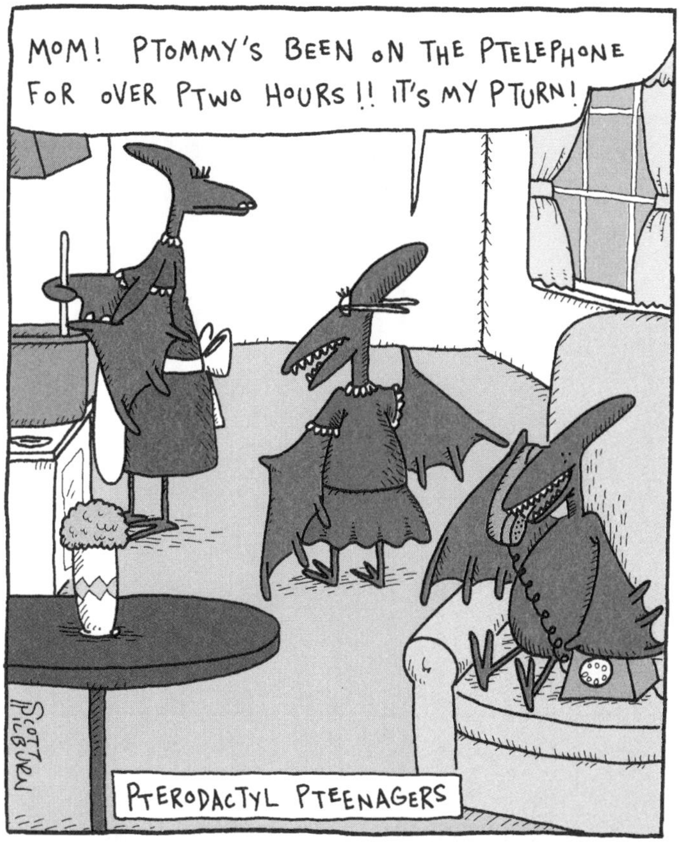
MOM! PTOMMY'S BEEN ON THE PTELEPHONE FOR OVER PTWO HOURS!! IT'S MY PTURN!
SCOTT HILBURN
PTERODACTYL PTEENAGERS

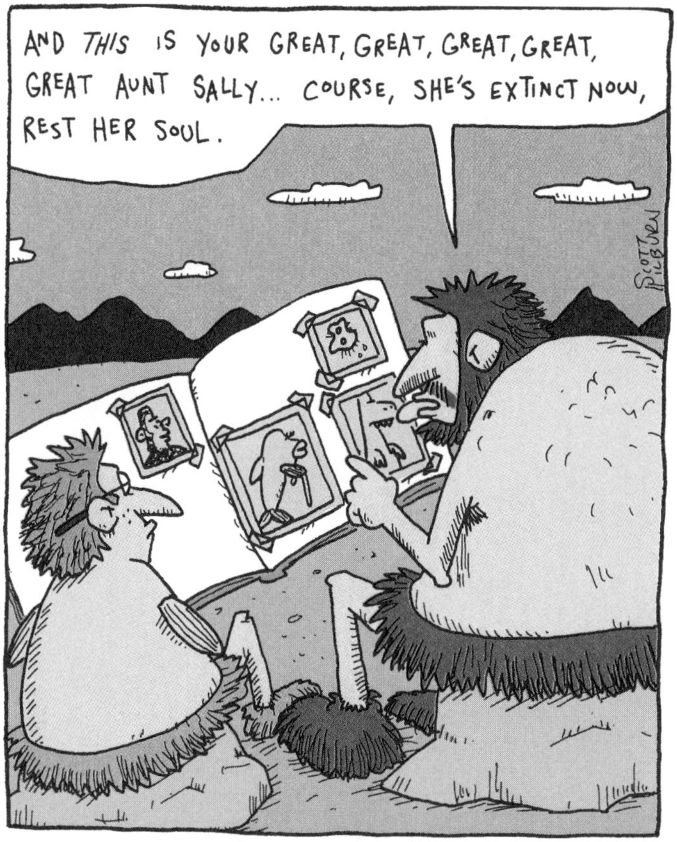
AND *THIS* IS YOUR GREAT, GREAT, GREAT, GREAT, GREAT AUNT SALLY... COURSE, SHE'S EXTINCT NOW, REST HER SOUL.
SCOTT HILBURN

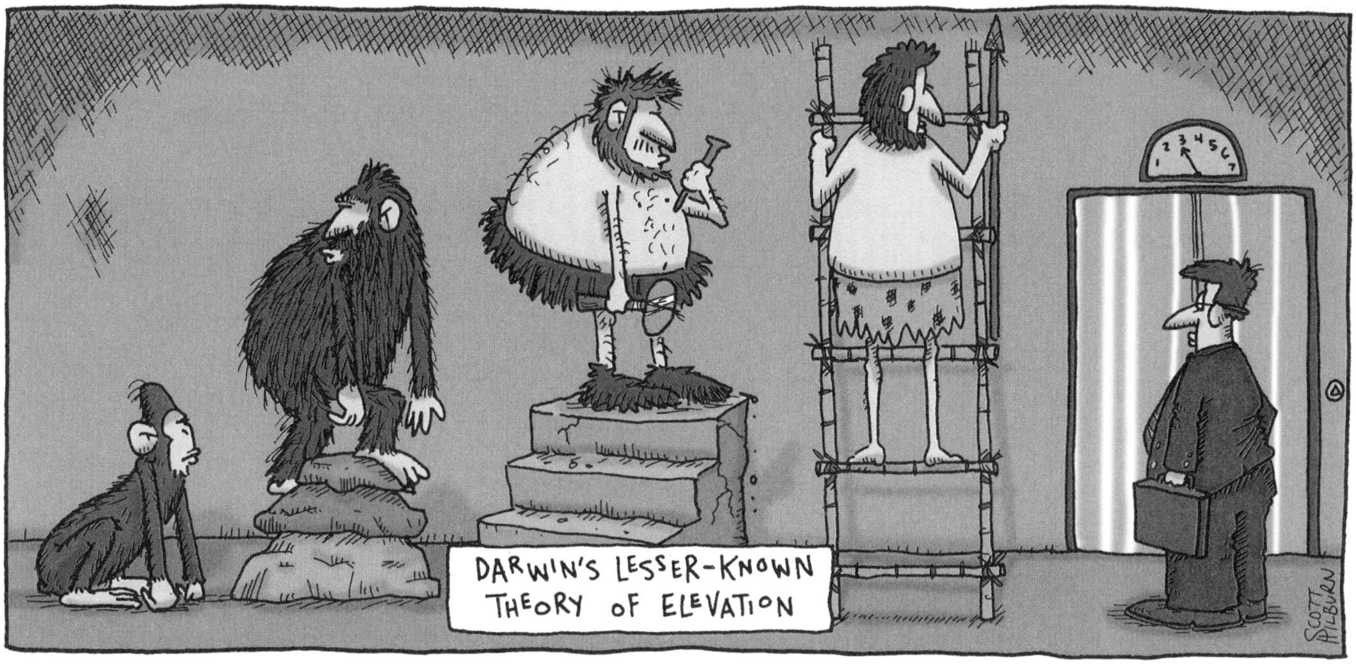
DARWIN'S LESSER-KNOWN THEORY OF ELEVATION
SCOTT HILBURN

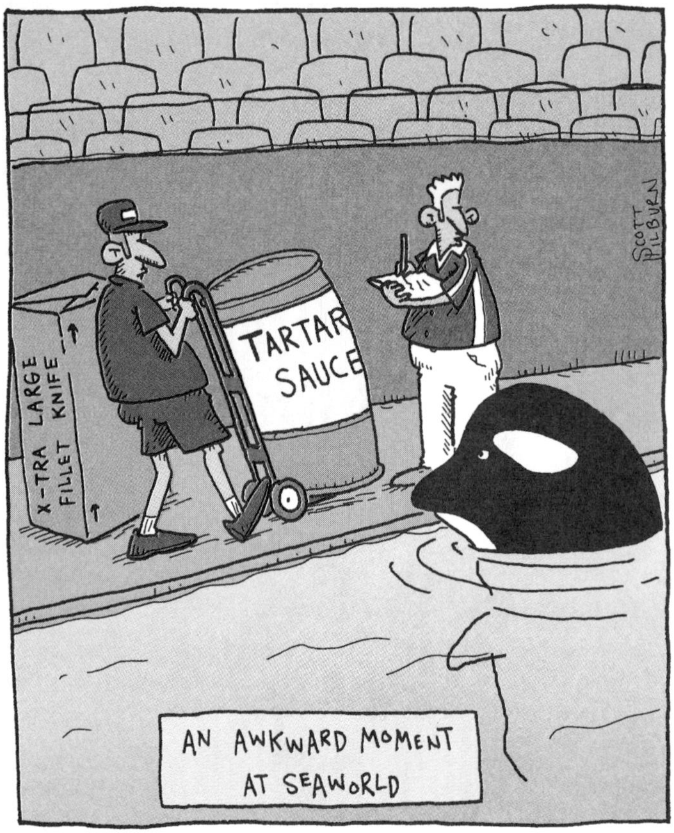
TARTAR SAUCE
X-TRA LARGE FILLET KNIFE
SCOTT HILBURN
AN AWKWARD MOMENT AT SEAWORLD

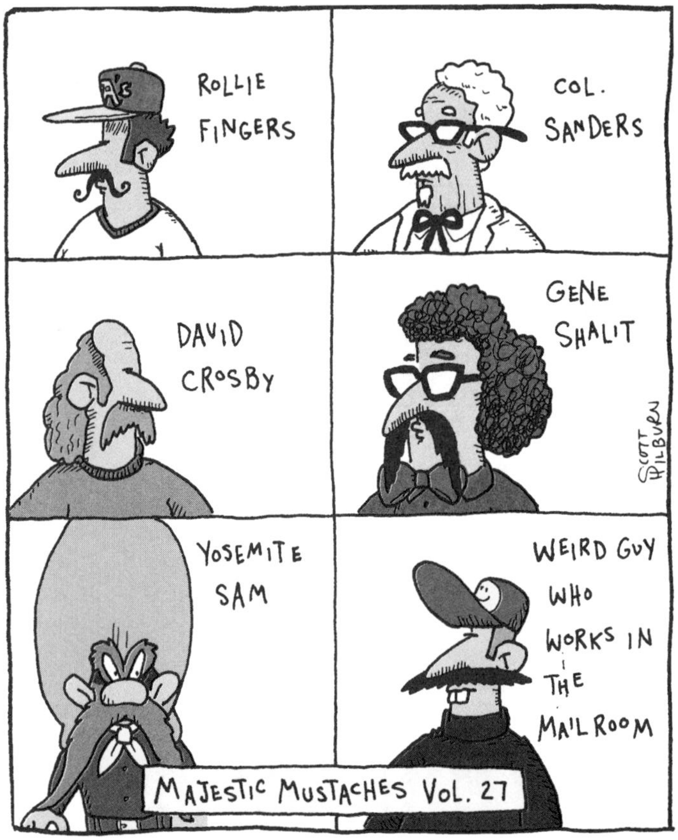
ROLLIE FINGERS
COL. SANDERS
DAVID CROSBY
GENE SHALIT
SCOTT HILBURN
YOSEMITE SAM
WEIRD GUY WHO WORKS IN THE MAILROOM
MAJESTIC MUSTACHES VOL. 27

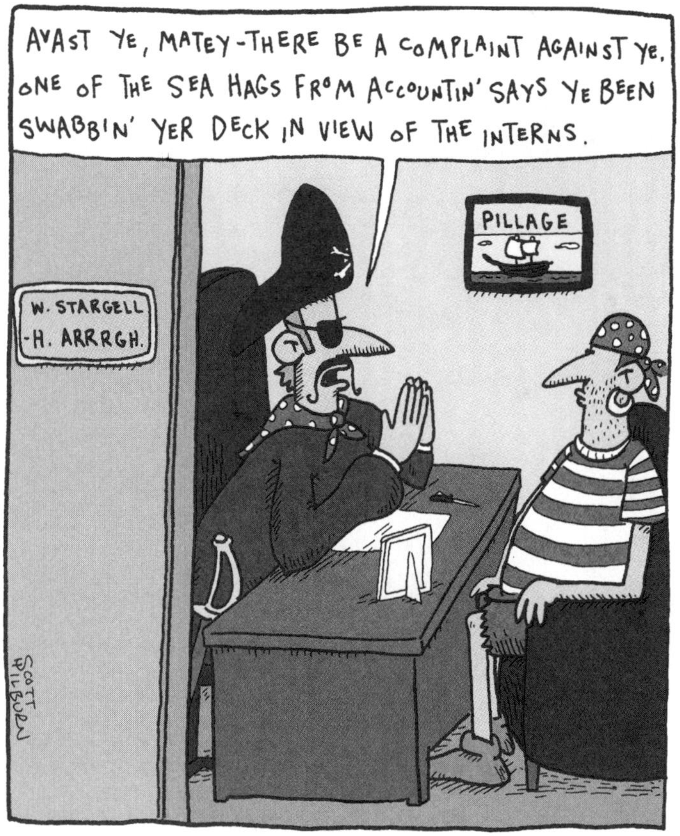
AVAST YE, MATEY-THERE BE A COMPLAINT AGAINST YE. ONE OF THE SEA HAGS FROM ACCOUNTIN' SAYS YE BEEN SWABBIN' YER DECK IN VIEW OF THE INTERNS.
PILLAGE
W. STARGELL
-H. ARRRGH.
SCOTT HILBURN

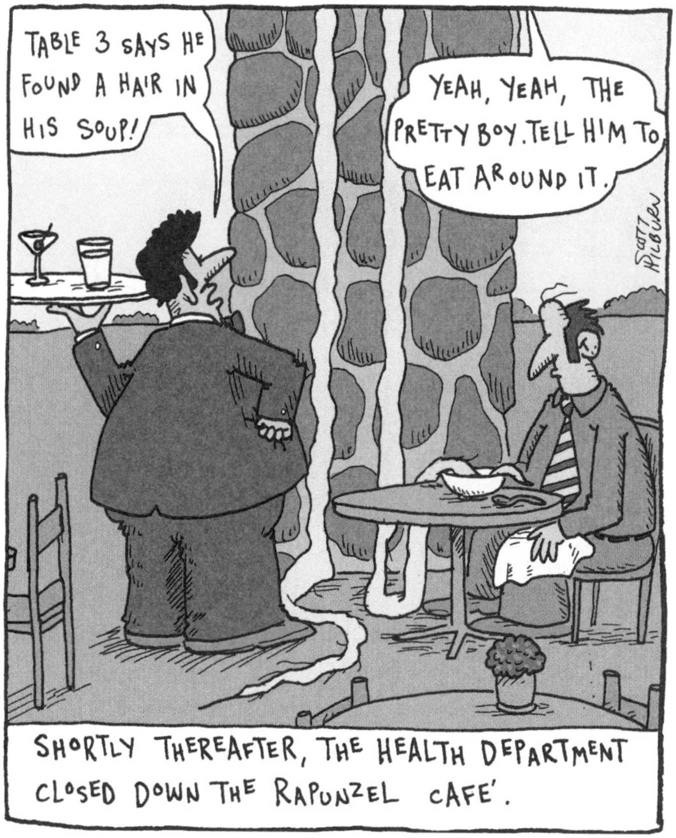
TABLE 3 SAYS HE FOUND A HAIR IN HIS SOUP!
YEAH, YEAH, THE PRETTY BOY. TELL HIM TO EAT AROUND IT.
SCOTT HILBURN
SHORTLY THEREAFTER, THE HEALTH DEPARTMENT CLOSED DOWN THE RAPUNZEL CAFE'.

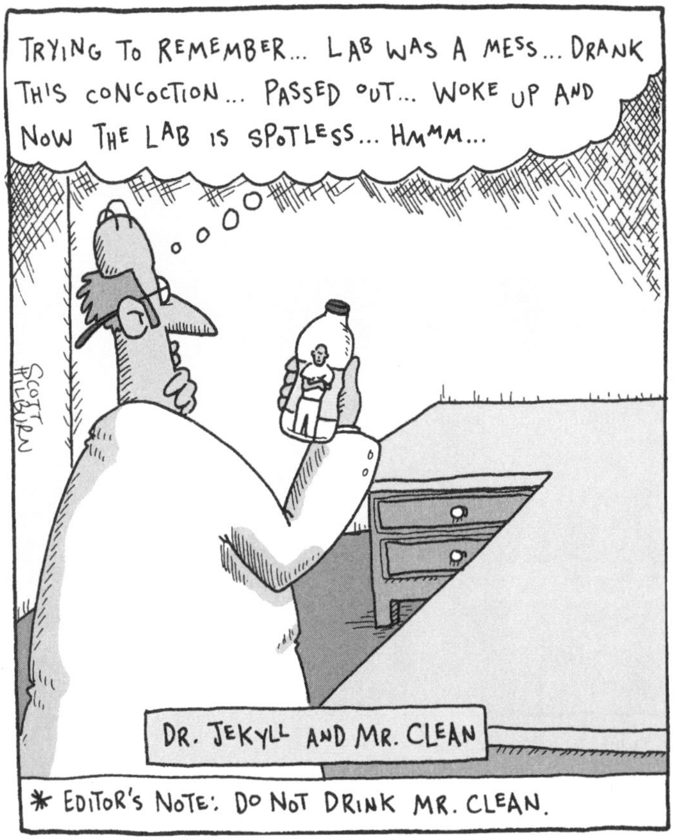
TRYING TO REMEMBER... LAB WAS A MESS... DRANK THIS CONCOCTION... PASSED OUT... WOKE UP AND NOW THE LAB IS SPOTLESS... HMMM...
DR. JEKYLL AND MR. CLEAN
* EDITOR'S NOTE: DO NOT DRINK MR. CLEAN.
SCOTT HILBURN

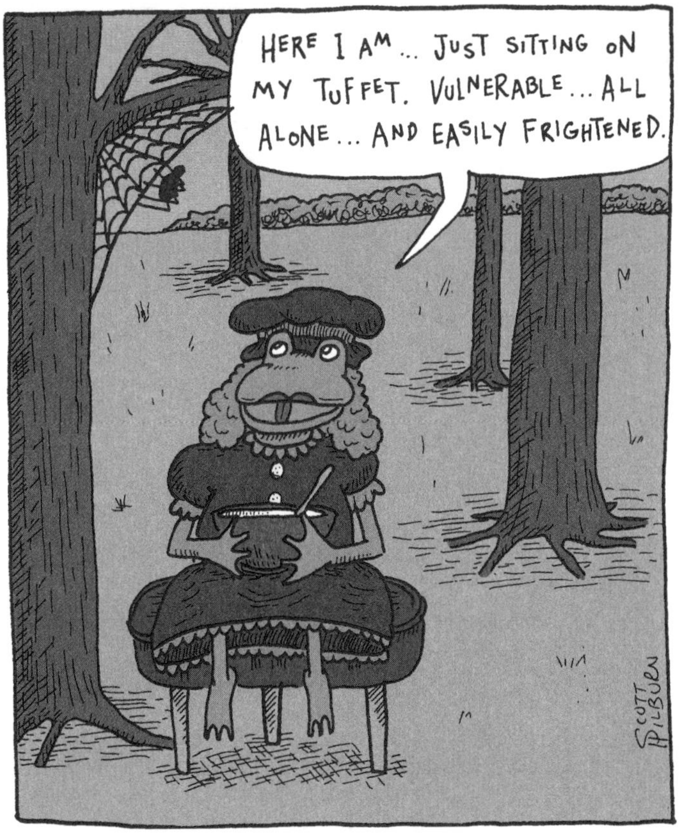
HERE I AM... JUST SITTING ON MY TUFFET. VULNERABLE... ALL ALONE... AND EASILY FRIGHTENED.
SCOTT HILBURN

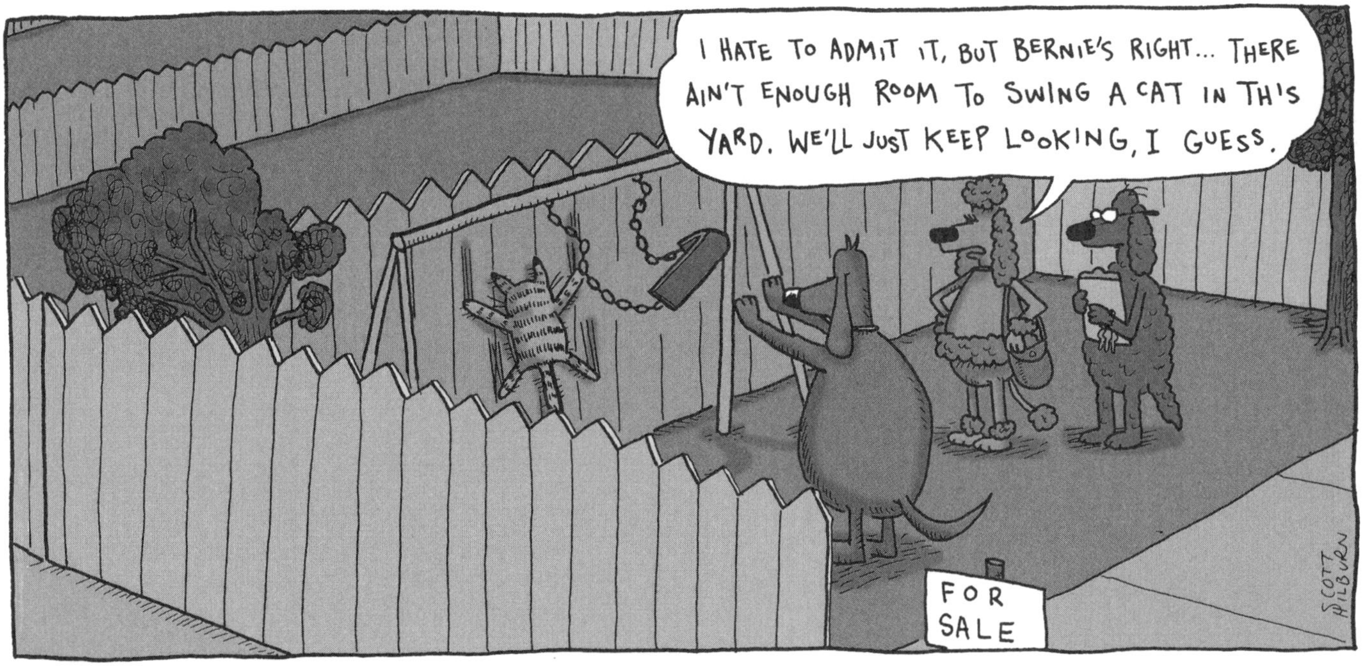
I HATE TO ADMIT IT, BUT BERNIE'S RIGHT... THERE AIN'T ENOUGH ROOM TO SWING A CAT IN THIS YARD. WE'LL JUST KEEP LOOKING, I GUESS.
FOR SALE
SCOTT HILBURN

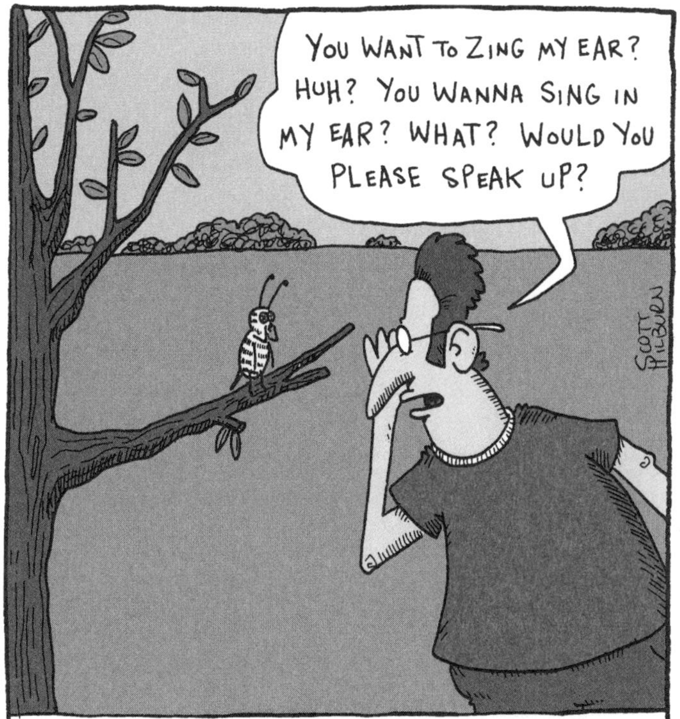
YOU WANT TO ZING MY EAR? HUH? YOU WANNA SING IN MY EAR? WHAT? WOULD YOU PLEASE SPEAK UP?
SCOTT HILBURN

NAÏVE TO ITS UNCONVENTIONAL APPROACH, WYATT IS VICTIMIZED BY THE RARE AND ELUSIVE MUMBLE BEE.

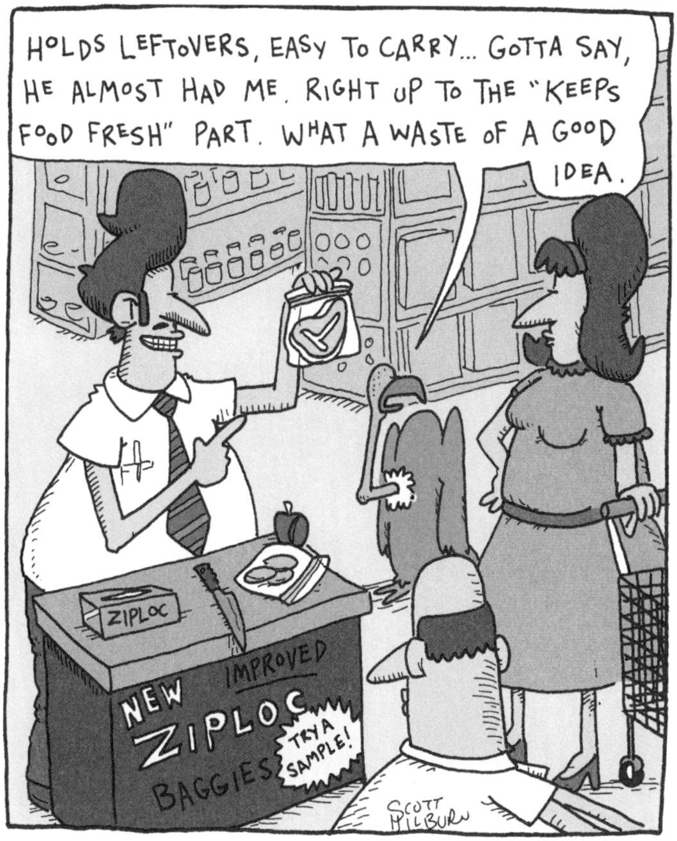
HOLDS LEFTOVERS, EASY TO CARRY... GOTTA SAY, HE ALMOST HAD ME. RIGHT UP TO THE "KEEPS FOOD FRESH" PART. WHAT A WASTE OF A GOOD IDEA.
ZIPLOC
NEW IMPROVED ZIPLOC BAGGIES
TRY A SAMPLE!
SCOTT HILBURN

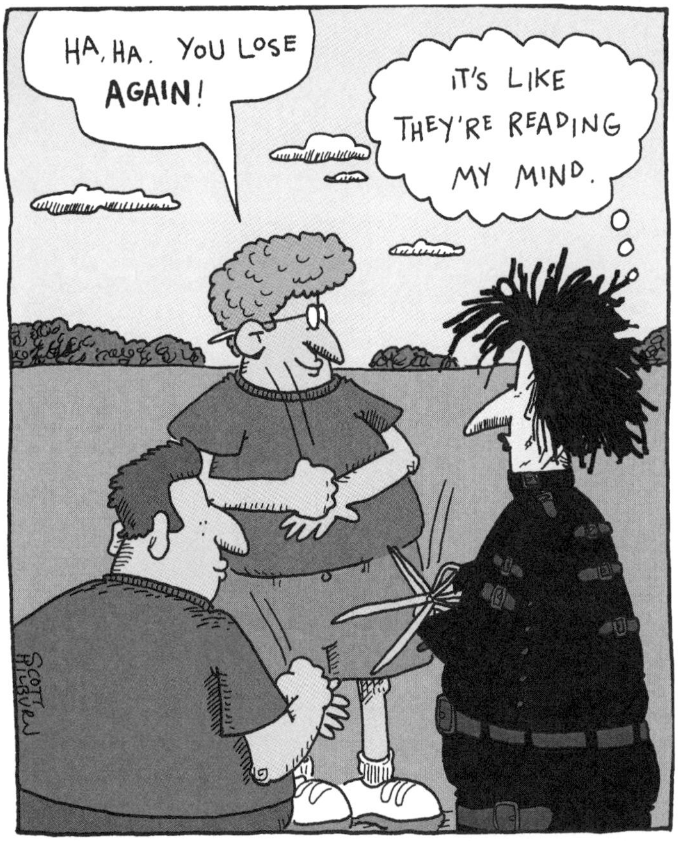
HA, HA. YOU LOSE AGAIN!
IT'S LIKE THEY'RE READING MY MIND.
SCOTT HILBURN

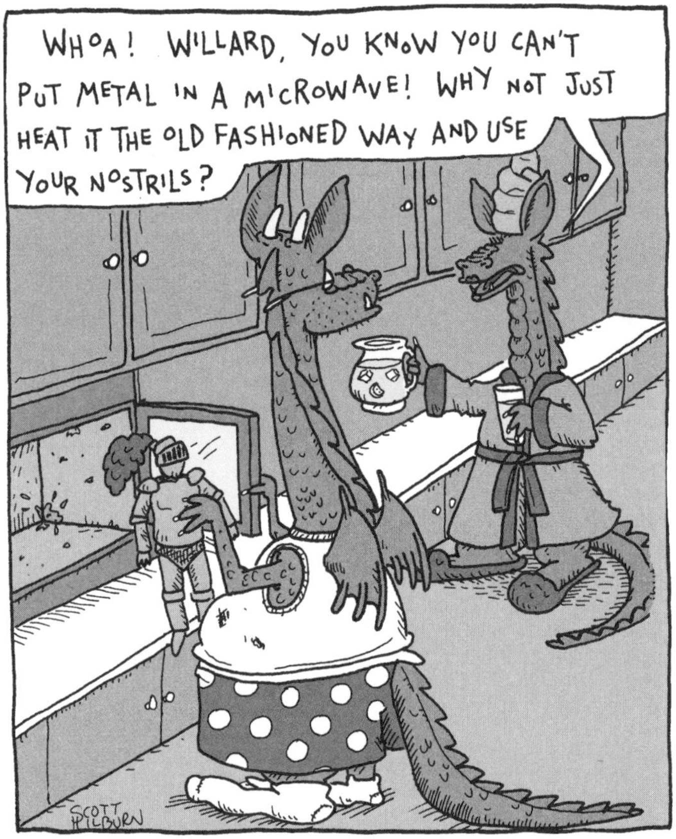
WHOA! WILLARD, YOU KNOW YOU CAN'T PUT METAL IN A MICROWAVE! WHY NOT JUST HEAT IT THE OLD FASHIONED WAY AND USE YOUR NOSTRILS?
SCOTT HILBURN

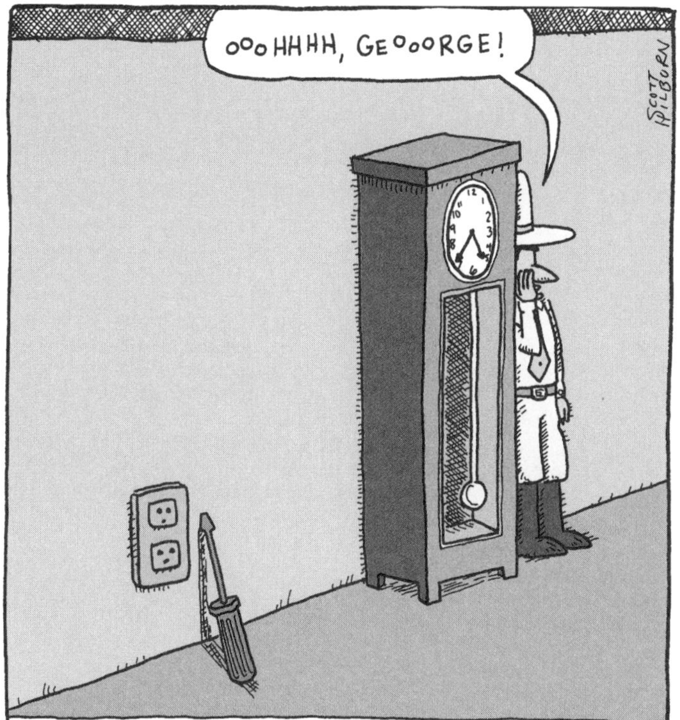
OOOHHHH, GEOOORGE!
SCOTT HILBURN

THE MAN IN THE BIG YELLOW HAT REMEDIES GEORGE'S CURIOSITY ONCE AND FOR ALL.

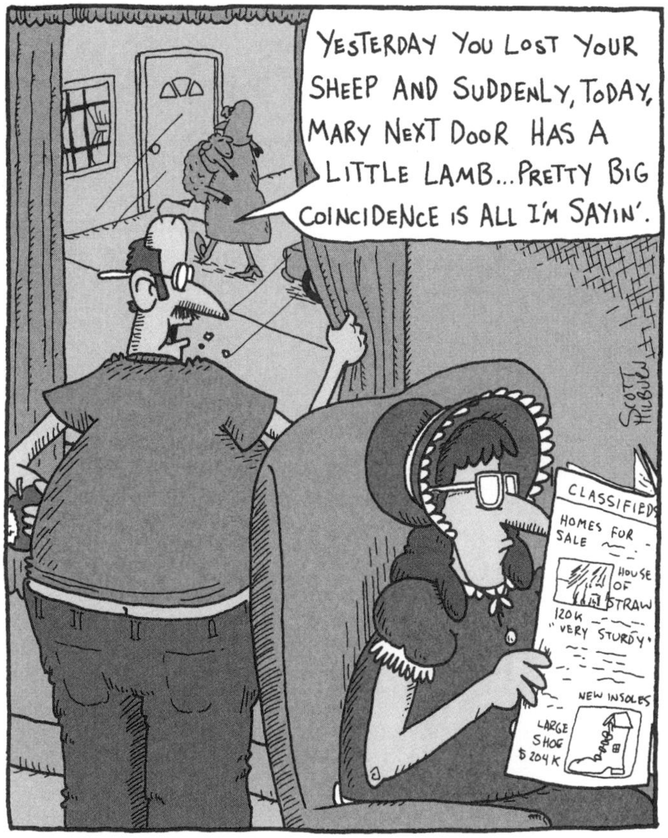
YESTERDAY YOU LOST YOUR SHEEP AND SUDDENLY, TODAY, MARY NEXT DOOR HAS A LITTLE LAMB... PRETTY BIG COINCIDENCE IS ALL I'M SAYIN'.
CLASSIFIEDS
HOMES FOR SALE
HOUSE OF STRAW
120K
"VERY STURDY"
NEW INSOLES
LARGE SHOE
$204K
SCOTT HILBURN

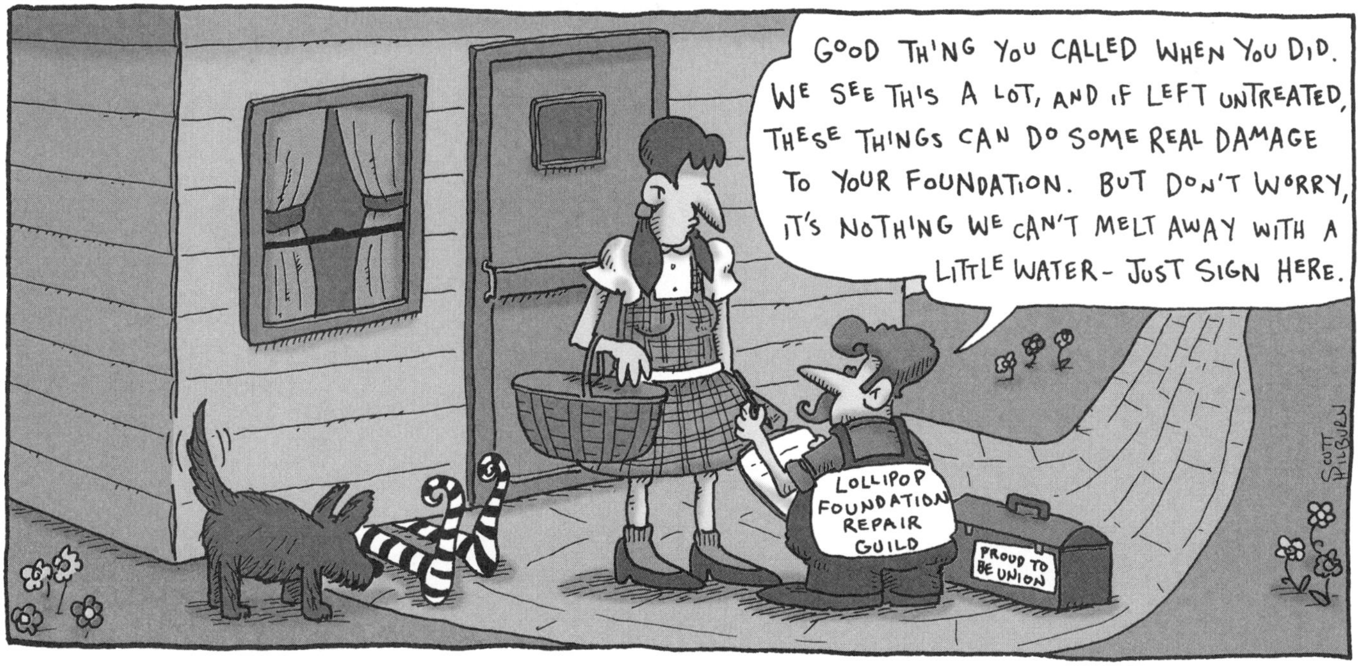
GOOD THING YOU CALLED WHEN YOU DID. WE SEE THIS A LOT, AND IF LEFT UNTREATED, THESE THINGS CAN DO SOME REAL DAMAGE TO YOUR FOUNDATION. BUT DON'T WORRY, IT'S NOTHING WE CAN'T MELT AWAY WITH A LITTLE WATER- JUST SIGN HERE.
LOLLIPOP FOUNDATION REPAIR GUILD
PROUD TO BE UNION
SCOTT HILBURN

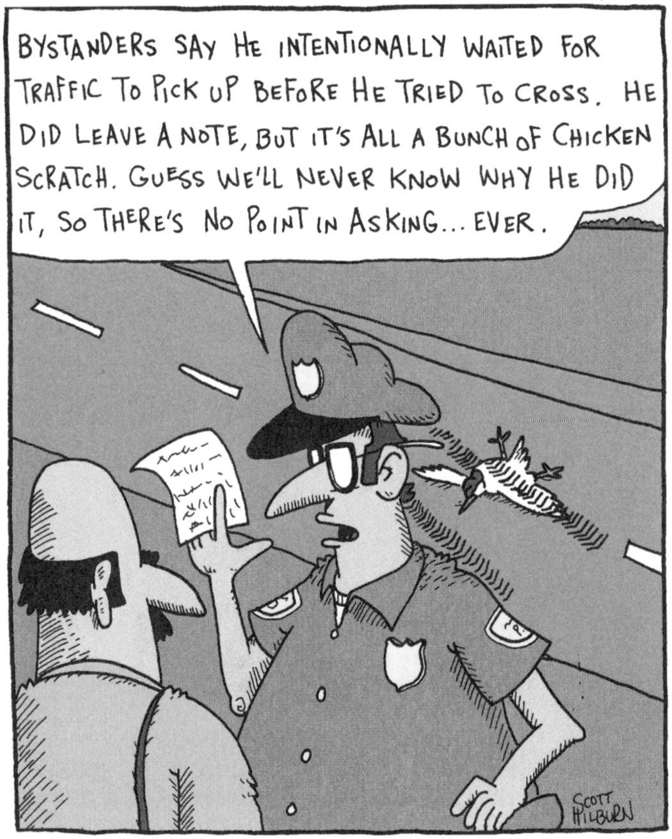
BYSTANDERS SAY HE INTENTIONALLY WAITED FOR TRAFFIC TO PICK UP BEFORE HE TRIED TO CROSS. HE DID LEAVE A NOTE, BUT IT'S ALL A BUNCH OF CHICKEN SCRATCH. GUESS WE'LL NEVER KNOW WHY HE DID IT, SO THERE'S NO POINT IN ASKING... EVER.
SCOTT HILBURN

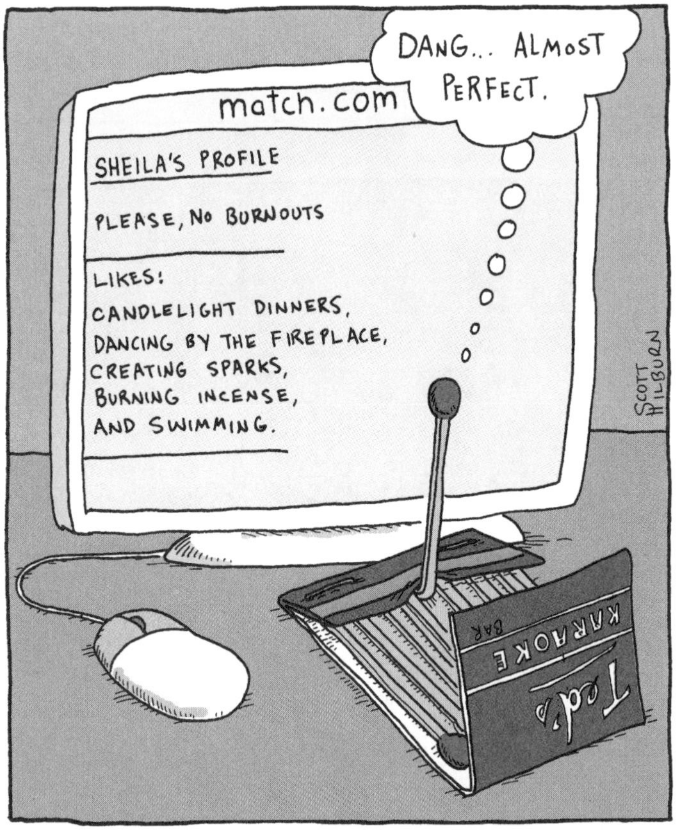
DANG... ALMOST PERFECT.
match.com
SHEILA'S PROFILE
PLEASE, NO BURNOUTS
LIKES:
CANDLELIGHT DINNERS,
DANCING BY THE FIREPLACE,
CREATING SPARKS,
BURNING INCENSE,
AND SWIMMING.
Ted's KARAOKE BAR
SCOTT HILBURN

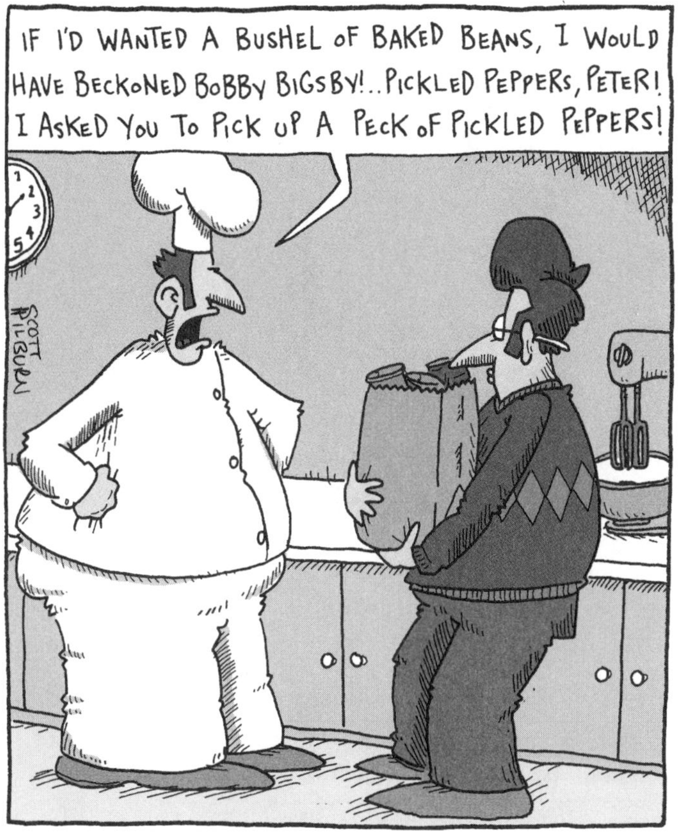
IF I'D WANTED A BUSHEL OF BAKED BEANS, I WOULD HAVE BECKONED BOBBY BIGSBY!.. PICKLED PEPPERS, PETER! I ASKED YOU TO PICK UP A PECK OF PICKLED PEPPERS!
SCOTT HILBURN

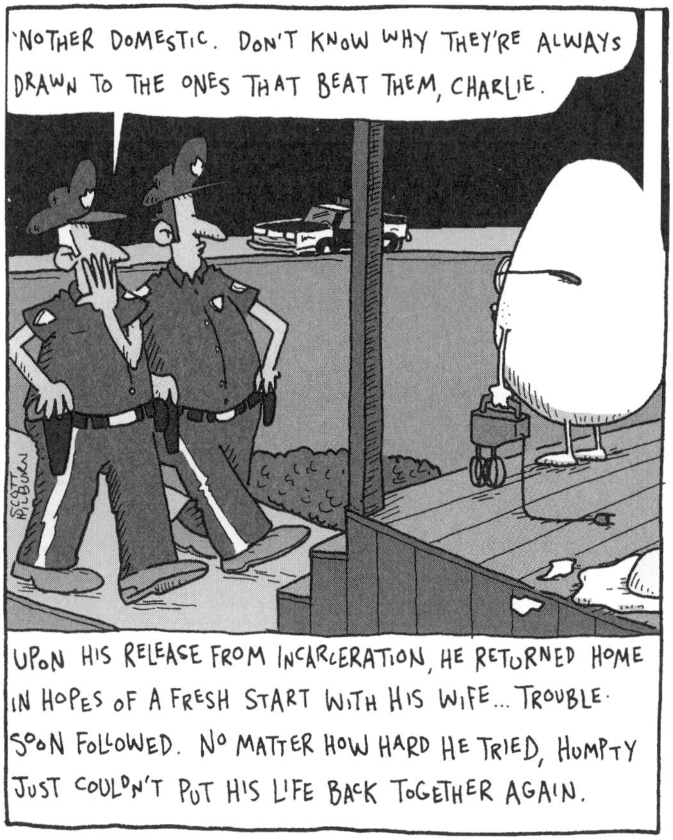
'NOTHER DOMESTIC. DON'T KNOW WHY THEY'RE ALWAYS DRAWN TO THE ONES THAT BEAT THEM, CHARLIE.
SCOTT HILBURN
UPON HIS RELEASE FROM INCARCERATION, HE RETURNED HOME IN HOPES OF A FRESH START WITH HIS WIFE... TROUBLE SOON FOLLOWED. NO MATTER HOW HARD HE TRIED, HUMPTY JUST COULDN'T PUT HIS LIFE BACK TOGETHER AGAIN.

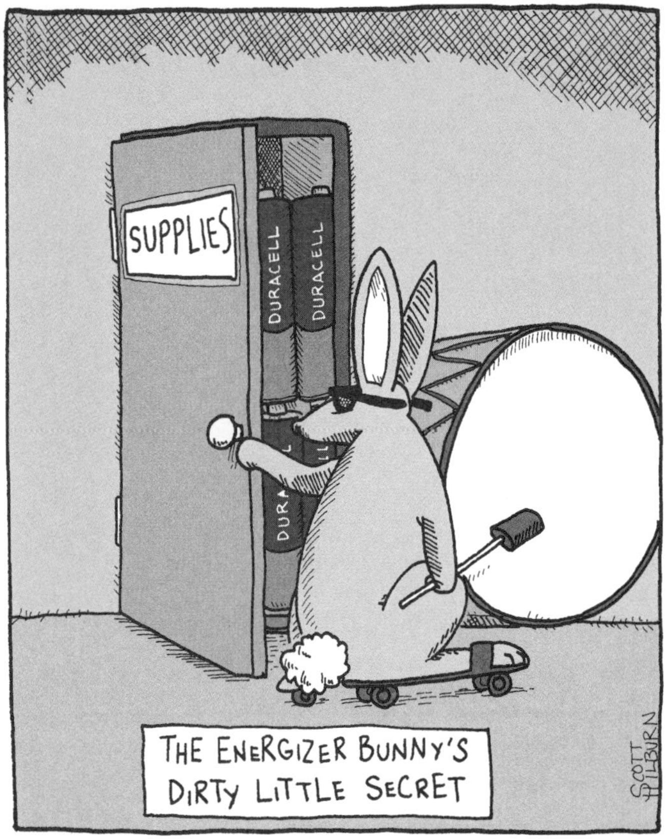
SUPPLIES
DURACELL
DURACELL
SCOTT HILBURN
THE ENERGIZER BUNNY'S DIRTY LITTLE SECRET

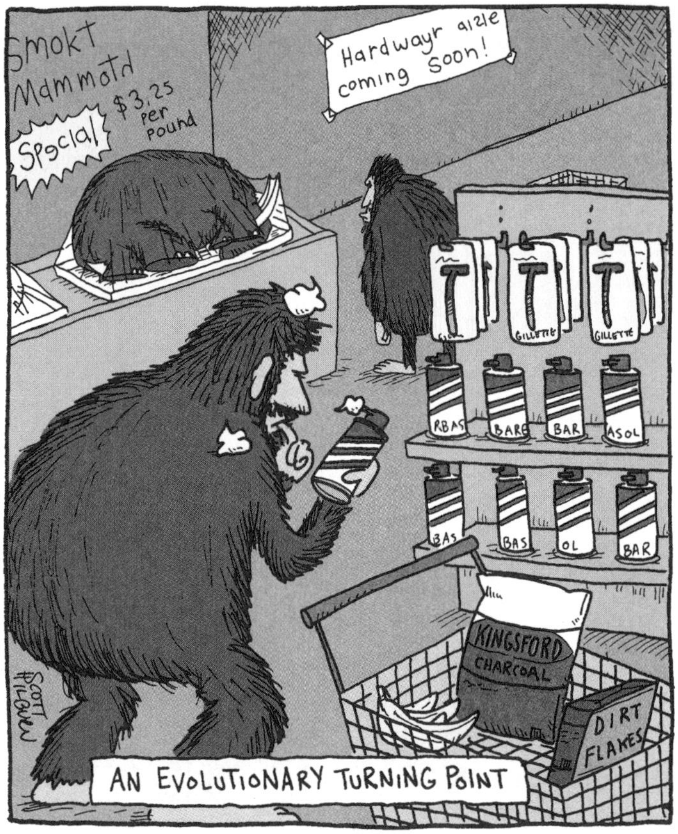
Smokt Mammoth
Special
$3.25 per pound
Hardwayr aizle coming Soon!
KINGSFORD CHARCOAL
DIRT FLAKES
SCOTT HILBURN
AN EVOLUTIONARY TURNING POINT

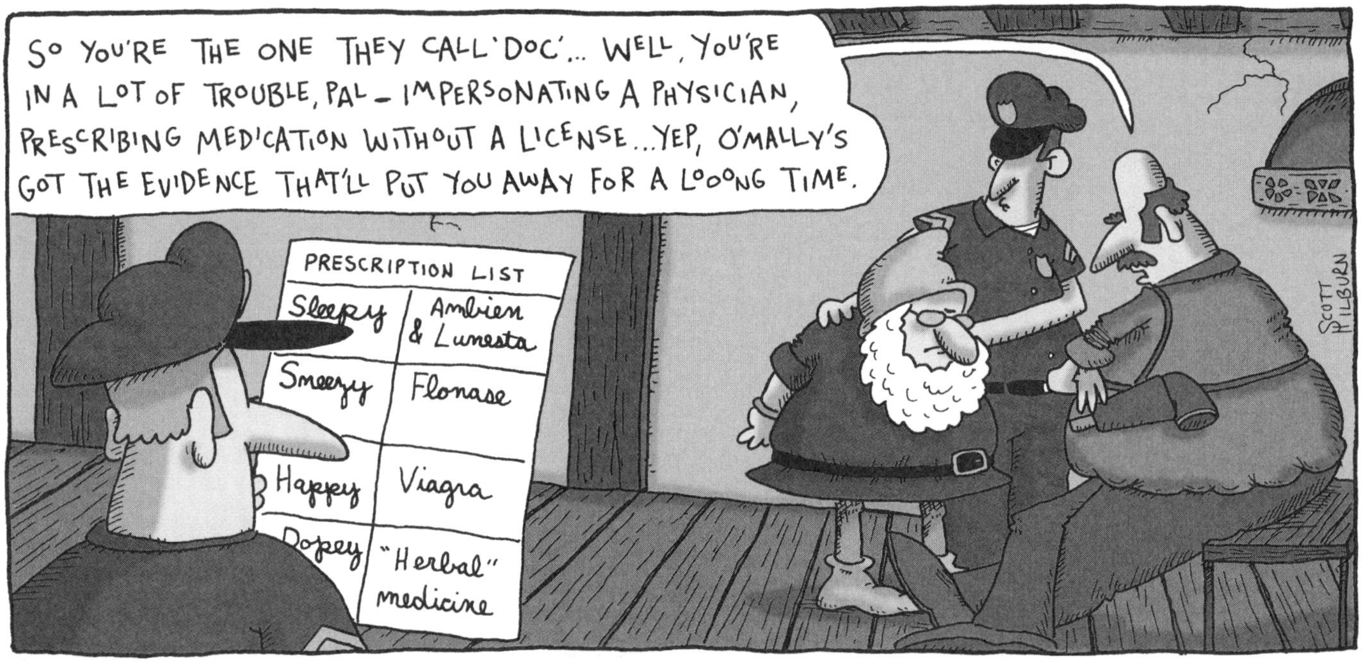
SO YOU'RE THE ONE THEY CALL 'DOC'... WELL, YOU'RE IN A LOT OF TROUBLE, PAL – IMPERSONATING A PHYSICIAN, PRESCRIBING MEDICATION WITHOUT A LICENSE... YEP, O'MALLY'S GOT THE EVIDENCE THAT'LL PUT YOU AWAY FOR A LOOONG TIME.
PRESCRIPTION LIST
Sleepy – Ambien & Lunesta
Sneezy – Flonase
Happy – Viagra
Dopey – "Herbal" medicine
SCOTT HILBURN

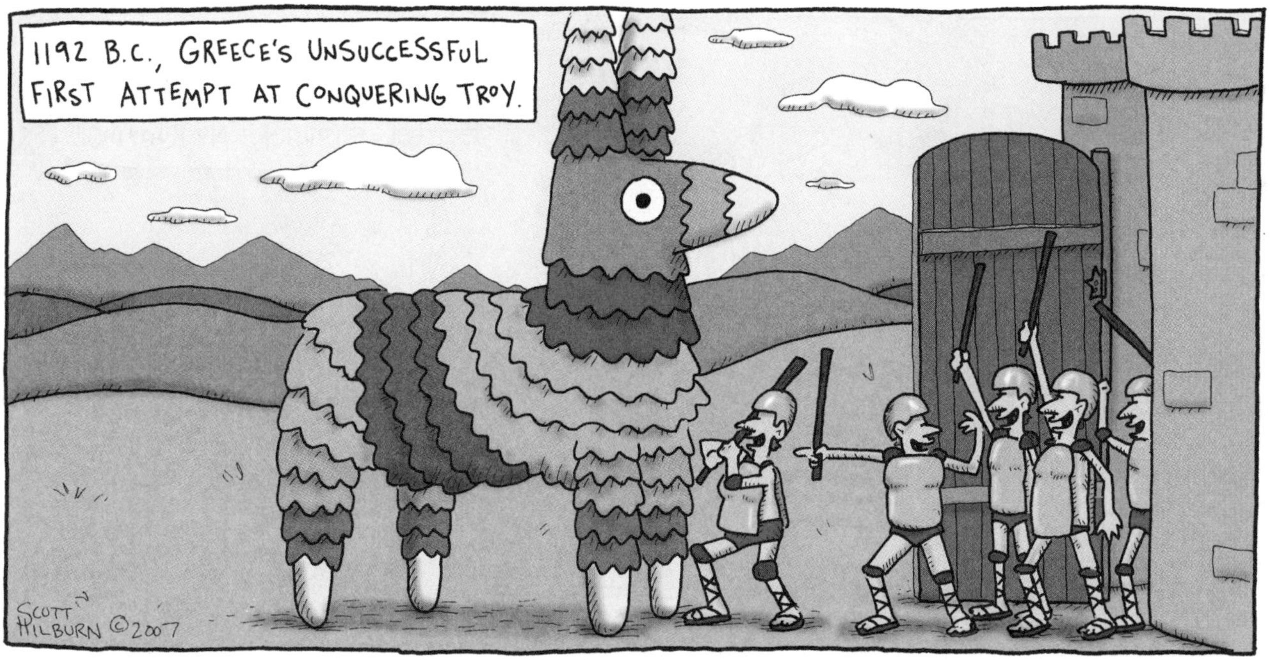
1192 B.C., GREECE'S UNSUCCESSFUL FIRST ATTEMPT AT CONQUERING TROY.
SCOTT HILBURN ©2007

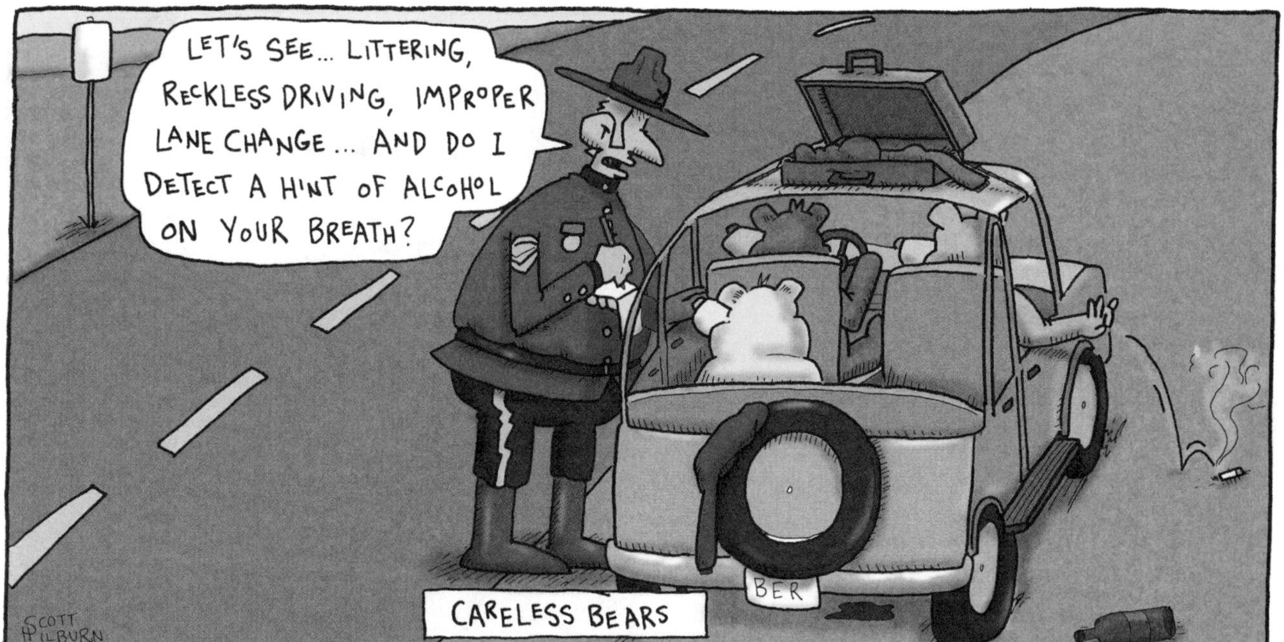
LET'S SEE... LITTERING, RECKLESS DRIVING, IMPROPER LANE CHANGE... AND DO I DETECT A HINT OF ALCOHOL ON YOUR BREATH?
BER
SCOTT HILBURN

CARELESS BEARS

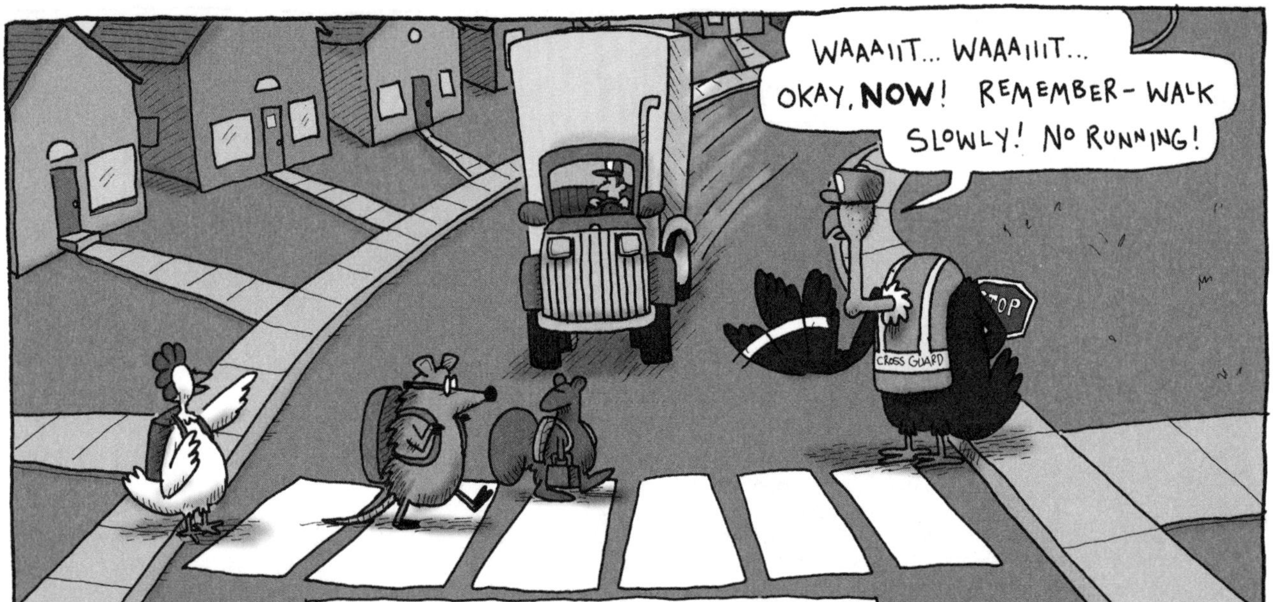
WAAAIIT... WAAAIIIT... OKAY, NOW! REMEMBER- WALK SLOWLY! NO RUNNING!
CROSS GUARD
STOP
SCOTT HILBURN

WHY DIDN'T THE CHICKEN CROSS THE ROAD?

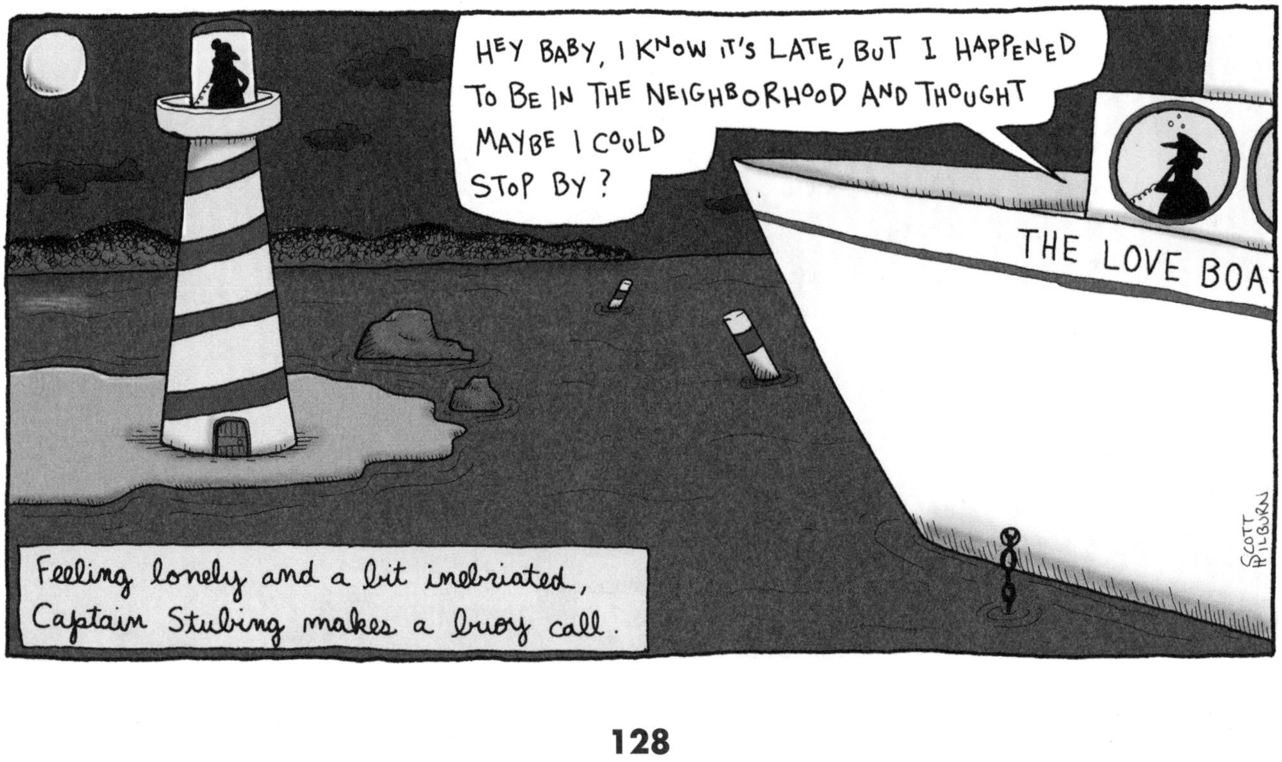
HEY BABY, I KNOW IT'S LATE, BUT I HAPPENED TO BE IN THE NEIGHBORHOOD AND THOUGHT MAYBE I COULD STOP BY?
THE LOVE BOA
SCOTT HILBURN

Feeling lonely and a bit inebriated, Captain Stubing makes a buoy call.